Exploring Intimate Life Styles

BERNARD I. MURSTEIN is Professor of Psychology at Connecticut College where he focuses on theories of marital choice, theories of marriage adjustment, interpersonal attraction, and the history of love and marriage. He has authored more than a hundred publications, including *Theory and Research in Projective Techniques*, *Handbook of Projective Techniques* (Ed.), *Theories of Attraction and Love* (Ed.), *Love, Sex, and Marriage Through the Ages*, and *Who Will Marry Whom? Theories and Research in Marital Choice*. He is a Fellow of the Clinical and Personality and Social Psychology Divisions of the American Psychological Association, Past President of the Society for Personality Assessment, and former Fulbright Professor at the Université de Louvain.

EXPLORING INTIMATE LIFE STYLES

Bernard I. Murstein, EDITOR
WITH CONTRIBUTORS

SPRINGER PUBLISHING COMPANY
NEW YORK

Copyright © 1978 by Springer Publishing Company, Inc.

Springer Publishing Company, Inc.
200 Park Avenue South
New York, N.Y. 10003

78 79 80 81 82 / 10 9 8 7 6 5 4 3 2 1

Library of Congress Cataloging in Publication Data
Main entry under title:
Exploring intimate life styles.

    Contributions based on papers originally given at a
Connecticut College symposium held Nov. 13-14, 1975.
    1. Family — United States — Congresses. 2. Marriage
— United States — Congresses. 3. Unmarried couples
— United States — Congresses. 4. Sex in marriage —
Congresses. 5. Collective settlements — United States
— Congresses. I. Murstein, Bernard I. II. Connecticut
College.
HQ536.E96   301.42 '0973   77–27272
ISBN 0–8261–2380–5   ISBN 0–8261–2381–3 pbk.

à Danielle, ma grande fille

Contents

Preface

T HIS BOOK represents a collection of original papers focusing on nonnormative life styles. Most of the important variant forms either within or outside monogamy are covered. The general aim was to provide a theoretical, or review paper on a topic by an established authority in the area* as well as a paper by individuals who had participated in the variant form or who described the experiences of those who have lived such a form.

In the interests of space, where the experience was fairly common (singlehood, cohabitation) or where it proved difficult to obtain suitable manuscripts within the time limits and financial restrictions of the symposium (swinging), only the review/theoretical chapter appears. In addition, there is a chapter by James Ramey that makes predictions for the immediate future and an epilogue by the editor. I have also written brief introductory commentaries for each topic.

The book, written in nontechnical language, may serve as a supplement for psychology, sociology, or home economics courses on marriage and the family, adult development, or human behavior. Its broad coverage and extensive review of several areas will appeal to some professionals, and its lack of jargon will make it easily readable by the layman.

---

*Most of the authorities were selected with the aid of a questionnaire sent out to a number of leading authorities on marriage asking for names of outstanding authorities in the area.

Acknowledgments

T HE ACHIEVEMENT of the Connecticut College Symposium on Changing Intimate Life Styles has been a cooperative enterprise in the
fullest sense of the term. Nancy MacLeod and Betty Morrison gener-
ously contributed in countless ways to the preparation and smooth
functioning of the program. My esteemed colleagues, Otello Desiderato, Ann Sloan-Devlin, Philip Augustus Goldberg, Steven Gunn,
Rabbi Peter Knobel, John MacKinnon, and Nelly K. Murstein provided
lodging for the participants. Professor Desiderato was also kind enough
to give my manuscript (the Epilogue) the benefit of his incisive and
pungent criticism. Fran Scholl was a super girl friday as was Heather
Tatten, who also did the art work for the program.

Although in the economic recession, which coincided with the holding of the Symposium, it was apparent that our program would have to
be run on a shoestring, it appeared at one point that there was not even a
shoestring of support. In the knick of time a quartet of "angels" appeared to supply the financial wherewithal to enable the Symposium to
survive: Richard Allen, president of the Connecticut College student
government along with the student government; Oakes Ames, president of Connecticut College; Mr. and Mrs. Adrian Goldman; and John
MacKinnon and the Psychology Department of Connecticut College. I
am truly indebted to them.

Last, but surely not least, my thanks to the participants. None was
paid for his or her efforts, and indeed many paid most of their transportation costs in order to participate. I hope that the experience the
Symposium gave them proved as rewarding an experience as their
contribution was for all of us at Connecticut College.

Contributors

Sterling E. Alam

Sterling E. Alam is assistant professor of gerontology at the University of Illinois. A former clergyman, he has appeared in numerous symposia focusing on communes, the future of the family, and deviant behavior. Among the papers he has delivered are "A New Venture in University Family Studies," "Middle-Class Communes: A Case Study and Research Proposal," "Children in Communes," and "Endings are Beginnings: A Guide to Alternate Lifestyles."

Vern L. Bullough

Vern L. Bullough is professor of history and director, Center for Sex Research at the California State University at Northridge, and adjunct professor at the School of Public Health, University of California, Los Angeles. He has authored numerous books including *Man in Western Civilization; The Scientific Revolution; The Subordinate Sex; Sexual Variance in Society and History; Sex, Society and History;* and the forthcoming *Sin and Sickness and Sexual Freedom* and *Women, Sex, and Prostitution.*

Michael P. Burk

Michael P. Burk recently completed his individual studies M.A. in identity studies. Although quite young, he has participated in a number of colloquia on the position of homosexuals in society. These include "Perspectives on Homosexuality" and "Aspects of Homosexuality." The present paper was presented recently at the Midwest Sociological Society in St. Louis.

Carol, Duane, Charlotte

Carol, Duane, and Charlotte have been living together for a number of years and have spoken to a number of groups about the strengths and weaknesses of such arrangements. They also help to publish and write for *Joy-Us,* the official newsletter of Future Families of the World.

Larry L. Constantine

Larry L. Constantine, instructor in psychiatry at Tufts University, is a practicing family therapist in Acton, Massachusetts, and along with his wife, Joan M. Constantine, is regarded as a leading researcher in the field of group marriage. During several years of research they found more than a hundred group marriages and corresponded with and studied more than thirty. In addition to their book, *Group Marriage,* and a recent monograph, *Treasures of the Island: Children in Alternative Families,* the Constantines have published widely in various journals and books.

Jacquelyn J. Knapp

Jacquelyn J. Knapp is currently a clinical psychologist at the Human Resources Center, Inc., Daytona Beach, Florida. Author of the first doctoral dissertation on open marriage, "Co-marital Sex and Marriage Counseling: Sexually 'Open' Marriage and Related Attitudes and Practices of Marriage Counselors," she also has presented papers at national and international conventions on "Emerging Marital Styles," "Intimate Friendship," and "Alternative Marriage Styles." Related published papers include "Some Non-monogamous Marriage Styles and Related Attitudes and Practices of Marriage Counselors" (*Family Coordinator*), and "An Exploratory Study of Seventeen Sexually Open Marriages" (*Journal of Sex Research*). Underway is research concerning personality profiles of spouses choosing nontraditional marriage styles.

Roger W. Libby

Roger W. Libby, a sociologist and social psychologist, is currently a research associate in sociology in the Department of Sociology, State University of New York at Albany. His research interests include the socialization of sexual attitudes and behavior from an interdisciplinary perspective and life styles of adolescents and young adults. In addition to numerous articles, his recent works include *Marriage and Its Alternatives* and *Sexuality Today and Tomorrow*, which he coedited. He is also the editor of the journal *Alternatives: Marriage, Family, and Changing Life Styles*.

Judith Fischer Lyness

Judith Fischer Lyness is assistant professor of human development at the Pennsylvania State University in the Division of Individual and Family Studies. Dr. Lyness has written papers on cohabitation and on heterosexual intimacy. Her current interests include the development of intimacy in adolescence, sex-role aspects of interpersonal relations, and intervention programs for the promotion of enhanced interpersonal skills in adolescence.

Eleanor D. Macklin

Eleanor D. Macklin currently serves as assistant professor in the Department of Family and Community Development at the University of Maryland in College Park. Her most recent research has involved study of the changing sexual attitude and behavior patterns on the college campus, with particular attention to the phenomenon of nonmarital cohabitation. She edits the *Cohabitation Research Newsletter*, was the author of an article on heterosexual cohabitation among unmarried college students which appeared in *Psychology Today*, and is broadly recognized as the leading specialist in the world on cohabitation.

James W. Ramey

James W. Ramey is the founder and current director of the Center for the Study of Innovative Life Styles; senior research associate, Center for Policy Research; board member and chairman, Executive Committee, Rockland Broadcasters; and consultant, U.S.C. Medical School Center for Health Services Research. He has published three books and over eighty monographs, articles, and chapters in books and professional journals in the areas of administration, health sciences, communication, innovation, privacy, education, and marriage alternatives. His most recent book is *Intimate Friendships*.

Roger H. Rubin

Roger H. Rubin is associate professor of family and community development at the University of Maryland. He has authored numerous professional writings on interpersonal life styles, families and income maintenance, and black family life. In addition, he has been an active participant in family life organizations.

David J. Ruth

David (a name he uses professionally rather than his full name) is a social psychologist who did his undergraduate and graduate work at Harvard University studying small group behavior and phenomenology. He came to the Twin Oaks Commune to do preliminary work for a doctoral dissertation on small groups in communal situations and stayed to become manager of publications and social science editor of *Communities Magazine*.

Robert G. Ryder

Robert G. Ryder is dean of the School of Home Economics and Family Studies at the University of Connecticut. He has published many papers over the past fifteen years including "Separating and Joining Influences in Courtship and Early Marriage" (*American Journal of Orthopsychiatry*, 1971) and "Notes on Marriages in the Counter Culture" (*Journal of Applied Behavioral Sciences*, 1973).

Wendy and Burt

Wendy and Burt have been married for six years and have an open marriage. Burt is a clinical psychologist. Wendy is a family therapist. They have been active in lecturing and writing about the open marriage concept.

Robert N. Whitehurst

Robert N. Whitehurst is professor of sociology at the University of Windsor, Ontario. He is coeditor of *The New Sexual Revolution* with Lester A. Kirkendall, *Renovating Marriage* with Roger W. Libby, and *Marriage and Alternatives*, also with Roger W. Libby. He is a clinical member of the American Association of Marriage and Family Counselors, the National Council on Family Relations, and various other sociological organizations. His current research involves a study of divorce in Canada. He also maintains an interest in changing life styles involving heterosexual long-term relationships.

INTRODUCTION

[1]

THE INSTITUTION of marriage has been in evidence since the onset of recorded history and, no doubt, long preceded it. Currently, however, not only is traditional marriage being attacked, but the very institution of marriage is being accused of perpetuating inequity between the sexes, limiting the development of outside relationships, and, thus, inhibiting the individual's fullest realization of his or her interpersonal freedom and growth. In addition, the existence of government regulatory powers to define and supervise the conditions of marriage has been called suppressive and an inducement to fostering a tendency to regard the spouse as a possession rather than as an independent human being. In short, marriage has been classified by several writers as an anachronism.

On the other hand, most people remain convinced that despite its shortcomings, marriage is not only an integral part of society, but is the best form of relationship that has been devised for meeting the needs of men and women as well as those of society.

A number of writers have capitalized on the agitation surrounding marriage to publish books with such sensational titles as *The Death of the Family* and *Is Marriage Necessary?* Such books give a false impression of the viability of marriage and the family. There is no evidence that the family is dying, and whether marriage is or is not necessary is beside the point. Marriage — some sort of marriage — seems to be preferred by the vast majority of people. It is also evident that people are increasingly discontented with the traditional style of marriage with sex-assigned

1

roles, loss of single identity in favor of couple identity, and a restriction of opportunities to interact with others except as members of a "couple."

The major question family researchers ought to concern themselves with, therefore, is What kinds of intimate life styles will further individual growth, allow for adequate socialization of children, and meet societal needs?

This book, with a few exceptions (see Preface), is divided into papers dealing with each of the variant forms of life styles on a theoretical or review basis and on an experiential basis. The aim is to assess the strengths and weaknesses of each variant form in order to estimate its function in present-day society and its viability for the near future. In some cases it has been possible to go beyond this global goal and to suggest what kinds of persons might profit from a given variant style and what kinds of persons might find such a style unappealing or disastrous.

The book is divided into three sections: The first section, Chapters 2 through 7, deals essentially with variants within marriage although not all of the participants in the variant forms are legally married, and not all communes contain subgroupings of married persons. The second section, Chapters 8 through 10, deals with variants involving unmarried persons. The third section (Chapters 11 and 12) deals with prognostications for the future. Each topic is introduced by comments by the editor.

There is a great deal of diversity among the writers and sometimes their writings differ on a number of points. But there seems to be unanimity on one central issue. Traditional marriage with a nonworking wife, no divorce, and sexual exclusivity within marriage is losing its ideological appeal, though it would be premature to call it a *rara avis*. The reader is invited to pull up a crystal ball and, based on the data presented herein, peer along with us to see if we can pierce the fog obscuring our knowledge of future intimate life styles.

CONTRACTS

[2]

THE NEED for and viability of contracts prior to and during marriage is a topic rapidly increasing in importance among workers in the field of marriage. What is not clear yet is the value of such contracts. Ryder argues well against contracts as providing a modus operandi for everyday life. Let me add that there is no question in my mind that individuals with "contract mentalities," or, as I have referred to them elsewhere individuals high on exchange-orientation (Murstein, Cerreto, and MacDonald, 1977; Murstein and MacDonald, 1977), are individuals who are generally dissatisfied in marriage. Yet I believe that Ryder does not give adequate credit to the virtues of contracts, particularly in marriage.

Contracts possess the virtue of stating in precise terms just *what* the individuals will do (e.g., if Matthew wishes to drink whiskey, he will move out of the house to a separate residence), and they communicate the *intensity* of his wife Matilda's feeling about his drinking (I don't want to live with a drunkard any longer). Thus the consequences of his continued drinking are unequivocal.

Another beneficial use of contracts occurs when a specific thorny issue is interfering with the relationship of the couple. The wife may complain about not getting any help in the kitchen, but the husband may say that he has to take care of many things for his wife including the constant transportation of her fading automobile to the dealer for repairs, which always involves long waits. In a quid pro quid arrangement, husband may agree to help out in the kitchen twice a week if wife will be partially responsible for her own car. If this contract can be honored successfully over a period of time, confidence in oneself and

3

the partner may lead to an ability to solve other problems, either by further contract or by discussion. ,

I do wish to reiterate the distinction between contracts and a contract mentality. Contracts may be a way out of an impasse. "Contract mentalities" lead to an attempt to regulate much of couple life by agreement and regulation. For reasons discussed fully in the above cited references, this sort of attitude generally leads to marital unhappiness.

REFERENCES

Murstein, B. I., Cerreto, M., and MacDonald, M. G. "A Theory and Investigation of the Effect of Exchange-Orientation on Marriage and Friendship." *Journal of Marriage and the Family* 39 (1977): 543-48.

Murstein, B. I., and MacDonald, M. G. "The Relationship of 'Exchange-Orientation' and 'Commitment' Scales to Marriage Adjustment. Unpublished Manuscript. Connecticut College, 1977.

Androgynous and Contract Marriage

ROBERT G. RYDER

THE TERM contract marriage has been acknowledged recently. It has been used generally to describe marriages in which the rules of the state are to be replaced or supplemented by a more private and more personalized contract between the two spouses. Androgynous marriage is a term that has been used for some years, e.g., Osofsky and Osofsky (1972), to describe marriages which are not organized on the basis of gender (c.f. Bird, 1970). Responsibilities and privileges are divided on some other basis than the sexual identity of the two spouses, and there is an effort to provide the two spouses with some equality of status. If these two topics, contract and androgynous marriage, belong together in the same essay, it is because a contract or other formal agreement, whether initiated before marriage or after, seems often to have been employed in order to move a marriage in the direction of androgyny. Androgyny has probably been the most popular motivation expressed in the substantive content of individualized marriage contracts.

This essay is not intended to be a dispassionate review of the relevant literature, or a report of new research. On the contrary, it has a thesis to advance. Agreeing that the present legal status of marriage and its embroilment in exploitative sex roles constitute a situation crying for improvement, it will argue that improvement can be approached best by doing less rather than more in some respects, and that there are problems in trying to deal with serious aspects of human relationships by means of regulations. A marriage contract, it will be suggested, can sometimes make a bad situation worse.

Perhaps an anecdote or two will convey something of this general orientation. A few years ago, while employed by the federal government, I attended an interagency meeting dealing with research on human subjects. We met in the wake of an accumulated series of unhappy disclosures. There was talk of cancerous tissue having been grafted onto unsuspecting people, of life-saving treatment having been deliberately withheld from individuals with syphilis, of psychosurgery having been done to people who were difficult to manage, and of people having been terrified out of their wits, all in the name of science. The solution to abuses like these was to be that in the future, informed consent was to be required before an individual could be made the subject of social or biological research. This was, and is, a foolish idea. It is fine enough as an ethical principle, but as an unrelenting regulation, filled with detailed specification, it is a regulatory substitute for dealing with the basic problem of trust and trustworthiness.

Looking back a little further, I grew up in a reasonably rough eastern city, in the days when one's relationship with the law seemed less involved with legalistic niceties. It was said that if a police officer became angry with a person, that person might get dragged into an alley and beaten up. That, however, would have been the end of it. The contemporary version of the same story has the police officer doing about the same thing, but then arresting the person for assaulting an officer. Similarly, people were often held in jail without being charged for a few hours or perhaps overnight, and then released. These days, a person held that way would be likely to complain to a lawyer, so the police, perhaps anticipating such a complaint, might be more likely to file formal charges.

The point there is not to look wistfully back at the days when life was less complicated, but simply to note that attempts to correct genuine evils by expanding legalisms that do not really change the basic situation in which people work, can easily turn out to have either no effect, or an effect opposite to the one intended. In general, it appears that as the level of social trust has progressively diminished over the years, as this society has become more aware and less tolerant of injustice, an attempt has been made to correct these injustices by expanding bureaucratic, regulatory "safeguards" which fail. As is well known to anyone who has done psychotherapy with obsessionals, attempts to control behavior with regulations almost always fail if not accompanied by a change of intention or a change in situation, and the more complex are the regulations, the more they fail.

What then can be said from this point of view with reference to marriage, and in particular to contract marriage? Consider first the legal situation presently provided by the state. Let us acknowledge, in fact let us insist, that it has some striking features that might reasonably motivate people to write their own contracts in an attempt to do better. Even without considering content, there are several features that couples might find objectionable. First, the present situation might be regarded as too binding and too vague. At present, people are in effect commited to a legally binding contract, and for some purposes they are commited for life. It might be thought that the antislavery provisions of the constitution prohibit contracts that cannot be escaped until death, but these seem not to apply to marriage. Too binding, or not, no one has the opportunity to read the marriage contract before signing it. It is not written down in any convenient place. In effect, one really does not know what one is signing.

Second, the marriage contract provided by the state can be changed after the fact without the consent of the married parties. If people move from one state to another, the contract to which they are obligated changes with the move, and spouses may discover that the contract they thought they had entered into originally is no longer the contract to which they are obligated. Even if they remain in the same place, the state legislature can at any time change the marriage laws, deprive the spouses of the contract they thought they had agreed to, and obligate them in effect to another contract that they might never have signed voluntarily.

A third objection does not deal so much with what the state does that is wrong, as with the fact that the state does it. Some couples might argue that marriage is a personal arrangement, and that therefore people should arrange it to suit themselves, rather than having the state make decisions for them.

It goes almost without saying that marriage laws also include content that many people find objectionable. For present purposes the most notable shortcoming is that marriage laws are seen as either facilitating or failing to prevent marriages being organized around the idea of people as property, with relationships structured according to gender. Any marriage law which specifies some obligations for husbands and others for wives, clearly mandates a system of sex roles and almost certainly mandates a traditional sex-role system. During the marriage, husbands may be required to provide money, but not child care or sexual services. Wives may be required to provide child care and sexual services, but not money. After divorce, the law is likely to enforce more or less the same division of labor, except for the wife being relieved of sexual responsibility. Even if distinctions as crass as these are not made, bolstering of the traditional sex-role system might be thought to be implicit in the law. Certainly there is no state, at the present time, which has marriage laws that treat traditional sex roles as a shortcoming or weakness.

There are thus several rational potential objectives for individualized marriage contracts. They might seek to provide clear and finite obligations and responsibilities instead of the vague and inconstant requirements of a frivolous governmental structure. They might seek to provide a pattern of requirements that corrects rather than perpetuates the substantive evils of the present system. And, they might help people take charge of their own lives, rather than having the state make significant personal decisions for them.

On the other hand, let me suggest, first of all, that there may be a range of things that a couple might agree to do in order to reach these objectives without entering into a contract. The word "contract" seems usually to be used, and in my view should be used, to refer to something more restrictive than simply all agreements. Even if used as a metaphor, with no real intent to fit a legal definition, "contract" connotes a certain degree of complexity, implies a formal and probably written statement, and suggests a set of quid pro quo's for the obligations that the various parties assume. A husband who promises to take his wife out to dinner if she will come and pick him up at work, may have entered into an agreement, but he has hardly entered into a contract in the present sense. Furthermore, an agreement pertaining to taking a spouse out to dinner might be sufficiently complicated, formal, and slavishly evenhanded so as to be a metaphoric contract in the present sense, but yet be only a contract in marriage, or pertaining to marriage, without being a marriage contract per se (see for example *Time*, 1972). This last term must surely be reserved for a contract which stipulates that set of basic obligations that define a relationship as marriage.*

If spouses want their marriage contract to be more than a metaphor, i.e., to be legally enforceable (c.f. Weitzman, 1974), does contract marriage become a way of returning power to the people? There is very little question here. It does not. The odds are very high that the contract will turn out to be legally unenforceable, in which case the apparent legality of the contract can be only misleading. Suppose for example two people make a contract that permits either spouse to have sexual relations outside of marriage. After having been married a few months, the wife decides to act on this particular portion of the marriage contract. The husband then discovers he cannot accept her actions as calmly as anticipated, or perhaps he never anticipated that she would act on that particular provision. He consults a lawyer, and discovers that "contract" or no "contract" he can sue for divorce on the grounds of adultery.

If however the contract is legally enforceable, it will be enforced by the same governmental structure the spouses attempted to supersede by writing the contract. Since there is no particular reason to expect a dramatic shift in the nature of judges sitting on state benches, one can hardly expect court decisions to support vigorously the substantive changes in social relations envisaged by the spouses in question. In any case, regardless of the sentiments of particular judges, turning back to the power of the state for enforcement is difficult to construe as people having power over their own destiny. A legally binding contract is based, in effect, on mistrust, and the only reason for it to be legally binding is to guard against the possibility that the partners will *not* be able to manage their own affairs. When that happens, some parental authority is supposed to take over and to see to it that justice (the parents' justice) is done.

If legally binding enforcement is not available, or is not wanted, what can be said about the effectiveness of marriage contracts, or contracts within marriage with more limited purposes? A well known marriage and family counselor described a particular case of an agreement that worked. In this instance, the wife complained that her husband threw

---

*The distinction between "marriage contracts" and "contracts in marriage" comes from Bernard I. Murstein, *Personal Communication*, 1976.

his clothes all over the bedroom floor, and would not pick them up. The husband's rejoinder was that he was tired at night, that it was a small matter for his wife to pick up the clothes, and that therefore she was being unreasonable. Both parties seemed to share the view that when the clothes finally became assembled in some convenient place, it was the wife's responsibility to clean them and prepare them for further use. The marriage counselor told them that they should get a plastic basket and put it in the bedroom next to the bed, preferably on the husband's side. The husband was then asked to agree that when he took his clothes off he would drop them in this basket, which would be right at hand. The wife in turn was asked to agree to be satisfied with the clothes being in this basket, and not to insist that they be in the clothes hamper located elsewhere. Both spouses promised to live up to the suggested commitments. The counselor described this as a successful case in which the agreement endured and was honored. Now, passing over the issue of whether a couple would really go to a marriage counselor over clothing on the floor without a more serious issue lurking in the shadows or being implied by the presenting one, and passing over the question of whether this agreement was too minimal to be called a contract, I suggest that what made this agreement work was not the fact that people agreed to it but rather that the counselor had caused a change in the situation.

Perhaps most readers can recall for themselves instances in which agreements that have had the effect intended, have included a change in situation that made compliance self-reinforcing, or that otherwise facilitated compliance, and which suggest that agreement per se without a situational (or motivational) alteration tends not to lead to enduring, intended change. I will content myself with one other illustrative incident, which is set in a commune. All the commune members agreed to clean up their dishes after using the kitchen facilities. Since the agreement applied to everyone, it was perfectly fair, and no one argued that it was unreasonable. On the other hand, almost no one honored it. After watching dishes pile up in the sink for perhaps a week at a time, two of the women finally took action. They smashed all of the dishes except for that small number necessary for one meal. Immediately, dishes began being washed three times a day, without fail. If anticipated sanctions are severe enough, perhaps sometimes even through the good offices of the spouse's lawyer, some agreements or contracts will be honored. Similarly, if the obligations required are sufficiently inoffensive, or are simply a statement of what people might do anyway, and do not fly in the face of long established habits (one thinks of the millions of men who cannot learn to close a toilet seat), then an agreement might be honored. But here too it may not be the agreement per se that has had the result. It may be the implied threat in one case, and the relative absence of resistance in the other.

Even if it is not legally enforceable, and even if a contract does not in and of itself greatly change behavior, it may still have positive effects. One intended consequence of a contract may be to communicate clearly between the two spouses concerning what they want from each other. Clarity of communication may indeed be highly desirable, and a contract might in fact contribute to it. It is moot, however, that clear communication is in itself adequate justification for the more elaborate contractual statements, considering that there may be other ways for wants and intentions to be made clear.

Contracts may also serve a reassuring function in giving people more confidence about what to expect in their future relations. The other side of this particular coin is that reassurance may not be much of a benefit, if it is based on expectations that turn out to be false. Expectations may turn out to be false either because a contract is not honored, or in spite of the fact that it is honored. For example, a marriage contract consists by definition of mutual obligations to be honored in an imagined future situation, i.e., the marriage. If the actual marriage situation turns out to be substantially different from the one imagined, the effects of the contract as lived may also turn out to be quite different from the effects anticipated.

Can contract marriage ever contribute to its substantive goals? In particular, can it ever generate androgynous marriage? Of course it can; but that may not be the typical outcome. The way in which individualized contracts seek androgyny seems typically to be by a process of specifying who shall do what, and when. Indeed, the detail required really to "insure" fairness and equality to both parties can get to be so excessive that for this reason alone both spouses might eventually throw up their hands in despair and retreat to conventional living. Reading some published material (Coffin, 1972) in which a reported contract divided child care into a 3:00 to 6:00 P.M. time period, and a 6:00 to bedtime period, and Saturday vs. Sunday, the image conjured up of rotating responsibilities seems distinctly tiring. Since at best the pull of conventionality is unrelenting (Kafka and Ryder, 1973), and is a constant hazard for those who lead their lives in some different way, it may be unwise to make that different way be any more work than necessary.

The issues mentioned so far are, however, secondary. A fundamental objection remains whether marriage contracts are legally enforceable or not, whether they are honored to the letter or not, and whether they actually change behavior, clarify communication, and provide appropriate reassurances, or not. The actual content of individualized marriage contracts may include long and unedifying lists of specifications including who should be responsible for doing what. There may be details of quid pro quo's specifying the penalties for various transgressions. In effect—and this is the really fundamental objection—the relatively but deceptively simple promise to love, honor, and perhaps obey is replaced by a more lengthy list of more concrete specifications to the extent that disagreement and mistrust with regard to the present system lead to the heightened legalization that has the same sort of unintended consequences here as elsewhere in our bureaucratized society. It is at least possible that instead of more rules, people need more trust and less legalism.

In terms of androgyny, to specify some slavishly equal set of obligations or obligatory sex-role reversals perpetuates at least part of the evil of conventional sex roles and may even add to it. The detailed specification of sex-role equality can serve to increase rather than decrease the extent to which the partners are caught up in issues of gender, and decrease rather than increase their propensity for dealing with each other as individuals. It is doubtful that there is any way a set of detailed specifications can honor people's individuality, even if compiled on an individualized basis. For one thing, people change, and hence their arrangements need to be made simple enough and open enough to permit that change. Even with no commitment to continue indefinitely, arrangements that attempt to specify equality in great detail carry with them some inevitable dehumanization, since people can easily become so embroiled in living up to a collection of "oughts" that they forget the point of it all. And the point of it all, I would hope, is to permit people to relax and be happy, and to be free from feeling oppressed and unnecessarily burdened.

There is a case of a man who hired a wife in the same way one would hire any other employee (Van Deusen, 1974). In fact, this woman was not really a wife, just someone who was paid to perform certain specified household tasks. Her duties were to cook and do housework, to provide x number of hours per evening of companionship (five days per week), and to sleep alongside her employer. Many of us might agree that this was putting far too much business into a personal relationship, but at least some things were clearly removed from the sphere of obligation. The man in this relationship reports that having been freed of the obligation to be loving and tender, he found paradoxically enough that this became the warmest and most real relationship of his life. One would imagine that neither party would expect this kind of relationship to be permanent. Perhaps the woman might retire from this rather unusual occupation and use her accumulated savings to hire a partner of her own, presumably someone who would cook, do housekeeping, and provide companionship for her. After all, is this not the American way? The real point here is, however, that whatever interpersonal success was achieved seems to have been a consequence of having an area of personal relationship from which obligation was definitively excluded.

Marriage contracts in which people seem to go to extraordinary lengths to guarantee exact fairness between the two partners seem to be extreme examples of arbitrary regulations intruding on the realm of the personal. As each of us really knows, there is no such thing as exact fairness when one is dealing with wants or caring. Caring, by definition, refers to a kind of bestowal that does not seek equal repayment.

Nonetheless, various tasks do have to be performed in physically maintaining a household, caring for children, and dealing with the outside social and economic world. Suppose it is true that a contract may be a step toward the bureaucratization of family life, moving arrangements in the direction of a complicated and legalistic balancing act. It does not follow that people should simply not worry about task and responsibility allocation, or that present conventional patterns are desirable. Far from it. Perhaps allocation of tasks and responsibilities should simply be kept as uncomplicated and undistracting as possible, consistent with necessary things getting done and people not being put into impossible or unnecessarily unpleasant positions.

The simplest of all arrangements is of course when a person lives alone. Either that person does what needs to be done, or it is not done, and in neither case does it become an interpersonal issue (passing over those cases in which a man lives alone but has a woman friend who conveniently comes over to do the housework). A person who lives alone may not be free of interpersonal complications, but it may be a little less likely for such a person that personal and relationship issues get to hide behind issues of who cooks the food or carries out the garbage.

However, when two or more people share the same household, tasks and responsibilities must be allocated in some way, and some of the conventional ways, e.g., the joint checking account, can be quite problematic.

A joint checking account can be almost asking for trouble because it can mean one person accepting the impossible responsibility of maintaining a balanced budget and paying bills, without being able to control the outflow of money. Another impossible situation occurs when one partner assumes total responsibility for keeping the living quarters neat, and the other partner habitually bedecks the place with clothing, cigarette ashes, and a variety of other odds and ends. It is probably unwise in general to accept responsibility where one does not have the authority to carry out that responsibility.

Another problem in simply dividing up tasks between spouses is that some tasks are so invested with high or low status, or high or low power, that for one person to own them completely leads inevitably to distress. Housekeeping is again a case in point. Another, for many people, is earning money.

The situation becomes complicated to the point of creating problems when tasks are not simply divided between spouses, but are shared or alternated, or responsibility is alternated. When sharing is done in an informal way between two people who see things in more or less the same light, it can be a small matter. But if the people involved do not see eye to eye, the process of formalizing can become excessive. If full responsibility for some major task alternates, really extensive costs can develop. For example, if employment for money rotates between the two spouses on a yearly or some other basis, the lifetime earnings of the couple are almost certainly going to be reduced by a substantial amount. If meal preparation is alternated more frequently than grocery shopping, meal preparation can become quite annoying. It may be here too that the least organization one is comfortable with may also be the best organization.

Really the same general point has been made for contract marriage, androgynous or not, and androgynous marriage, contract or not. The point has been that the organization of tasks and responsibilities should be kept as simple as possible, and that the legal structure pertaining to marriage should be kept as simple as possible. In either case the intention is to leave the maximum amount of time and energy for better things. For some couples, this may mean not only avoiding the unnecessary addition of complications and legalisms, but working to reduce those complications and legalisms presently applied to married couples whether they like it or not. Concretely, some may wish to make serious changes in the marriage laws, or even to repeal them, which would certainly be one way to acquire the power over their marriages now held by the state. Short of eliminating marriage laws, a couple might simply ignore them. Spouses might marry each other by mutual pledge, or by religious service, and leave the state out of it. Clearly, attempts to change, eliminate, or ignore aspects of present laws may be very difficult, or lead to serious ultimate consequences; but then the same statement can also be made about attempts to succeed at contemporary, legally conventional marriage.

Assuming that in one way or another spouses have and will continue to have at least some say in the obligations to which they will be subjected, and in decisions regarding task and responsibility allocation, and assuming that the decision-making process itself does not become so complex as to be a dominating presence, the actual content of obligation or task allocation decisions is perhaps not the most important thing. To make a really radical assertion, perhaps what counts most is not what people do, but how they feel. To put it another way, the satisfaction or annoyance accompanying a particular task is likely to be at least in part a matter of the meaning of that task, what the task allocation seems to imply about one's status or worth. If it is clear that a task allocation does not have this sort of implication, then the allocation is less significant. By the same token, if two people have strong feelings about each other's value and capabilities, as well as about their own, a great emphasis on task allocation may be pointless. If people feel good about themselves and each other, task allocation may be largely a distraction or a necessary evil. If people feel badly about themselves and each other, no amount of task allocation is likely to correct the situation. The main thing ultimately must be whether or not people can really relate to each other as individual human beings. If they can get beyond feeling in terms of the roles society places on them, as well as the alternate roles they might create, then the rest will not be quite so important.

REFERENCES

Bird, C. *Born Female*. New York: David McKay, 1970.
Coffin, P. "Marriage Experiments." *Life* (April 28, 1972): 41–46.
Kafka, J. S., and Ryder, R. G. "Notes on Marriage in the Counter Culture." *Journal of Applied Behavioral Science* 9 (February 3, 1973): 321–30.
"New Marriage Styles," *Time* (March 20, 1972): 56–57.
Osofsky, J. D., and Osofsky, H. J. "Androgyny as a Life Style." *Family Coordinator* 21 (1972): 411–18.
Van Deusen, E. *Contract Cohabitation*. New York: Grove Press, 1974.

ANDROGYNY

[3]

IT IS DIFFICULT not to be touched by the piercing honesty of Judith Lyness. She does not deal in academic polemic but in the coin of "earned" wisdom. Roles that sound exciting as abstract conceptions may be counter to the individual's needs once they manifest themselves. Thus Lyness discovers belatedly that she is interested in a maternal role if not the exploited role of "mother." In an androgynous marriage she gains a new perspective on the problems of the househusband, discovers that the role of nagging housewife is not indigenous to women but to that of being a houseperson, and in the end remarks that "to be truly liberated is not to switch roles but to be in touch with one's own needs." Femininity is the inner self. Female is the role played.

Although androgynous attitudes on the part of both members of a couple potentially should yield more flexibility in meeting household needs, a call for rigid adherence to changing household responsibilities at specified intervals may run counter to the best interests of the couple. What is needed is the freedom to choose, not a forced need to be democratic. Finally, as her own candid observation in her epilogue indicates, androgyny does not guarantee compatibility and permanence. Marriage is a very complex relationship, hardly reducible to equally shared responsibilities.

An Experiential Report of Androgynous Spousal Roles

JUDITH FISCHER LYNESS

Introduction

THE WORDS "androgynous spousal roles" describe as well as any words might the kind of relationship my partner and I have been living and developing during the past three (or more) years of our ten-year marriage. In this report, I shall try to describe the meaning this kind of relationship has had for me by contrasting it with a traditional marriage as well as by describing some of the feelings I have about this form of relationship. Gender and identity, roles and consequences are discussed with the assumption throughout that choice and responsibility are important aspects of any relationship.

Although this is a report on androgynous spousal roles, it is not so much a description of how these roles may be carried out as it is a personal journey through time and inner space. The discussion is oriented more toward explaining why and how we have come to androgynous roles than it is to providing a recipe for "successful" androgyny. Androgyny came slowly after an attempt first at a traditional relationship and then by switching these traditional roles, or role reversal. Although I worked and/or attended graduate school for the first six years of our marriage, my partner was considered the breadwinner, and we held other traditional attitudes and goals. Then we experienced several years of role reversal. In the past year we have begun to work out a more androgynous, or to use the term preferred by my partner, "sex-role independent" life style. Thus, over the nearly ten years of our marriage we have undergone many changes in roles, attitudes, and goals and we have changed in what we understand of ourselves. Most of all there have been a greater appreciation and awareness of that inner self which too often had been distorted and too frequently had been dismissed, if perceived at all. This achievement of an inner listening had made an androgynous role experience not only more desirable for us, but more likely as well.

The report is not a prescription for social change, nor is it a survey of changing marital styles. Androgyny is one way through which people may work out a relationship, but it comes complete with its own difficulties and its own strengths, and the relationship I describe is no exception. I do not believe androgyny is the answer to social problems with sex roles nor is it the solution to personal discontent. It is a way to learn about oneself and others. It is a way to risk change with uncertain and even surprising outcomes.

Gender

The sex of my partner is male, my sex is female. In this aspect we represent a traditional heterosexual pairing. Thus, it may be that the comments and reflections in this report are limited to heterosexual pairs. Yet I think it is likely that the sex of the partners in an androgynous relationship may be an irrelevant variable in dealing with identity, work, and sexual roles.

Identity

In the traditional marriage myth, maleness and masculinity, femaleness and femininity are virtually synonymous. The identities and the roles played were assumed to follow from the gender of the partners. Outside of the traditional marriage, various pairings such as androgyny in roles and identity are possible. The androgynous role reflects aspects of the male role and the female role (or neither, depending upon your point of view), and the androgynous identity combines masculinity and femininity. In the relationship I describe, androgyny in both roles and identities appear together, although that may not be true for others and has not always been the case for us.

I see myself as assertive, often competitive, sensitive, and easily influenced by emotions in some situations. I see my partner as decisive, sportsminded, sensitive, and often passive. Many people other than ourselves would demonstrate such a mixture of masculine and feminine traits, yet it has taken me a long time to accept the androgynous in me and to be comfortable with it. In working out sex-role independence, my partner has created the conditions under which he, for the first time, can be comfortable with roles.

As a young person I acted the "tomboy" but also babysat, cooked meals, and shared housecleaning chores. I was an avid reader and it was in the realm of fantasy that I found my first contact with the masculine. I identified with the male characters who played such a leading role in the books I read, typically science fiction, mysteries, and westerns. It never occurred to me then that the males' adventures could not apply to me because I was female. At the same time it never occurred to me to seek out books by women or books about girls. I rejected women's books because I rejected femaleness if it meant femininity.

My mother worked, at first as a secretary, but her artistic talent and her energy soon found her a career as a Madison Avenue copywriter. My younger sister and I seemed to take different things from our mother's enjoyment of work. Back then, I think my sister was uncomfortable with our mother's role and rejected it for herself. She married young and wanted most to be a successful housewife, although lately she's been changing and finding new directions for herself. If I appreciated anything in my mother, it was that she enjoyed her work. This appreciation was not without ambivalence, because in the late fifties and early sixties mothers were supposed to stay home and enjoy it.

Our father had different impacts on us as well. I gained approval from my father for my grades in school; my sister earned his approval more for extracurricular activities such as cheerleading and sewing. His different responses to us may have been influential in terms of the directions followed—I to graduate degrees and she to a young marriage.

My teenage preferences and attitudes were puzzling. I was not very feminine but I was not masculine either. I experienced myself as a misfit in the social world but felt committed to this conglomerate identity as right for me. I had no label then for what this identity was and I experienced some pain in having it, not knowing that it could lead me to the emerging world of androgyny.

To what extent do I perceive choice about the identity I have? It could be argued that this identity was determined by those childhood events I have described. Those events were no doubt influential, but the choice has been mine. There were very strong forces working to disengage me from my androgynous identity. For instance, my mother and sister insisted that I had to be feminine if I was to have (male) friends. I chose to defend the experience I had of myself, however incoherent it might have been, rather than accept the path they offered of manipulation and compromise leading to an acceptable feminine identity. There have been other choice points and I think that through the years I have consistently held to this androgynous identity when it was unknown and socially unacceptable, and now when it may be socially distinguished.

My partner reports himself as follows: he does not define himself in terms of sex roles; he finds that traditional masculinity was a role he tried as an adolescent, including motorbike and leather jacket, but that he felt incomplete. His sense of more completeness in his identity came about when he began to parent. He feels that our son needed nurturing which he did not see me providing. He felt that if our son was to get that nurturing then he would have to provide it. And he did. This parenting, along with other later changes in our lives, seemed to allow him to be open to and comfortable with his own androgyny. This independence from stereotypes has been part of his achieving a life more congruent with his goals, most importantly, this goal of independence.

So neither my partner nor I came to androgyny easily. There were times in our lives when those nonstereotyped aspects of ourselves were alienating. I can only speculate that it may be somewhat easier now for people to be in touch with and accepting of themselves especially with concepts such as androgyny to help pull it together. Often now there is social support for androgyny for adults, particularly women. But our children, who need clarification and support in the working out of their identities, typically find confusion and support for the traditional. If we are not afraid to risk androgyny for ourselves, we need not be afraid for our children. They are probably more androgynous than we are willing to see.

Roles

In the traditional marriage the husband has a career and works at that career, bringing in the money that supports "his" household. The wife works in the home carrying out household and parenting tasks. Their sexual relationship is such that he initiates sexual relations and she performs her wifely duty. Exclusivity in sexual relations is expected, although a double standard may operate such that if he fools around he'll be forgiven if he promises never to do it again. Birth control is her responsibility with his consent. He is the instrumental decision maker, she is the expressive facilitator of harmonious family relations.

Like many who married almost ten years ago, I believed the stereotype on one level while rejecting it on another. I believed he *should* work, but that I *chose* to. It was not for several years that I was willing to commit myself to a career. The household tasks were my responsibility, but he helped me, and I was grateful!

In carrying out our roles I suppressed my inclinations toward decision making, dealing with the choices by deferring to my partner instead. He very agreeably made choices "for me." I attempted to "manage feelings" to ensure harmony by meeting my preception of his emotional needs, a perception that was rooted in stereotypes not reality. It seemed perfectly obvious that when his needs were met, then mine would be met as well. I did not understand when I failed.

The conflicts in me were many, and at one point early in our marriage I wrote a poem of which I'll cite a fragment to illustrate the conflict and my sense of failure:

> I'm so tired, wrung out, warring
>   factions pressed together
> a slice of cheese, no holes
>   to escape
> fighting, giving up, resuming
>   but tired
> continual alienation, seeking
>   what cannot be:
> controlled self. There is none,
>   each part goes its way
> I listen to the dialogue
>   and wonder and panic
> at what is me and what
>   is not me . . . .

I had tried very hard to succeed in a traditional marriage and I did not. Although my partner experienced much the same feeling, I cannot say that there was any dramatic overnight change. The change was gradual. First one area of the traditional was discarded, then another, as we tried to find ways to live together that would meet the growing awareness of what our needs really were as opposed to what we believed they should be. Sometimes we went so far from the traditional that I found myself uncomfortable, and we gradually moved away and are still moving from the role reversal we tried for awhile.

If there was any turning point in our roles away from the traditional, it came when I began my first full-time faculty position. At that time I work, but that I *chose* to. It was not for several years that I was willing to role of houseperson. This almost complete role reversal lasted about a year and then he worked at substitute teaching while continuing his houseperson activities. In order for this reversal to be effected we both had realized changes in ourselves and in our goals. I came to see myself as not a person who worked but a person who was excited by a professional career. My partner had realized that he did not achieve satisfaction in working, and that he valued less the material goods for which the job was a means to a consumption-oriented end. We are still changing and redefining our relations with each other, and no doubt this changing will continue as long as we are in touch with ourselves.

I hesitate to describe the way we have divided up the work and household and other responsibilities because I do not believe that the way we have worked things out is a "should" for others any more than the traditional was a "should" for us. But the experiences we have had with our divisions of responsibility may serve to illuminate some of the difficulties involved in change.

For the present, then, the way I understand our relationship is as follows: I have a career to which I am committed and I work at it on a full-time basis. My partner does not wish to work at a job he would not enjoy but he expects to work at something. In the recent past he has worked as a substitute teacher. He does most of the child care, roughly half of the evening meals, and usually the laundry. We both work at housecleaning on a sporadic basis.

The financial aspect was a difficult problem for us for some time in that we had been used to pooling the money we each brought in and then taking out for personal expenses as needed. This began to be a problem for me when I wanted to spend some of the money without having to account to him for it, and without feeling guilty about spending money on my needs. And it was a problem for my partner in that he wanted to get the bills paid, without feeling that my spending would threaten these plans. Now we have a monthly household budget to which we each contribute in proportion to our income. The rest of the money we earn after we give the household its money is our own. In this way I manage "my" money without guilt and my partner can count on an unjeopardized household budget. Much of the tension over spending priorities has been dissipated, with each of us feeling more personally responsible and autonomous in our financial affairs.

Personal Consequences

The arrangement I described above may sound very reasonable, even desirable to those women who believe they would like a career and to those men who believe they would not. Yet I would maintain that the end result is not as important as what happens to you in getting there. The stereotype of the traditional marriage has the man achieving satisfaction through his work and the woman finding fulfillment in her maternal activities. But as men and women have been pointing out, men have discovered little in the way of satisfaction, and women have failed to feel fulfilled. Personal consequences of androgyny for men and women could involve both satisfaction and fulfillment. I tend to feel satisfied when I have worked through a problem to an insight that reorganizes the way I think about myself. Fulfillment is the energy released in the self-chosen freedom to be me. Actualization is a term which covers both satisfaction and fulfillment, and more. It comes through risking growth and change. And it must be worked at. For there are times when insights do not come, I sometimes forget that freedom is chosen and must be rechosen, and I must remind myself often that I am not perfect. The challenge for me is not in trying harder, but being open to trying "different" when trying harder is not appropriate (cf., Wheelis, 1973, on the distinction between trying harder and trying different). There have been a number of surprises in trying different.

One of the first surprises was the discovery that I was not as liberal nor as liberated from stereotypes as I thought I was. Second, I found that many complaints, resentments, etc., stem from roles and not individuals, and finally, I discovered that a social climate holding role reversal in high regard can be just as stifling to change as a social climate valuing the traditional.

When I accepted my first faculty job I could answer very glibly the inevitable question, "What will your husband do?" with "Anything he chooses." It took awhile but I finally recognized that my feelings were not in concert with my liberated idea about what he could do. For he chose not to work. And when I expressed discomfort with this, I heard that I could not expect him to do this, that, or the other thing, just to work at a job. I was angry but refused to recognize my anger because it did not fit with my view of our liberation from traditional roles.

Now I understand the situation in different terms. I believe each of us is responsible for ourselves and jointly responsible for our son, though we may mutually agree to define our separate areas of that responsibility. I am not uncomfortable with his choosing to do as he wishes, but I am uncomfortable with the thought of being responsible for him in the name of his liberation. The issue is not so much what he does, but who is responsible for what he does. And I know that I am not. And for me, the issue is the same. I am responsible for what I do or do not do.

At times I believe I did not act on that responsibility for myself, such as at home, and I lost a sense of myself as independent and competent. I think I went so far to leave room for my partner to operate in his new role as houseperson that I cut myself off from things that I enjoyed. Thus, I have reclaimed some home related responsibilities. It is not because he did not do them well, or that he did them too well, but because I needed to be more involved with the care and feeding of myself. To be truly liberated is not to switch roles but to be in touch with one's own needs and to care about them and to be responsible for them, to care about the other's needs but to recognize that the partner is responsible for meeting his or her own needs.

However, as my partner has pointed out, he cannot meet all of his own needs, and he can meet some of mine. But he cannot meet all of my needs nor can he meet even some of them all of the time. Yet the partnership to him implies his meeting some of my needs. I tend to view the meetings of needs not as an obligation (i.e., a responsibility) but as an outcome of a self-conscious choice. At times this may be a relatively easy choice when characteristics of one partner actually fit with and meet the needs of the other. But each of us changes with time and to continue to express these need-meeting aspects requires a choice to do so or a choice to explore altered patterns, since the partner may have changed too. Not to choose is to assume an obligation with all the hidden and often destructive calculations of what is expected in return.

So, the first surprise was to find that I had to redefine liberation. In the second surprise, when the roles people play are similar, I found that it matters neither who plays the roles, nor whether they are male or female, for the problems transcend the players. A woman in a fairly traditional marriage might complain that her partner never picks up his clothes. My partner and I have had the following exchange:

HE: Why didn't you put your clothes in the hamper before I did the wash?
ME: Why didn't you tell me you were going to do a wash?

Thus, when I happen to be playing a traditional male role I might sound like the "typical" husband and vice versa when my partner plays a traditional female role. It is not that I have become more masculine or he more feminine, but that the situation elicits stereotyped responses, and we become as embroiled in these patterned exchanges as any traditional couple.

A final surprise for me was the enthusiasm of others for our choice of life style (the role reversal). We had moved to a new community, and a reputation had preceded us. At first the attention we received, particularly from women, was quite flattering. Women told me I had it made with a partner who did all the housework. More recently, increasing numbers of men have told my partner how they're finally catching up with him, or he's really on to something, knows how to live, etc. I allowed the approval of others to take on coercive aspects, in that I denied my own negative feelings and any doubts that I had for far too long. I developed a strong commitment to continue the role reversal in the face of mounting evidence of tension and unhappiness in me.

In trying new ways of relating, it is nice to hear that others think you are doing the right thing, and it is flattering to think that others regard your life style as the way marriage should be. But my inner voice is more important and the one I have to live with. The support of others is important but there is a kind of support I most appreciate and that is the warm acceptance of a friend who cares about me and my feelings. It is the support for my inner experience which I find most valuable. I had social approval for the role reversal but personal doubts. Finally, I listened to me. The experience of listening to myself was a personal revolution in that it involved a dramatic change in my orientation toward myself and others. It released an exhilarating amount of energy as I chose to be me. I wrote about that moment of change in the form of a poem:

> I sat alone
>> looking out the window
>>> for someone
>>>> to come
>>> listening for someone
>>>> to call
>>>>> and
>>> feeling despairing
>>>> and
>>>>> lonely.
> I had my illusions
>> of what I wanted

from him
I had my delusions
    that friends would come
        to rescue me
            from
            my unhappiness,
but no one did.
I stared unseeing out the
    black window
that was the bottom
    of my
    life.
And I sat thinking
    I don't need
        my illusions
    I gave up depending
        upon others
            for my needs,
And I set myself free.
No one had come to
    rescue me
        so,
    I did it
        myself.

In summary, the personal consequence for me of androgynous roles has amounted to an inner exploration, a learning to be really with my feelings, to recognize them, to be responsible for them, and to set myself free of roles defined by others, be those roles traditional—or the reverse.

Social Consequences

In preceding sections I have alluded to some of the social consequences I've experienced with friends, children, and colleagues. There have been interesting reactions from colleagues and potential employers, not always positive. One job I applied for several years ago sent back a letter telling me they were not interested in people in hippie attire, long hair, or "Bolshevik" beards! What was more remarkable was that their form letter reply did not consider that a woman might apply for their job. There have been discouraging instances where I have been stereotyped in the traditional way: I attended graduate school on a full-time basis, yet I had potential employers wonder what I was going to do with our child if I worked and some people have assumed that I was not mobile because I was married.

At the same time my partner has faced some difficulties, one of which was balancing my need for more sharing of the economic work roles with his needs for a good environment in which to work. And he has found reverse stereotyping from potential employers wondering about his longevity on the job if he didn't have to work. One potential employer suspected he would just quit if the going became tough or he didn't like the job. Another interviewer was leery since I was in a mobile occupation and my partner might quit if I were to accept a job elsewhere. My partner had a librarian cross out "houseperson" on his library card application and write in "unemployed." I could have been a houseperson, but he was unemployed!

Colleagues have tended to be fairly careful about what they say, yet some subtle indications of possibly negative feelings have been expressed in questions such as "Has he found a job yet?" One colleague suggested (in jest?) that I should throw my partner out if he didn't work. Reactions such as these contributed to a teeth-gritting determination to make role reversal work no matter what.

Other colleagues have had very different reactions from those described above, such as the men who feel that perhaps there is an alternative to a career after all. At the very least, my partner appears to serve as a stimulus to others to consider possible alternatives in their lives. Some have come to very thoughtful conclusions about themselves, finding that academic competition is not for them, even after becoming full professors. They are dropping out, but seemingly in ways that further and reflect their sense of responsibility toward themselves and their concern for others.

There exist other men who use our situation as justification for desiring to continue a traditional relationship while ceasing to carry out any responsibility. They see only that which seems attractive: my partner does not work at a career. They fail to see that which is less attractive: that he carries out the household responsibilities. They are, in effect, saying they are no longer responsible for themselves.

In encountering this sort of reaction I finally began to see more clearly how I really felt about the issue of responsibility. To see reflected back to me this version of ourselves led to a sudden illumination of our situation. My reaction to the reflection was so unambivalently negative that it opened me to an understanding of the negative feelings I had about our role reversal. It led to my own determination to be more responsible for my own needs and less responsible for my partner's. For just as I see that he is not fragile, neither am I helpless.

Earlier I described the social approval of friends for our role reversal and indicated that I in turn valued those friends who related to me beneath the surface of what I did to what I felt. One of the aspects of acceptance of androgyny is the change in my relations with other women. I see a similar change in my partner's relations with other men. During the time of our traditional marital relationship we also maintained more or less traditional relations with friends. I was not close with women and my partner's closeness to male friends was devoid of physical contact. I realized that I had no women as close friends and I wanted to change that. As I became more comfortable with my own identity, I felt I could be more open and loving toward other women.

It was easier for me to say I wanted women friends than it was for me to find any. It wasn't that there were no women willing to involve themselves in friendships with me. It was I who held back. Now I am able to overcome that hesitancy thanks, in part, to the persistent loving regard of one friend. She had to work very hard to be my friend and to help me overcome the ambivalence I had, but we made it.

Not all of the friendships with women have worked out. There have been some painful disappointments. There are women who seem unhappy with what I represent to them. Yet I cannot give back my Ph.D. or drop out of my career or in other more subtle ways become what they need because they are uncomfortable with the way I am. Nor can I use those friendships that have not worked out as a justification for denying there can be closeness with women. I can remain open to those that can be.

In my partner, acceptance of an androgynous identity means he is now more open about his feelings when he is with other men. He seems to be warmer toward them and able to act on his warm feelings. They can hug him and he can hug them in return. We are finding that some old friends with whom we've had traditional friendships are people with whom we now have closer, less guarded, and less competitive, relations as we discover in mutual disclosure that we all have changed.

Both we and our friends have spent some time dealing with the consequences of androgyny for our children. We want our children to be independent and nonsexist. Sometimes our child, now eight, is independent to an extent that is surprising, even challenging. The nonsexism is more difficult. At times it has been dismaying to see the extent to which he adheres to the masculine stereotype in his values when his father does not. And this is in the context of a very close and very warm father-son relationship.

The father-son relationship is one encouraging sign that he may not become trapped in the masculine mystique, and there are others. Although he seems to value male friends more, he does not reject female friends. He plays with both boys and girls at an age when many are dividing into same-sex play groups. As I write this, his best friend is a nine-year-old girl who plays Little League. He apparently sees his parents as androgynous. A Draw-Your-Parents drawing he did showed us as interchangeable and without recognizable stereotyping. And our son shows an awareness of sexism. Faced with learning religious prayers he confided that he thought that what he was learning was sexist. When asked what he meant he replied that the Hail Mary was sexist. And he had the good sense to refrain from sharing his discovery with the Sister.

In general, then, I see that our son is in a good place. While he has adopted some outward signs of the masculine stereotype, which no doubt have great survival value in school and with friends, he has not rejected gentleness, nor his own feelings for girls as friends. He does not accept uncritically what comes through the culture. He is capable of perceiving sexist attitudes and behaviors and he seems to view his parents' roles accurately and with acceptance.

But to be an androgynous parent seems to have been more difficult for me than to be an androgynous spouse. I have had a long search to find a way to parent that is comfortable for me. Originally I experienced the birth of our son as an intrusion. I was going to graduate school, writing a master's thesis, about to move to a larger apartment, and a few months away from a full-time job when he was born. I found myself constantly exhausted in spite of my partner's help. There seemed to be few rewards for mothering. No one had told me that babies did not even smile for at least a month, that it was a lot of work. And he wouldn't even cuddle in the rocking chair I had bought with cuddling in mind. It seemed to be mutual rejection. When my partner began to do more and more parenting I felt relief, as long as I clearly was the "mother." But eventually I was not clearly the mother. My partner was.

As with chores around the house, eventually I realized that I had cut myself off from something I could enjoy. So, now I am more directly involved with our son, doing more child care and in particular, not being too busy to be able to put something down and really listen to him. Now we can cuddle.

Societal Consequences

The changes toward androgynous roles that I have described have not been easy. There have been no role models, no guidelines, no helpful hints from those who have gone before. It will remain difficult for some time as long as our culture values masculinity more than femininity and sees androgyny as a threat to the social order. But perhaps it has been beneficial to pursue these sex-independent roles without a program, timetable, or list of do's and don'ts. The achievement of androgyny has had to come from within. In the testing and the changing which we have experienced we have found that just as traditional marriage did not work for us as a couple, neither did role reversal.

What might be the impact on society of androgynous spousal roles? I wrote at the outset that I did not see our relationship as constituting a prescription for social change. This may have seemed an incongruous statement to find in a report about androgynous spousal roles. Perhaps by now that statement has been clarified. Each couple needs to find its own way in a relationship, perhaps even out of a relationship if the partners perceive no way to live together. The process I have described is not uniquely suited to the androgynous. But for the possibly 30% of the population who have androgynous identities (Bem, 1975; Spence, Helmreich, and Stapp, 1975), the adoption of a sex-role independent life style may be a matter of survival.

If the society we live in wished to promote stable liaisons, that is, ones that will continue at least through child rearing in growth promoting ways, then the society must also indicate reasonable expectations for the people who enter such relationships. There is change, there is sometimes fear of admitting the change to yourself and to your partner. There are discoveries that you have fantasies you did not know you could have and there is reluctance sometimes to risk vulnerability in sharing these fantasies. There are difficult choices with uncertain outcomes, but not to risk brings certain discontent. And there may be a great discrepancy between the way things "should" be and the way you experience them. The voice to listen to is your own.

Just as liberation for individuals begins when they listen to and act on their inner experience, the society may become liberated from blindly acting on its "shoulds" if it would listen to and act on the needs of its members. What I need is recognition and support for the search and process of finding how to live in ways that work for me and my partner and our child. I think this would involve a greater openness in the society, a change in its institutions to promote greater diversity and acceptance of that which is different, and a real effort to end sexism, be the target male or female. The result could be a more open people, a people who could sort themselves in different ways according to their needs, a more diverse people with energy and vitality. When people liberate themselves they also free themselves to experience all the energy that went into maintaining the stereotype. The energy is their own to use on themselves to work out their lives.

Summary

I have described many of the changes in myself as well as in my relationship with my partner and with our child. The two themes or assumptions that have tied together the experiences are choice and responsibility. No matter how influential the situations, the individual is left to choose her or his own experience of it. Each person is responsible for herself (or himself). Caring for the other is possible only when you have cared for yourself. When you have taken care of your own needs, then you are most free to really care for another's.

I cannot predict the future changes in our relationship any more than ten years ago I could have predicted our present. I know there are no guarantees that we will change in the same ways, but I know we will change. We can only go with these, facing as honestly as we can the implications of these changes for ourselves

In the process of living our relationship, there have been many different images representing myself, my partner, and our relationship. Sharing these images may serve to unify the changes I have described and the themes I have tried to illustrate. At an early point in our relationship I saw myself and my partner as birds. I was a huge, hovering bird, wings flapping. He was a great snowy owl, remotely perched on a high tree top, every so often hooting wisely. At a later time I was a mermaid and he was the stone sea wall. My partner agreed he could be the stone sea wall but denied the pitchforks I saw embedded in that wall waiting to impale the mermaid. Still later I saw myself as a turtle lumbering up a mountain, a heavy shell upon my back. The mountain represented societal expectations and the shell was my partner. Then I transformed that turtle and its burden into a slender but muscular couple, hands joined together, bathed in sunshine, bounding up that mountain. Their steps were as though they were in the lighter gravity of the moon instead of the heavier gravity of earth. Now I am back to birds, a metaphor of androgynous roles. We are eagles, we touch base on the mountain, we can fly over it or around it. We can leave it if we choose. We can glide in the thermals, we can dive and soar around the cliffs and crags. We are not anxious when one is ahead, the other behind. We are free of the mountain. We choose to fly together, touching wings, but we are separate beings.

Epilogue

A year has passed since I wrote "Androgyny." There have been many changes since then in our relationship, most visibly a separation. We agreed to help each other in the transition, and to divide everything roughly equally, including custody of our son. So this year, our son is living with his father in Colorado, next year he returns to live with me in Pennsylvania. And I find the separation from my son perhaps the most difficult adjustment of all. Questions to respond to in this epilogue include: Why the separation? and, Does this mean androgynous spousal roles cannot be worked out?

In answer to the first question, I'm not sure I know why we separated in any coherent, explainable fashion. There seem to be many theories and explanations. Basically, I guess we did not find a way to meet some important human needs for comfort, acceptance, and understanding. There was, finally, an unwillingness to risk any more in the relationship with each other.

Does our separation mean that androgyny in marriage cannot work? No. No more than staying together would index that it had worked. Relationships have difficulties, some soluble, some not soluble but tolerable, and some, possibly intolerable. And relationships have a history (as ours was described in my chapter). This very history seems to have obscured the attraction we have for each other, and, with our consent, has precluded a future together. A paradox is that I find he is a person I would be attracted to today if I had just met him.

One way of looking at this paradox is that some of his initially attracting qualities were moderate: a sense of the absurd, a cynicism, a rebelliousness against the Establishment. But extreme, carried out, lived with, they were qualities with which I really was not comfortable even though I probably colluded with him in their expression. My motives were complex, but included a vicarious component: a desire to experiment through him.

I perceive another complexity of motive: a way in which I hid aspects of myself from him, primarily out of fear of receiving his ridicule or anger. Yet I wanted him to accept me, a me he couldn't know because I didn't trust him with that knowledge. I believe I had good reason to hide aspects of myself since early in our relationship he had ridiculed some of these traits I had dared to show and he did betray confidences. (Perhaps I was overly sensitive and too ready to generalize that one or two instances constituted a permanent situation, but I was not willing to chance much again.)

These aspects of myself I refer to are qualities I discovered to be important to me and which I wished to express overtly. More simply there was a thought: if only I am rid of his negative reactions (or him) I can be me. I wanted to have this sense of an integrated self. But I was afraid to try without some sign from him in advance of an unconditional acceptance. There was no advance sign. I lost hope that he would ever welcome and encourage this integration. And I refused to risk trying it in front of him.

In the attempt to carry out the more androgynous roles, I think there was some sabotage by him, perhaps unintentional, but leaving that effect. For example, when I took my turn at cooking or child care he was there to direct it, to control it (or at least to try to control it), so that it seemed I was doing these things for him. He seemed unwilling or unable to take on an outside-the-home worker role. Role reversal seemed to continue and that was not what I wanted. On one level there was agreement by him to carry out my vision of the androgynous roles; but I suspect the fact that it was my vision doomed the experiment from the start. There was something in our relationship, in him, that rebelled against meeting needs I requested him to meet. In some sense, I think he saw me as the Establishment. This situation presented me with an insoluble bind: if I expressed my needs, he refused to meet them, saying he couldn't respond to "demands"; on the other hand, if I refrained from stating my needs, they went unmet through his ignorance (or ignoring, I'm not sure which) of what they were. He did not ask me, nor did he give freely of what I needed.

As individuals, I believe we both can achieve androgynous roles, but not in relation to each other. There was not enough good will, concern for the other, or willingness to risk, not because we didn't have these qualities, but because the history of our relationship, the past, interfered too greatly with the present.

As I pointed out in the chapter, I do not believe that there is a foolproof process or formula for working out a human relationship. The person to listen to is yourself as you experience your relationship. As other people begin their relationships in different places and with different experiences perhaps the androgynous roles will emerge. This process requires much effort, good will and risk, but I hope it can go forward, for others and myself, without overwhelming pain.

REFERENCES

Bem, S. L. "Sex Role Adaptability: One Consequence of Psychological Androgyny." *Journal of Personality and Social Psychology* 31(1975): 634–643.
Spence, J. T., Helmreich, R., and Stapp, J. "Ratings of Self and Peers on Sex Role Attributes and their Relation to Self-Esteem and Conceptions of Masculinity and Femininity." *Journal of Personality and Social Psychology* 32(1975):29–39.
Wheelis, A. *How People Change.* New York: Harper Torchbooks, 1973.

OPEN MARRIAGE

[4]

THE ARTICLES by Knapp and Whitehurst and Wendy and Burt clearly indicate the nonconventional approach to life of individuals involved in open marriages, similar to the backgrounds and approaches of swingers and individuals in group marriages. Like these other groups, those in open marriages showed strong sexual interest early in their lives. Their own marriages seem to be secure and enriched by their experiences. The nagging question that remains is, How select are the samples of Knapp and Whitehurst? Is their present contentment the lot that would befall the majority if they, too, opened their marriages, or do they rather represent a paltry, few survivors of a kind of relationship which would shatter the marriages of the vast majority who tried it? Only further investigation will clarify this issue.

Another notable finding is the absence of signs of bizarre personality in the psychological tests administered to the participants. Although some might imagine that participants in open marriages as described in these pages must be pretty "disturbed" individuals, the data of *these* participants offer no support for such a conclusion. Unconventional, without a doubt, but *different* is not necessarily maladjusted.

Another interesting finding is the fact that women seemed to be the active, dominating figures in these open marriages, whereas the men were more passive. This finding is similar to the personality profiles of men and women in group marriages reported by Constantine and Constantine (1973). Why this should be is uncertain. One possibility is that since men possess more power in our society (Murstein, 1976), the average man, if he inclines toward nonmonogamy, may choose clandestine adultery and the double standard in which the masculine ego is

34

unthreatened; consequently, only in marriages in which the woman is very strong may it be possible for the woman openly to demand and achieve equality. Not surprisingly, such women turn out to be more successful in their extramarital interpersonal ventures than their husbands.

The data, a brief sunshower in a desert of ignorance, only whet our appetites for further information. Is open marriage a mutual venture, or one in which the stronger threatens the weaker with divorce if he (she) doesn't comply? Why is it that open marriage strengthens some marriages and serves as a catalyst for the disintegration of others? Hopefully, the coming decade will answer these and similar questions.

REFERENCES

Constantine, L. L. and Constantine, J. M. *Group Marriage: A Study of Contemporary Multilateral Marriage.* New York: Macmillan, 1973.

Murstein, B. I. *Who Will Marry Whom? Theories and Research in Marital Choice.* New York: Springer Publishing Company, 1976.

Sexually Open Marriage and Relationships: Issues and Prospects

JACQUELYN J. KNAPP AND ROBERT N. WHITEHURST

O CCASIONALLY in the social sciences, researchers exploring a relatively new phenomenon disagree on definitions or descriptive terms, leading to a bewildering multiplicity. Recently we have experienced an overabundance of sometimes confusing terms such as "open marriage," "open-ended relationships," "intimate friendships," "commitment with freedom," "self-fulfillment within marriage," "opening-up marriage," and so on, all referring to certain types of emerging nontraditional interpersonal living styles.

Particularly confusing is the phrase "open marriage," coined by Nena and George O'Neill in their best-selling book (1972). Often misinterpreted, their description of open marriage emphasized role equality and flexibility — a peer relationship — and the potential for each spouse to grow separately rather than suggesting or promoting sexual openness.

While the O'Neills did not recommend outside sex, they did not advise people to avoid it either, maintaining a noncommittal neutral position that extramarital relationships are not integral to open marriage but *may* be included if the couple has the necessary trust, identity, and open communication. Thus, actualized outside sexual relationships are not necessary for the marriage to be "open."

In their research the authors found that almost all respondents equated open marriage with *sexually* open marriage, in which one or both spouses have openly acknowledged independent outside sexual relationships with satellite partners who maintain their own residences. Such patterns usually but do not necessarily develop out of O'Neill-type open marriage, with role flexibility, equality, open communication, trust, etc. existing in varying degrees. When nonlegally married couples agree to have other nonsecret sexual involvements, their arrangement may be referred to as a *sexually open relationship*. The key characteristic of both sexually open marriages and relationships (SOM/R) is a mutual agreement not to be sexually exclusive but to expand the boundaries of emotional, physical, and social relationships to include other people in addition to the primary mate.

The sparse research that exists on either open marriage and relationships (OM/R) or those that are sexually open tends to emphasize couples' sexual behavior and its consequences, a bias not unusual in our sex-obsessed society. This chapter attempts to present and integrate data and implications from two completed studies by the authors on *sexually* open marriage and relationships and to speculate as to the long-term viability of this nontraditional life style.

Whitehurst's Study

Whitehurst (1974), in examining the self-reported living patterns, attitudes, and feelings of couples involved in both SOR and SOM, related a number of social factors to the increasing potential for experimentation with alternative marriage forms, particularly sexually open relationships within and without marriage. As morality becomes increasingly relative, the community no longer has unequivocal answers or sanctioning power over social deviants. There are increases in personal alienation, urban anonymity, individual mobility, and open talk of marital variations and sexual freedom. At the same time we have decreasingly effective social controls through the traditional agents of family, religion, and general community. Forces are no longer squeezing people into preordained life styles, set by outside authorities and sanctioned by these agencies. The resulting normative vacuum allows greater experimentation, reliance on support networks of close friends, and variety-filled living styles, including SOM/R.

Subjects

Through references from others Whitehurst located and gave questionnaires to thirty-five couples, twenty-three legally married and twelve not legally married, who defined their marriages or relationships as sexually open. The data presented are for the total sample, since response patterns for the two groups were not significantly different.

Age of respondents ranged from twenty to sixty-two. Their residences, primarily urban and suburban, were in both Canada and all major geographic regions of the United States. Most respondents were upper-middle-class professionals or career people who were influenced toward SOM/R by the O'Neills' book, Robert Rimmer's novels, liberal friends, therapy groups, and the general dissatisfactions of isolated urban life and conventional marriage. The majority said they were atheists or agnostics, and a significant number were Unitarians or humanists who viewed living a full life as their sacred obligation. Several couples had had limited and brief group marriage experiences. A distinguishing feature of the various life styles was that all outside dating was done on an individual basis.

Respondents saw SOM/R as a compromise way of living which merged freedom to pursue personal growth and autonomy with commitment and security. Rejecting the restrictiveness of traditional marriage, they sought variety, complexity, romance, courtship, and even problems to keep things lively. SOM/R appeared a way to have role equality and structure in ongoing evaluations of gender-role performance.

General Characteristics

As active seekers of utopian ideals and interpersonal complexity, respondents appeared intellectually committed to sexual openness. The complexity sometimes exacted a price in uncertainty, anxiety, and a degree of emotional pain. These were not experienced as totally undesirable, however, since they resulted in high levels of communication, mutual problem solving, and ongoing excitement. Tranquility and even stability in the primary relationship were at times traded for personal growth and ego-enhancement from outside relationships, but the emotional discomfort was associated with growth and positive change, according to a "pleasure-pain formula," and therefore accepted.

In addition to relationship complexities and inevitable anxieties, some other common experiences were significantly increased feelings of self-esteem and an overall positive evaluation of the meaning of SOM/R. Virtually no one had any desire to return to conventional types of relationships. Sexual problems *per se* were relatively rare. Respondents seemed more natural and less rigid in their views of sex, which was considered fun and vital, than conventional persons who might approch sex less playfully. Few sexual double standards were reported, the women's liberation movement being a major influence and impetus for refining gender roles and equal status arrangements.

Women seemed to have an easier time making outside contacts which led to sexual relationships, and as a result they had more outside partners than the men in the sample. Unlike the North American feminine stereotype, these women were not passive or hesitant to express their ideas, needs and goals to men who interested them. The male respondents, in contrast, were more traditional and conservative than the females to begin with and had to do the most changing and adapting to the sexually open life style. In sum, sexual openness was to some extent favored by the female respondents, who appeared to be the primary benefactors.

As the O'Neills suggested, loyalty and fidelity became redefined in terms of relationship primarily rather than mate ownership or exclusivity. With intimacy extended beyond the primary pair, the mate became the *most* significant but not the *only* significant other. The result was a paradoxical situation: The primary bond became simultaneously more *and* less important. Contrary to usual Western-type thinking about love and the experience of polarities, these couples reported a concurrent development of both intensification or closeness and a sense of apartness with the primary other. Whether this occurred as a self-fulfilling prophecy or not is unimportant. They believed the primary bond was enhanced by increased freedom. If they experienced themselves as closer to each other, that was their reality, the validity of which cannot be questioned, even though it challenges our cherished belief that love can be good only with one person at a time.

In light of such unconventional views and behavior, it appeared that judgment of the success or failure of sexually open marriages or relationships cannot be based upon pair longevity or lack of stress, conflict, or confrontation between partners. Instead, success evaluations must be based upon insiders' views in terms of overall self- and couple-satisfaction — especially through enhanced self-feelings and a sense of integration with the larger world.

Problems

The problem most unique to SOM/R seemed to be the limited potential for honest social interaction and friendship beyond the most intimate relationships. Confidants had to be chosen with great care or else there was the risk of exposure and rejection. Many found it painful to have to exclude more conservative friends, relatives, and coworkers from knowledge of the sexually open life style. It was difficult to accept the fact that their views and behavior probably would be rejected within their own larger social networks.

Although none of the couples had formal written contracts outlining their ground rules, all had verbal agreements which required continuous accommodation and renegotiation. Each couple had to work out their own commitments regarding the options available as they related to others and the degree of openness with which they felt comfortable. Reaching agreement often required intense, honest communication and endurance that Whitehurst speculated would be too difficult for many people conventionally reared in a jealous, possessive, male-dominated society.

Jealousy most often involved fear of loss and lingering feelings of possessiveness or desire to control the mate. Though they worked toward equality, occasionally partners discovered they had a different commitment to or involvement in SOM/R which led to conflict, particularly in regard to sharing free time. The partner "left out" might experience resentment and loneliness. This was usually not a serious problem, however, since most respondents had careers, many interests, strong individual lives, and outside partners to occupy free time.

The women complained that their primary male partners or spouses, in spite of generally heightened communication resulting from the life style, sometimes backed away from intense emotional discussions and escaped into work, sports, or all-male activities. In addition, the women often felt that household division of labor wasn't truly equal; that the men lacked motivation to enlarge their share of the everyday tasks; or that the men too frequently had lower standards of neatness and cleanliness.

Sometimes freedom and openness were abused, as in the case of one couple who used outside relationships as a means to escape each other. When the primary relationship bond either was not solidified first or was neglected, and sexual openness was used to try to keep the relationship from falling apart, openness did not work to the benefit of the couple. When a person acted out his or her aggressions and hostilities against a primary partner through an intimate relationship with someone else, the process became destructive rather than liberating.

Whitehurst concluded that SOM/R is not advisable for people who are not emotionally equipped to handle freedom for self and primary others, time alone, complex interrelationships, high intensity communication, or the inevitable struggle of possessiveness versus autonomy.

Benefits

As mentioned, the problems of SOM/R were viewed as inevitable and accepted or tolerated within a framework of personal growth and relationship enrichment. Respondents were enthusiastic in extolling the benefits of the way they lived: Increased openness led to newly discovered feelings about themselves and their relationship to the world; with enhanced self-esteem came increased relationship-esteem and closeness; and as they opened up to new experiences they felt less isolated and more personally fulfilled.

Explicitly or implicitly, many evaluated sexual nonexclusiveness for themselves on the basis of questions such as: Is life more fun, interesting, and varied? Do I feel more zest in living? Most answered yes, though few seemed to succeed in achieving stability in a primary relationship with an ego-satisfying outside relationship. Nevertheless, respondents expressed no regrets at having entered SOM/R, which they continued to see as a viable mode of life. They placed extremely high value on their personal growth experiences and were unwilling to return to or move toward a traditional life style.

Knapp Study

Within the context of rapid cultural change in the visibility and vocality of sexual nonconformists, Knapp (1976) has hypothesized a movement toward increasing rejection of traditional male-female relationships. She conceived of SOM/R as ramifications of our moving, as Robert and Anna Francoeur suggest, from a "hot-sex culture," to a "cool-sex culture."* The traditional hot-sex marriage is closed and typified by rigid roles, unequal statuses, and possessive exclusiveness, while nontraditional cool-sex marriage is open and promises role flexibility, spouse equality, and open companionships.

Knapp (1974, 1975a, 1976) studied seventeen legally married couples who defined their marriages as sexually open. Two initial selection criteria were used: One or both spouses had had or were currently having outside sexual relationships, and, second, they indicated that they preferred independent functioning rather than exchanging partners as in swinging. As the research progressed it became evident that additional characteristics were common across couples: emotional involvement with satellite partners was generally accepted; nonspouse partners lived in their own homes; prospective partners did not have to be selected from certain groups or predetermined populations; and goals such as social and intellectual sharing, personal growth, and increasing one's ability to love and communicate were pursued in addition to sexual pleasure.

Subjects

Knapp's couples, eleven from north-central Florida and six from eastern Kansas, were located primarily through referrals from mutual acquaintances. Everyone contacted to participate in the study agreed to do so. Each respondent answered fifty-one open-ended and forced-choice questions regarding personal history, open marriage attitudes, and sexual experiences. In addition, thirty-one respondents took two personality tests (The Myers-Briggs Type Indicator** and the Clinical Analysis Questionnaire†). Two respondents took only the Myers-Briggs. Because there were no significant areas of difference either in background or sexual experiences and attitudes, results are presented for the total sample rather than the separate Florida and Kansas groupings.

---

*The Francoeurs characterize *hot sex* as "male dominated, double standarded, intercourse-obsessed, property-oriented, and clearly stereotyped in its sexist images and models." *Cool sex* is described as "egalitarian, single standarded, sexually diffused, and oriented towards intimacy and open, synergistic relations with persons" (Francoeur and Francoeur, 1974, pp. 34 and 39).
** I. Myers. *Manual for the Myers-Briggs Type Indicator.* Princeton, N.J.: Educational Testing Service, 1962.
†K. Delhees and R. Cattell. *Manual for the Clinical Analysis Questionnaire.* Champaign, Ill.: 1PAT, 1971.

Respondents, all Caucasians, averaged just over thirty years of age with a range of twenty to forty-eight years. Fifty percent of their occupations, including that of student, were academically related. Annual income varied from $3,000 to $40,000. Everyone had completed high school, seven had some college, seven had bachelor's degrees, nine had master's degrees, one had attended law school, one was a physician, and four had Ph.D.s. Eighteen were oldest children in their families of origin, and five were single children. The majority reported having no particular religious beliefs in the traditional sense, though they described themselves as concerned with spiritual aspects of being. Ninety-four percent of the females and 88 percent of the males reported having sexual intercourse prior to marriage. Ten of the couples had a combined total of nineteen children, ages two to fifteen. Length of marriage ranged from one to twenty-two years, ten couples having been married from one to five years and four couples between eleven and fifteen years. Five males and two females had been previously married and divorced. Five couples had participated in marriage counseling. Outside sexual relationships had been one of several difficulties leading to counseling for six people, with only one female indicating that it had been the primary problem for which she sought help.

Sexual Behavior Pattern

All of the wives and fifteen of the seventeen husbands had been or were currently involved in open outside sexual relationships. In eleven of the seventeen couples the wife was first to have outside sexual experience, and in three additional instances she was responsible for arranging a shared first outside experience together with her husband and close <u>friends</u>.

Wives again prevailed in the extent of outside activity, having eighty-one satellite partners or 57 percent of the combined total while their spouses had sixty partners, 43 percent of the total. The women had more satellite relationships in nine of the marriages, husbands had more in five instances, and three couples had the same number of outside partners. When one partner had considerably more outside contacts than the spouse had, there tended to be more stress in the marital relationship. In one instance when the wife was sexually active outside and the husband had no other relationships it led to severe marital strain based on the husband's fear of impending loss. In a similar situation, however, the husband agreed with his wife's views of marriage and simply felt too busy himself at that time to get involved in comarital complexities.

About two-thirds of the sample, males and females equally, had primarily experienced deep friendship or affection with their satellite partners; eight additional persons stated their most common experience had been sex with love. Length of relationships varied from a month or less of active sexual involvement to one or two years or more, seventeen people describing long-term relationships with varying degrees of personal commitment to the nonspouse partners.

Most couples emphasized that they did not have to share all the details, thoughts, or feelings about the additional relationships, though they were strongly against lying to the spouse or withholding information when asked for it. They also stressed the importance of treating outside partners, who were sometimes very "inside" in importance, with about the same respect, care, and concern they tried to show the spouse. It was not unusual for spouses and outside partners to get together to discuss problems or mutual interests or engage in joint decision making.

The respondents' children were mostly under ten years of age. Perhaps because their parents' nontraditional marital style was not very visible, they had not raised any questions that would indicate worry or even curiosity about what their parents were doing when they went out or had friends over. Respondents did emphasize that they wanted to share their feelings and beliefs about marriage as soon as the children were mature enough to understand the deliberate rejection of traditional values and standards, but they had not yet done so.

Ground Rules

Informal verbal contracts seemed to evolve as problem areas developed, though three couples had agreed upon sexually open marriage contracts before marriage. The "rule" with the highest priority was honesty in relationships, followed by acceptance of emotional involvements that did not interfere or compete with the primary marital relationship, and freedom for each spouse to pursue separate interests. In addition, couples had explicit expectations regarding the need for discretion, time sharing, and avoidance of potentially stressful outside relationships, such as those with a close relative of the spouse, with someone obviously emotionally disturbed, or with persons themselves involved in disruptive marriages. It was highly desired that spouses or primary mates of outside partners know and approve of the additional relationship, as usually was the case. Maintaining secret relationships and investing energy in clandestine meetings were generally unaccept- able and even repulsive to the respondents, who repeatedly stressed the value of openness in living one's convictions.

Fourteen couples had agreed to a flexible, non gender-based role structure in the family. Household tasks were either performed by those who especially enjoyed doing them or were rotated. Three couples by mutual choice followed traditional divisions of labor, these wives seem- ing to prefer such an arrangement and not feeling it had been "forced" upon them.

Advantages and Disadvantages

The most frequently reported benefits included: better fulfill- ment of personal needs; the excitement of new experiences, both social and sexual, leading to feelings of increased vitality and enjoyment of sex with the spouse; an eventual lessening of jealousy and possessiveness; freedom and security together; and the opportunity to be fully oneself with no further need for role playing.

Seven respondents could think of no particular disadvantages of SOM as they were living it. Others mentioned jealousy; time-sharing problems; occasional resentment over the importance of an outside partner that had resulted from differing expectations of the various people involved; difficulty finding private meeting places; and living with the realization that one's beliefs or behavior might be threatening or offensive to significant others with differing values.

Twenty-two respondents reported increased satisfaction with their marriages after becoming involved in SOM. Four said there had been no significant changes (things were OK before and OK now), and one husband felt decreased satisfaction. For three couples the question of increased or decreased satisfaction was not applicable since they had decided to have sexually open marriages prior to marriage. Twenty- seven stated they had no desire to return to sexual monogamy and that for them being unmarried might be a better alternative than traditional marriage.

Motivations

Twenty-nine persons indicated that they preferred SOM be- cause it enabled them to live their personal philosophies or beliefs. Almost as many said it helped them to meet unfulfilled emotional/

physical/intellectual/social needs and as a result to reduce pressures in the marital relationship. Since two people can never hope to satisfy all of each other's needs directly related to happiness and well-being, they reasoned that outside relationships (social or sexual) have the potential to relieve pressure within the marriage and provide a broader base for need-fulfillment and happiness. To them marriage which excluded meaningful intimacy with anyone else in the world simply did not make sense. With only two exceptions, respondents' awareness of unmet needs and acceptance of a definite philosophy of SOM preceded their outside sexual involvement. This philosophical acceptance was followed by varying degrees of emotional acceptance and intellectual-emotional integration. Manufacturing a philosophy to rationalize already accomplished sexual behavior was not typical of this group.

Personality Factors

Contrary to some mental health professionals' opinions that persons engaging in extramarital sexual activity are acting out or displacing hostilities or narcissistic needs or that they are neurotic, immature, promiscuous, maritally maladjusted or psychopathically deviant in addition to sexually inadequate or aberrant, Knapp (1974) found that on the basis of their scores on the Clinical Analysis Questionnaire her respondents as a group could not be judged as significantly more neurotic, antisocial, or personality disordered than the general population of the United States. If anything, they were less neurotic and anxiety-prone and more self-assured and nondefensive.

More important in descriptive terms were the results of the Myers-Briggs Type Indicator (MBTI). In brief, the MBTI is a self-report personality inventory which elicits preferences on four dichotomies: Extroversion-Introversion (E-I), Sensing-Intuition (S-I), Thinking-Feeling (T-F), and Judging Perceptive (J-P). The end result is a "type" of four letters, one from each dichotomy, with corresponding descriptions for each of the sixteen major categories and their subdivisions (Myers, 1962).

Since MBTI data from the seventeen SOM couples are presented in detail elsewhere (Knapp, 1974, 1975b), a brief summary will suffice here. Seventy-two percent of the sample fell into one of three categories: the extroverted intuitive (ENFP, 39 percent), the introverted intuitive (INTJ, 18 percent), and the introverted feeling type (INFP, 15 percent). The preference that all three of those types have in common is intuition (N). Intuitives tend to be individualistic, independent, oriented toward possibilities, high academic achievers, creative, nonconforming, stimulated by complexity and chaos, initiating, inventive, relatively indifferent to what others say and do, imaginative at the expense of observation, and willing to sacrifice present realities for future possibilities. While estimations place the number of intuitives in the general population at about 25 percent, they made up 88 percent of the sample, most closely resembling standardization groups of highly creative artists (Myers, 1962).

The majority of respondents also chose feeling over thinking (i.e., preferring to make judgments on the basis of personal values rather than impersonal logic) and perceptive over judging (i.e., being open, spontaneous, and adaptable rather than exacting, critical, and decisive). They were fairly well balanced between extroverts and introverts, unlike the general population which supposedly has about 75 percent extroverts. Extroversion-introversion was found to be statistically unrelated to initiation of the first outside sexual activity, though gender of the initiator, female, was highly significant. Interaction of the two variables, E-I and gender, was also found to be insignificant.

Based upon a composite of the group's predominant characteristics as indicated by their MBTI preferences, we can hypothesize a modal type, of person who is more inclined to try SOM. Such persons would be imaginative; future-oriented; individualistic; willing to take risks to explore possible new ways of relating to others; caring little for convention; and willing to defend personal views and values with determination. Open to new experiences, they would tend to use enthusiasm and idealism to influence others. Rather than being destructively antisocial or lacking in social conscience, they would be deliberately nonconforming, variant rather than deviant, and socially innovative. While not as concerned about socially prescribed morality as the average person, they would be strong believers in their personal ethical systems. If current trends persist, such persons would be females more often than males.

If further research upholds the personality trends observed in this small sample, then certain types of people indeed might be attracted to SOM and be more able to manage such a complex life style successfully.

Overview of the Two Studies

While the results of these two early studies obviously cannot be generalized to a larger population, they are of considerable value in attempting to acquire a descriptive handle on sexually open marriages and relationships. The combined sample of 104 respondents, 40 married and 12 unmarried but pair-bonded couples from across the United States and Canada, provide quite homogeneous data in regard to the participants' backgrounds, motivations, experiences, insights, values, problems and hopes for the future, and rejection of traditional monogamous marriage.

Based upon these data, the authors hypothesize that two polar types of couples may be attracted to a sexually open life style: (1) those who have high levels of conflict and dissatisfaction in their primary relationships and either are divorce-bound or searching for an alternative to divorce, and (2) those who have established and are maintaining strong, stable, primary relationships in which there is a high degree of mutual affection, respect, understanding, and agreement regarding choice of life style.

The high-conflict, stressful marriages, a minority in the sample, usually had one spouse, most often the wife, who wanted a sexually open, nontraditional arrangement while the husband preferred a less extreme, more traditional relationship socially and/or sexually. One such husband expressed his preference for "good old-fashioned uncomplicated secret affairs" and found his wife's openness emotionally difficult to handle. In most of the stressful marriages there was also an intellectual-emotional split in acceptance of SOM—in their heads they totally agreed with the philosophy and *wanted* it to work for them, but emotionally their gut-level reactions were fear, anger, and resentment. Role strain and basic personality conflicts, perhaps aggravated by the additional pressure of outside relationships, were also evident, as in one couple where the husband was a traditionalist and strong intuitive thinking type while his wife was a sensing-feeling type who believed strongly in sexual freedom.

As an interesting aside, Knapp received referrals to six couples as potential participants from a colleague in a northern Florida city. Before she could arrange to meet with them and administer the questionnaires, most of the couples had separated and were filing for divorce. Had they become involved in the study they might have provided valuable data about divorce-bound couples and their involvement in SOM. As Whitehurst noted earlier, SOM as a Band-Aid usually did not succeed in holding an already shaky marriage together, and if the relationship were fragile or immature to begin with SOM may very well have been the catalyst that blasted it apart.

The majority of the marriages were relatively satisfactory, low-conflict ones, and some could be labeled exemplary. The latter couples conveyed a sparkle and extraordinary vitality along with other common characteristics: (1) mutual devotion; (2) the ability to integrate outside relationships with the primary one so that each seemed to benefit the others; (3) facility in expressing a cogent philosophy of SOM; (4) nearly equal social/sexual involvement of both spouses in outside relationships; (5) an equal conviction of the rightness of SOM for them so that one spouse did not have to exert pressure on the others to accept a nontraditional marriage; and (6) achievement of intellectual-emotional integration with relative ease. When SOM seemed most successful, the couples had not reshaped themselves to fit a nonmonogamous marriage style, since it suited them as they already were. Prime examples are the couples in which at least one of the spouses had been previously married and resolved never to have a traditional marriage again, forming their open-marriage contracts before the second marriage.

Sexually open marriage appeared to be especially attractive and beneficial to the women in both samples for a number of stated reasons: (1) They acquired essentially equal social/sexual rights with the men, eliminating the usual double standard; (2) The threat of secret affairs was virtually eliminated, and open outside relations were seen as much less threatening to family stability and integration since the noninvolved mate retained some input and control; (3) Role structures tended to become flexible so that the women no longer were solely responsible for household maintenance and child care; (4) Having independent outside relationships allowed them to adjust their own social and sexual paces, which often exceeded those of the males; (5) Each person was able to express affection to and receive affection from more sources, a need the women said was often unfulfilled to some extent in their primary relationships; and (6) There was some relief that they no longer had to be the only persons required to satisfy all of their mates' needs. Being the primary initiators and beneficiaries of SOM/R, women thus tended to invest more interest and energy in nourishing and maintaining their nontraditional life styles than the males, who had relinquished some of their traditional advantages.

Both researchers were struck with the efforts of each couple in their respective samples to achieve a harmonious balance between commitment to the primary relationship and freedom to function independently and experience others outside the primary relationship. Knowing this was a thin line to walk, respondents nevertheless persisted in their search for the best of both worlds, convinced that marriage or nonmarital commitment need not be a social or emotional prison.

Future Outlook

Predictions about the future for SOM/R or any other kind of nontraditional living style must be based upon current trends and consideration of long-term changes in the social climate.

According to the 1970 U.S. Census (Ramey, 1975), there is evidence that both males and females are postponing first marriages. At the same time divorces have doubled since 1965, the current rate in Florida being 66 percent, and the number of nonmarried cohabitors in the U.S. is probably well over six million. With 35 percent of the adult population single, widowed, divorced, or separated, and 60 percent of all married women employed full-time outside the home, only about 18 percent of the population remain in traditional nuclear families, the institutionalized norm in our society. Another ideal, backed by legal sanctions, is sexually monogamous marriage, though evidence would indicate that in actual practice the majority of marriages are non-monogamous (Kinsey, 1948; Gebhard, 1969). Thus, since the end of World War II we have slowly shifted away from our unquestioning adherence to a monolithic value system regarding marital and family behavior and moved toward increasing pluralism or other choices and more freedom in making those choices.

As this trend continues, Whitehurst's earlier observations of a normative vacuum resulting in increased experimentation and variety become even more salient. Given the current trend toward greater variety in marriage and relationship styles, the prominence of SOM/R among all the various alternative styles must be evaluated and then weighed against traditional marriage, which still prevails in the public image as the ideal or prototype.

Whitehurst sees male-female inequality and closed monogamy as still being deeply entrenched in our society by early socialization and custom. Only a select minority of people can presently tolerate negative sanctions, imposed by middle-class morality, and complex interpersonal stresses. The need exists for considerably more network support through positive sanctions of law, customs, and community acceptance before SOM becomes more stable and functional. There are indicators, however, especially in the larger cities, that societal barriers may gradually be giving way. With increased visibility and success rates lending support to the viability of SOM, it may eventually become a more prevalent form for a greater segment of the upper middle class. At present, however, it is not seen as likely to replace secret affairs as the favored mode of extramarital sex for the majority of people engaged in nonmonogamous marriage, or to be any more important than a number of other unconventional marriage adaptations.

Knapp, in contrast, hypothesizes an increasingly important role for OM and SOM among other alternative styles and in opposition to traditional marriage based upon two of her research conclusions: (1) that more and more women are finally expressing their dissatisfaction with conventional marriage and taking the lead in establishing marriages based upon role equality with options for open outside relationships if desired, and (2) that people with certain definable types of personality are discovering that SOM especially fits their needs and personal philosophies of living. Given our social climate of rapid change and situational morality, it would seem that those who have been square pegs jammed into the round holes of traditional marriage are better able now than ever before to find appropriate reference and membership groups to support their marriage experimentation. Following the emergence of women's liberation, gay liberation, black power, Chicano power, and the American Indian movement, perhaps the next move out of the closet will be the marriage liberation movement!

Among the many alternate life styles, including swinging, group marriages, singlehood, single parenthood, homosexual unions, communal families, cohabitation, and aggregate marriages, open marriage with options for satellite sexual relationships would seem more viable than many others simply based on practicality. For example, group marriage and communal living both require a pooling of resources, an adequately large but low-profile residence, and extremely complex accommodation to the needs and idiosyncrasies of others who are physically present in the household or commune. Swinging, in the group party sense, requires considerable organization and a tolerance for exhibitionism and voyeurism. Homosexual marriages have a certain visibility, and they risk both legal and community sanctions, still bearing the stigma of sexual perversion and mental illness. In comparison, sexually open marriages have very low visibility, do not require special living arrangements, and are based upon the intactness of the marital unit. Children remain under the primary influence of their parents, and outside relationships may be formed and dissolved without major upsets in living arrangements or property settlements. When it works well, participants combine the security and specialness of the marital commitment with the freedom and individuality required for self-actualization. For these reasons and more, Knapp believes that SOM may become one of the most viable of alternatives.

How does this alternative measure against the heavy forces of traditional, male-dominated, publically monogamous marriage? At present, convention prevails, backed by the religious and educational superstructure of society. Futurists are predicting radical changes in those social forces, however, as technology and population bring about unthought-of changes and adaptations in an increasing spiral. This process may leave marriage as we have known it in a state of relative chaos for some time to come, but out of chaos can emerge diversity and perhaps tolerance for differences. It may not be too iconoclastic to predict increasing openness in alternative living styles with sexually open marriages in the vanguard—while simultaneously realizing that predictability itself has become unpredictable, and the future is anybody's fantasy.

REFERENCES

Francoeur, A., and Francoeur, R. *Hot and Cool Sex: Cultures in Conflict.* New York: Harcourt, Brace, Jovanovich, 1974.

Gebbard, P. In Hunt, M., *The Affair.* New York: World, 1969.

Kinsey, A., Pomeroy, W., and Martin, C. *Sexual Behavior in the Human Male.* Philadelphia: Saunders, 1948.

Knapp, J. *Co-Marital Sex and Marriage Counseling: Sexually "Open" Marriage and Related Attitudes and Practices of Marriage Counselors.* Doctoral Dissertation, University of Florida, 1974. Ann Arbor, Mich.: University Microfilms, #79–19, 352.

Knapp, J. "An Exploratory Study of Seventeen Sexually Open Marriages." *Journal of Sex Research* 12 (1976): 206–19.

Knapp, J. "Some Non-Monogamous Marriage Styles and Related Attitudes and Practices of Marriage Counselors." *The Family Coordinator* 24(1975): 505–14.(a)

Knapp, J. "The Myers-Briggs Type Indicator as a Basis for Personality Description of Spouses in Sexually Open Marriage." Paper presented at the First National Conference on the Uses of the MBTI, Gainesville, Fla., October, 1975.(b)

Myers, I. *Manual for the Myers-Briggs Type Indicator.* Princeton, N.J.: Educational Testing Service, 1962.

O'Neill, N., and O'Neill, G. *Open Marriage.* New York: Evans, 1972.

Ramey, J. "Legal Regulation of Personal and Family Lifestyles." Paper presented at the Fourth International Conference of the Unity of the Sciences, New York, November, 1975.

Whitehurst, R. "Open Marriage: Problems and Prospects." Paper presented at the annual meeting of the National Council on Family Relations, St. Louis, October, 1974.

Our Open Marriage

A CCORDING to the O'Neills in their book *Open Marriage*,* an open marriage has the following qualities: Living for now, realistic expectations, privacy, open and honest communication, flexibility in roles, open companionship, equality, identity, and trust. We feel that our marriage has all of these qualities so we consider it an open marriage.

The O'Neills believe that couples with open marriages should decide whether or not to be open to outside sexual relationships. We faced that issue long before we were married and agreed that we did not want to put any restrictions on each other's relationships with other people. We valued the kind of growth possible through intimate relationships with others and didn't want to limit such growth.

So the term "open marriage" has two meanings when applied to us. The first is in the sense the O'Neills use the term—having the qualities described in the first paragraph above. The second sense is the way the term is used in Jacquelyn Knapp's chapter: being open to sexual relationships with other people. In this paper we are going to focus on the kinds of experiences we've had as a result of being open to sexual relationships with others. But we want to emphasize at the beginning that our interest is in *relationships* with others, rather than just *sex* with others. Our search is for intimacy, caring, and love—all of which can, but don't necessarily, involve sex. In this we differentiate our open marriage from old-fashioned swinging, where the focus was on sex devoid of deep emotions.

We met at a large midwestern university where Burt majored in

*Nena O'Neill and George O'Neill. *Open Marriage*. New York: Evans, 1972.

52

psychology and Wendy majored in education. During our courtship, we spent many dates in coffeeshops discussing books, ideas, and ourselves. One of our favorite types of discussion would begin with a "What if. . ." For example: "What if we get married someday, and then I find I want to have an affair with someone. How would you feel about that?" Neither of us could ever think of any objections we'd have. We just didn't anticipate feeling jealous. Our love grew slowly from casual friendship to deep friendship to romance. After a couple of years, we just moved in together to see how we felt about living with each other.

Our discussions about relationships took on deeper meaning as we became "a couple" in our thinking and in the eyes of our friends. We encountered the books of Robert Rimmer and really devoured them. His ideas—especially in *The Harrad Experiment* and *Proposition 31*— were exciting and made a great deal of sense to us. The more we read and talked, the more natural it seemed to love more than one person at a time. In fact, at the time we were falling in love with each other, we were each in love with another person. And somehow, that never bothered either of us or seemed at all unnatural. These other relationships, however, were never very intense and they faded into the background of our lives as we got to know each other.

We began discussing our ideas with friends, and found a number of them who were thinking along the same lines. We'd get together for casual evenings talking about all the possibilities of group marriage and nonexclusive love.

We had a golden opportunity to develop our ideas when a local mental health center, which was sponsoring discussion groups on marriage, decided to have one on group marriage. We knew the discussion leader, and we signed up along with some interested friends. So there we all were, around a conference table, with a video tape camera whirring so the psychiatrists could analyze our thinking on the subject. And we explored topics like possessiveness, jealousy, sex, and children. As the formal discussion series came to an end, our group had become close, so we decided to meet together every Saturday evening for a pot luck dinner and further exploration of group marriage. At first, our meetings were exciting as we fantasized about a glorious future as one big family. But problems started early. Some members wanted to start looking for a house immediately; others became uptight if they saw their spouse with an arm around another person. So one by one, couples and individuals dropped out of the group and it fizzled to an end.

After living together on and off for a couple of years, we talked more and more seriously about getting married. We felt under considerable pressure since we were both teaching school in small midwestern communities and knew that the discovery of our cohabitation would jeopardize our jobs. For Burt to lose his job would have meant the end of his draft deferment. Although Burt wanted to get married, Wendy had some doubts. She feared that institutionalizing the relationship might cause it to stagnate, but she was concerned about Burt's draft deferment and the deteriorating relationship with her parents since they had learned of the cohabitation. So after many hours of discussing what marriage would mean for us, we made the big decision.

We wrote our own ceremony and included in it phrases understood only by us which said that we would not have an exclusive or monogamous marriage. We had our minister say to us: "I ask if you can use your love not to create your own world, but to expand it, and never allow it to become exclusive, but rather a center core from which your love will extend outward to life and all of humanity." And in the ring exchange: "These rings are the symbol of unity, in which your two lives are now joined in one unbroken circle, in which wherever you go, you will always return unto the other to find your whole selves. Yet the ring is opened at the sides—symbolizing the expansion and growth of your union." To us, these lines meant that we would be a solid base of love and support for each other, from which we could venture out to explore life, love, and sex if we chose. We considered ourselves free as individuals. Our marriage was to us no greater commitment than our cohabitation had been. It was not a promise to love each other forever, but rather a statement that we loved each other today. It was not a promise to be together tomorrow; only a statement that we wanted to be together today. To us, it was a base from which we could grow in whatever individual direction we chose. As long as we each grew in roughly the same direction, we felt we would be together. And that's exactly what has happened during the first five years of our marriage.

On that wedding day in June of 1970, we were hoping to form a group marriage with another couple in the coming few years. We felt that the love and warmth and excitement between us was too good to keep to ourselves; it was too powerful not to allow it to grow and include others. After a summer of traveling, we settled down to life in the midwest. Burt was still teaching school, and Wendy was working on a master's degree. Many of our old friends were around, and discussions of group marriage and sex continued.

Our movement toward nonmonogamy began gradually. A turning point occurred on a friend's waterbed. We had invited two single friends over to dinner and they really hit it off. Later, the fellow invited us all over to his place to see his new waterbed. After jumping around on it for awhile, our two friends started slowly making love. At first, we felt a little awkward, but then decided to do the same. So we made love next to them, while we all bounced gently together on the waterbed. Afterward, we all felt warm and close to each other. We realized that if we had theorized about how it would be to make love next to friends, we would have talked for months and probably never would have gotten around to doing it. But because it just happened spontaneously, nothing could seem more natural or lovely.

Not long after the incident, we each decided to work toward Ph. D.'s, and were accepted by a large eastern university. So we moved to the east coast in 1971; Burt to study psychology, and Wendy, education. After our first year in our new home, we were feeling especially lonely. We hadn't found anyone interested in the concept of group marriage and neither had we developed any intimate friendships. After three years of supposedly open marriage we were still monogamous in practice. We were becoming increasingly curious to experience sex with other people. Our premarital sexual experiences had been pretty much limited to each other. Now we were wondering what we might have missed.

We had originally sought only a group marriage, and had totally rejected the idea of casual sex or swinging. But now the thought of using swinging to develop intimate friendships became more appealing. We finally came to the conclusion that swinging might be fun to try and at least would be an interesting experience. But we lacked the courage to make contacts by means of a swinging magazine or bar. Just at this time we learned of an organization that matched people with similar interests, including people who were swinging.

We contacted the matching service and were given the names of Jan and Ron, who had been swinging for twelve years. We arranged to have lunch together, and were pleased to learn that they were rather disillusioned with swinging and were seeking deeper relationships. We all seemed compatible, with similar values and interests. The next weekend we went out to dinner with Jan and Ron, and the following weekend they invited us to dinner at their house. We felt rather nervous, thinking that this might be the time when we would change partners for sex. The question of sex had produced a slight tension among the four of us, since we all expected it to happen eventually, but no one wanted to push it. That evening we did change partners, with the whole thing starting fairly spontaneously. We stayed at Jan and Ron's the entire night, and had a relaxed and happy breakfast with them late the next morning.

As we drove home, happy but exhausted from lack of sleep, we talked over the experience. For Wendy it had been sensuous and exciting. The touch of a new sex partner had generated an excitement and passion she hadn't expected. And she found Ron a fascinating person whom she wanted to know better. Burt had similar feelings. He and Jan had spent much of the night talking as well as making love, and he felt very close to her. He seemed to be falling in love with Jan as well as feeling a tremendous sexual attraction toward her.

During the following weeks, we got together with Jan and Ron often, sometimes as a foursome, and sometimes as separate "cross-couples." Ron and Wendy had long lunches and afternoon swims. They discussed themselves and the feelings that were developing between them. Burt and Jan neglected their work to be together as often as possible. Occasionally the four of us went to a concert together, or had dinner, or just discussed how things were going.

Almost from the beginning, there were some problems to work out. For example, Wendy felt uneasy because she saw Burt and Jan becoming intimate faster than she and Ron were. She feared that she and Ron might push their own relationship along too fast, trying to keep up with Burt and Jan. After a long talk on the subject, Wendy and Ron realized that they were each slow to trust others, slow to open up, and slow to develop relationships. Burt and Jan, on the other hand, felt a burning intensity in their relationship. Like the most naive and romantic of new lovers, they couldn't get enough of each other. The four of us finally decided that both relationships should proceed independently, each at its own level and pace.

But during the first few weeks, the problems were rather minor. We seemed to be developing an intimacy and honesty with Ron and Jan that we had never before experienced with another couple. After such a short time, the four of us felt like old friends. The feelings of affection developing among us seemed as if they would keep growing forever. And the strangest thing was how natural it all felt. Although we realized that the rest of the world would probably consider us crazy or immoral, we could only see four people who were coming to care for each other very much.

The excitement we felt during those weeks has yet to be duplicated.

Since that time, we have been intimate with other couples. But with Jan and Ron it was our first time, and we were starry-eyed and naive. We could see no major problems, and no reason why our intimacy and closeness would not continue to grow into a group marriage, with the four of us living together in bliss.

Only a few weeks elapsed before we noticed a crack in the façade of our dream castle. Burt and Jan were developing severe problems in communicating with each other. It produced mutual hostility, with long periods of silence between the two of them. The four of us had many long late-night discussions trying to understand why Burt and Jan were having so many problems with each other. The conflicts between the two of them were maddeningly complex and seemed to grow worse and worse. At the same time, Wendy and Ron were falling deeper and deeper in love and feeling increasingly frustrated that their spouses couldn't get along. Finally, Burt and Jan broke up completely, with deep mutual feelings of resentment. None of us ever quite understood why Burt and Jan could not get along and after many discussions on the topic labeled it a "personality conflict."

By this time, Wendy and Ron were very much in love, and continued to see each other for many months. Ron had a very difficult time, for Jan resented his continued involvement with Wendy. For a while Ron drifted away from Wendy to try and work out his own marital problems. Today, Wendy and Ron are still good friends.

The experience with Jan and Ron was extremely important to our growth both as individuals and as a couple. We felt emotionally drained afterward, but absolutely convinced that we wanted to continue an open life style. We also became much more realistic about the problems that outside relationships entail. Because we often see other people as either fearful about sexually open marriage, or else over-eager, with unrealistic expectations and fantasies, we want to discuss in some detail what we learned from our first extramarital encounter.

First, there were many unexpected joys. There was an intrinsic excitement in starting a new romantic affair. Even though our own marriage was very warm, loving, and satisfying, it had taken on a comfortable routine. Our new relationships brought back the thrill of youthful romance. If all of one's close relationships are established and secure, one can feel a lack of challenge and freshness. But if all of one's relationships are new and unsettled, one can feel insecure and emotionally overtaxed. We felt that the ideal situation for us included both the old relationship between us and a new one. To have the security and comfort of each other, plus a new, more fluid romance, gave us the best of both worlds.

Despite all the problems, we found the challenge of a four-way relationship irresistible. There was so much activity occurring simultaneously that our skills at relating were stretched and strengthened. After settled years with each other, and rather casual socializing with most of our friends, the challenge of intimate and intense relating was invigorating.

Perhaps the most important reward of outside relationships was the great deal we each learned about ourselves. We viewed ourselves reflected through the eyes of another, and noticed things we hadn't seen before. We found aspects of ourselves being drawn out by our new partners, aspects which had previously lain dormant. Sides of our personalities that seldom came into play in our own interaction were rediscovered. Burt, for example, experienced "Burt-with-Jan" and, by comparing this facet of himself with "Burt-with-Wendy," learned more about his potentialities and limitations. Thus, our self-concepts widened and deepened through our intimacy with others. We had never felt that two people could provide for all of each other's needs, and actually having an opportunity to meet more needs through outside relationships, as well as meeting the outside partner's needs, increased our awareness of what our own needs really were.

Just as we both grew as individuals, we also grew as a couple. We discovered things about our interaction together that we had never noticed. As we were each challenged in our new relationship, we turned to each other with greater energy and interest. It seemed that the more we loved, the more loving we had to share. And our sex life improved enormously. It became recharged with an intensity and excitement that had not been present for a long time.

But in addition to realizing the rewards of an open marriage, we matured and became more realistic about the pains of this life style. We understood at first hand the problems one must struggle with. We had few problems with each other, but many with our new friends. And the difficulties were of a far more complex nature than anything we had ever experienced. Each of us had to work out a relationship with our new partner, as well as with our partner's spouse. In addition, we each had to deal with any problems between the two of us. Thus, in a two-couple situation, there are three relationships in which each person is directly involved. In addition, each individual must contend with three other relationships of which she/he is not a part. For example, Wendy had to be sensitive to what was happening between Burt and Jan, between Burt and Ron, and between Jan and Ron.

Another problem we encountered was a great demand on our time. Even more serious, however, was the enormous drain on our emotions. The emotional investment is something that people considering an open life style should carefully consider. We both suffered hurt feelings in our relationships with Jan and Ron. We were upset by many things that were said and implied during our difficult days of adjusting to them. But we felt that we had chosen to risk pain as well as joy. We grew from our outside relationships more than we ever could have from monogamy. We continue to risk being hurt because we see pain as a frequent accompaniment of growth. Also, the hurt is lessened by always having the security of each other to return to. People starting from an insecure primary relationship or who are very vulnerable emotionally, however, have a lot to lose from outside involvements.

We also learned the difference between fantasy and reality. Prior to actually experiencing a sexually open marriage, our imaginations were filled with romantic fantasies. In reality, open marriage seemed very natural — just people relating to other people. It was like the rest of life — a mixture of joy and pain.

We've continued to live our open life style in the two years since meeting Jan and Ron. We've become close to several couples, with one couple in particular — Larry and Jennifer — remaining close friends for the entire two years. We met them just as Burt and Jan were breaking up. Our new relationship entailed many problems, many struggles, and many hard times. But we were also able to conduct it with greater maturity. We understood the importance of bringing problems out into the open early and discussing them. The major problems with Larry and Jennifer were the kinds of problems encountered in any intimate relationship — just learning how to get along with another person. We were less naively romantic—less in love with love. We allowed our emotions to grow more slowly and evenly, without the crises and midnight encounter sessions that had come to characterize our relationship with Jan and Ron. We're still close to Larry and Jennifer but we live many miles apart now. We learned more about ourselves from this relationship; we grew as individuals and as a couple.

We have also been involved in separate intimate relationships, with each of us finding our own lovers independently. One advantage of separate outside relationships is the ease of finding a compatible individual compared to finding a compatible couple. Also, relationships between two people are likely to be far less complicated than relationships among four people.

Our separate outside relationships, however, have posed some problems which were not as serious in four-way relationships. Jealousy (e.g., Burt not wanting Wendy to have an outside relationship) has occasionally been a minor problem. But when jealous feelings arose in one of us, the other was always so responsive that just talking over the feelings was sufficient to eliminate them. Envy (e.g., Burt wanting to have a relationship like the one Wendy had) was more of a problem. When one of us had no outside relationship, or had a less satisfying relationship than the other, she/he often felt envious.

Logistics were another problem. Finding a time and place to be alone with our lover was often a hassle. We sometimes felt a bit awkward when both of us were in the same apartment with one of our lovers. Burt, for example, would feel that Wendy and her lover wanted to be alone but would also feel left out if he were not included in their interaction.

Another difficulty was that often our lovers or potential lovers wanted a different kind of relationship than we did. Married people were usually interested in secret affairs. Single people, on the other hand, were often looking for a primary relationship, rather than a secondary one.

Comparing our responses to our outside lovers has been very interesting. Burt has always met Wendy's partners, and vice-versa. However, Burt has not always cared for Wendy's lovers, nor Wendy for Burt's. "What in the world does she see in *him?*" was a question that often went through our minds. At first, these differing tastes were a bit disconcerting. Then we realized it was only natural for Burt to be attracted to women who could fulfill different needs and desires than Wendy could, and likewise for Wendy's attractions.

With any open extramarital relationship, whether involving couples or individuals, we have experienced a number of general problems. First is simply how to meet other people interested in open relationships. One possibility is to try to find swingers who are actually interested in relationships, with sex being of secondary importance. Some of our most satisfying relationships were with people we have contacted through swinging bars or magazines, but who certainly did not fit the stereotype of the sex-obsessed swinger. Another approach is to simply move your "straight" friendships in the direction of greater and greater intimacy. Many people are very frightened of intimacy, however, especially physical intimacy. We have had several couples whom we had grown close to begin to back away when we started talking about group marriage or open marriage. Finally, there do exist several support groups for people interested in alternative relationship styles. These groups include Future Families of the World (FFW) in Washington, D. C., The Harrad Community in San Francisco, and Family Synergy, with branches across the country.

Support groups such as these are very helpful in meeting another general problem in open relationships, namely, where to go for help. There are no cultural norms or models for open relationships, and people contemplating or living such a life style often feel lost and confused about what they really want. Yet few psychotherapists or marriage counselors are sympathetic to the concept of extramarital openness. People in open relationships share with gay people the stigma of being labeled sick merely because they are deviant.

Because they are viewed as sick or immoral, and because most people in monogamous relationships consider openness a threat, people in open marriages are often very concerned about privacy. Loss of jobs or social ostracism can result from revealing one's open life style to the wrong people. Realistic discretion can sometimes be carried to extremes of paranoia. People in open relationships often feel isolated from their monogamous friends, from whom an important part of their lives must remain hidden.

Because there are no generally accepted ethical standards for nonmonogamous relationships, each couple must develop their own. Our own personal guidelines have evolved through our experiences, and are always subject to revision. About a year ago we attempted to put our moral standards into words. These four principles are ideals which we try to live up to, but don't always succeed:

1. *Autonomy.* Neither of us has the right to put demands on the other. Where we disagree, we go off separately in our individual ways. Or we try to compromise in ways that don't leave one of us resentful. If neither of these ways will work on an important issue, an ultimate resolution would be ending the marriage. That would be preferable to one of us giving up too much autonomy. Thus, we each have the right to have whatever relationships with others we want.

2. *The Primacy of our own Relationship.* We feel a deep commitment to each other, and do not want outside relationships to harm our own beautiful relationship. So far, it has only been deepened as we grow through intimate involvements with others. Others must accept that our own relationship is of primary importance.

3. *Honesty.* Open communication is essential to us. This means first

that we try to be totally open with each other—even when it hurts. It also means that we will not keep a confidence from each other. If someone wants to tell one of us a "secret," we warn that person that the secret will not be kept from our spouse.

Honesty to us also means that a sexual involvement with another person must be known to, and approved by, the other person's partner. We have each, regretfully, given up a potential lover because we rejected secret affairs.

There is one exception to the principle of honesty for us. We *will* keep each other's confidences from others. So, although Wendy will not keep her lover's confidences from Burt, she will keep Burt's confidences from her lover. This is, admittedly, a double standard of honesty, but there are many times that we want to tell each other something that we are not ready to tell a third person. It would inhibit the openness between the two of us to operate in any other way.

4. *Speaking for Ourselves.* We try to avoid getting caught in the middle between our spouse and a lover. If Burt is having problems with his lover, Wendy does not have the right to call up the lover and tell her what is on Burt's mind. To do so would probably only make things worse. Direct communication is likely to be much more effective and accurate than indirect communication through a third party. Thus, unless Wendy were asked by both Burt and his lover to operate as a kind of mutual facilitator, she would just encourage the two of them to work the problem out. Too often in the past, we have each resented the other for trying to interpret our feelings to others. Now if someone asks Burt how Wendy feels about something, he tries to respond, "Ask Wendy."

These standards are highly personal, hammered out through many hours of thought and discussion. We would never propose them as universal standards for everyone, any more than we would recommend open marriage to everyone. These principles may change in the future. But they reflect where we are now.

In the past years our thoughts on nonmonogamy have deepened as a result of our move to a new community. One of the most important things about our last two years was that we discovered Future Families of the World. FFW provided a great deal of support for our life style and we became close friends with many people we met through the organization. About six months ago, we completed graduate school and moved to New England to take jobs in our fields. Since leaving our FFW friends we have had considerable time to look with perspective over the past two years.

It now seems in looking back that we have evolved through a number of stages in our approach to openness. After leaving our first stage of romance and fantasy, we entered a second stage of exploration and variety. We sought to be intimate with a number of people, and were largely successful in achieving our aim. And we learned some invaluable things.

Again, we grew enormously as we learned more about ourselves. We also saw many people as they really were—beyond the façade of their "social" selves to their private selves. We observed the intimate relating of other couples and were able to improve our own relating. We saw life and love from many viewpoints.

But we have also learned that true intimacy is not possible with too many people at a time. One cannot be pulled in too many directions at once without spreading one's emotional energy too thin. So now we find ourselves entering a third stage in our open marriage. We are still seeking intimacy, but only with a limited number of people. We do not have the time or energy to be close to more than a few people at a time. We desire the kind of close relationships that last for many years. We've both become quite bored with superficial socializing. So quality of relationships has become more important than quantity. We don't care how many intimate relationships we may have in the future, we only care that those we have be satisfying and caring relationships.

We have come to view intimacy for what it is, and we realize that sex is not necessarily related to it. One can be intimate without being physically intimate, and certainly one can have sex without feeling. The ideal is both physical and emotional intimacy together, but we vastly prefer intimacy without sex to sex without intimacy. So our goal now is intimate friendships—with or without sex. Such an intimate friendship might eventually lead to a group marriage. But we have learned that the development of a relationship cannot be specified in advance. We have come to let relationships flow along their own course, rather than try to guide them along the path of our expectations. We no longer feel a need to decide that a relationship will lead to group marriage, or intimate friendship, or sex, or any other goal. Relationships just are.

We try to be careful not to let outside relationships take up too much of our time. We are both very busy career people with many personal interests such as meditation, yoga, ta'i chi, music, and reading. To each of us, time alone is essential to keep in touch with our inner selves. We often go off alone on walks for just this purpose. We also need to spend time with each other, continuously renewing our own relationship. We treasure quiet evenings at home just basking in each other's company, or quiet dinners out, or walks together hand-in-hand through the park. We feel a deep peace and contentment with each other, and turn to the other for enrichment and growth.

The only problems at present with our life style are finding people who share our values and deciding how open to be with the outside world about our life style. The secrecy issue has always been of special concern to us. In a sense, it is a contradiction to have a secret open relationship. Yet how does one share this part of oneself with another without seeming intrusive and pushy and threatening? For now, we have adopted a general working rule of not going out of our way to volunteer information about our life style. But on the other hand, we refuse to lie or be evasive about it.

We hope that we have conveyed three basic ideas in this chapter. First, sexually open marriage can contain great joy and growth. Second, sexually open marriage inevitably involves struggle and pain. Finally, like anything else, open marriage is not for everyone. If you use it to escape the problems in your own marriage or in yourself, you will probably experience little of the joy and much of the pain, and your primary relationship is likely to suffer. We think it is significant that we did not actually try extramarital sex until after we had lived together for five years. By then, we had worked out most of our major conflicts and had settled into a peaceful security with each other. If we had taken on the complexity of multiple relating at too early a time, the working out of our problems might have been slowed.

But you may be attracted to the concept of open marriage because you want to share the love you have with each other and because you want some newness and challenge to balance the stability you already have. If so, you may experience so much joy from openness that you will gladly risk the pain involved. This has been our experience.

Our final words are perhaps our most important. We think it is critical for people to accept each other, and to tolerate and attempt to understand different values. Monogamous people must realize that others can, for good and healthy reasons, choose not to be monogamous. But it is equally important for nonmonogamous people to recognize that others can, for good and healthy reasons, choose to be monogamous. Both are valid paths for different people. There is no one path for everyone, and by sharing our experience here we hope to emphasize the diversity of paths available for exploration and growth.

Addresses of Open-relationship Support Groups

Family Synergy
P.O. Box 30103
Terminal Annex
Los Angeles, Ca. 90030

Future Families of the World
P.O. Box 7574
Washington, D. C. 20044

Harrad Community
P. O. Box 6864
San Francisco, Ca. 94101

Questions Posed to Wendy and Burt by the Editor, and their Replies

1. Why do you think *you* were able to allow yourself to fall in love with more than one person at a time, whereas most others would not?

Well, for one thing, people are different. Our path is not someone else's. Many people just are not attracted to our life style.

Of those who are attracted to this life style, many do not practice it. A lot of people feel that it's morally wrong, or they fear the consequences. Consequences can include hurting or losing a spouse. Most of those who do allow themselves to love more than one person at a time do so secretly, for fear of the consequences. What makes us different is not that we allow ourselves to love others, but that we do so openly and with each other's encouragement.

Much of our ability to do this comes from the fact that we each feel relatively secure within ourselves. Wendy has an identity apart from Burt, and Burt has one apart from Wendy. If one of us died or left, the other person would, of course, suffer and mourn, but would survive. We each have an identity that would survive our relationship, and we could each find happiness without the other. Obviously, our first choice is to be together, but we know we could be happy alone. So the thought of possibly losing the other isn't as frightening to us as it might be to people who fear they cannot be happy without each other.

2. You mention that you are seeking enduring relationships, yet you emphasize that the *thrill* was a big rewarding factor. Does this suggest that after a while you would have to drop the new partner when their potential has dimmed?

No, of course not. For one thing, the kind of thrill present in very new relationships is nice, but nothing we feel a need for. Good relationships grow richer and deeper through the years; they are constantly changing. This change is in itself a thrill. There is much thrill in our own relationship, and probably always will be. It's also very exciting and rewarding, at the same time, to be involved in a different relationship that is at a different stage and growing in different ways. The real thrill comes from personal growth, and growth comes best from the slow change and maturation in long-lasting relationships; not from flitting from one relationship to another to experience budding romance over and over.

3. How did you manage to overcome sexual jealousy? How did you overcome envy when the other person was having a good time and you were alone? Do you really, in fact, overcome it or only suppress it?

Neither. When we feel it, we express it, and talk about it, and find a way to deal with it. We're not beyond feeling jealousy, envy, hurt, or guilt. Rather, we just accept feeling itself as being a part of life. To love is to feel hurt, to live is to feel sorrow, and to risk is to sometimes stumble and fall. And the hurts, the sorrows, and the stumbles usually contain the greatest potential for personal growth. Yes, we feel all of these things sometimes. But when we do, we express them to the other, knowing that they will be received sympathetically. And through facing these feelings, we grow and maintain better contact with our inner selves — giving us yet greater energy for more loving and more growing.

COMMUNES

[5]

COMMUNES are as American as apple pie. In 1843 when the commune movement in the United States reached its first peak, thirty-four communes were opened (Webber, 1959). Despite the rash of communes in the nineteenth century, few could be considered to be successful. The resurgence of communes in the 1960s and 1970s does not seem to have resulted in a higher ratio of success. Once again the hard lesson learned by earlier serious students of commune life had to be learned by the twentieth-century communards.

The movement, according to David, has slowed. Does this mean that communes function mainly as safety valves for the young who are readily frustrated by perceived injustice in the world? Was the recent renaissance of communes in part attributable to the Vietnamese war? David evidently hopes that communes will serve as models of how life should be lived. But without a greater impetus will a critical, necessary number be reached so that the movement can influence enough people (see Chapter 11)? It is my opinion that it would take an economic catastrophe plus a major increase in the number of communes before the communal style of life would play a major role in reshaping society.

Many of the idealistic myths of the commune have already been abandoned. The myth of a commune in which everyone did his or her "own thing" died with the pile-up of garbage and stacks of dirty dishes that no one was inspired to do. The myth of living off the land failed for most communes in the poor soil and the lack of sophisticated machinery, available markets, and skilled labor. The communes that succeed are those "that develop common purpose, and an integrating philosophy, a structure for leadership and decision making, criteria for

67

membership and entrance procedures, organize work and property communally, affirm their bonds through ritual, and work out interpersonal difficulties through regular open confrontation" (Kanter, 1973, p. 407).

Apparently few communes have met these criteria. Some of the problems in the commune described by Alam were adult differences over child care and extramarital intimacy and sex. Perhaps in the final analysis it was the lack of an integrating philosophy that caused this commune to be short-lived. Despite a brief existence, many members of short-lived communes have learned how to give, how to share, and how to accommodate. They have dealt with the universal dichotomy of neatness versus messiness, and have learned to live with jealousy; if parents, they may have had the opportunity to compare themselves with other parents. They learned to share domestic duties and abandon sex-typed roles. These experiences may be painful, but in retrospect, most individuals in communes have reported them as growth-promoting.

REFERENCES

Kanter, R. M. "Getting It All Together: Group Issues in Contemporary Communes." In *Communes: Creating and Managing the Collective Life,* edited by R. M. Kanter. New York: Harper & Row, 1973.

Webber, E. Escape to Utopia: The Communal Movements in America. New York: Hastings House, 1959.

The Commune Movement in the Middle 1970s

DAVID

History

I N ORDER to understand the contemporary communal movement, it is necessary, I think, to look first at some of its roots in the social environment of young people in the second half of the 1960s. Those years saw the full blooming of the Vietnam War, of demonstrations, police riots, urban race riots, and "campus unrest." In those years also there arose the "hippie" movement, the human potential movement, a new ecological consciousness, and the first flowering of Eastern religions in the United States.

For many of us the first twinges of doubt about the American political/economic system had come with the assassination of President Kennedy. The strength of those twinges was increased by the Warren Report and the "credibility gap" of the Johnson years; and, by the late sixties, the doubts became full-blown urges to revolt. As we became more sophisticated in analyzing the position of the United States in the world, we began to believe that wars like that in Vietnam were an inevitable cost of our high standard of living. We began to understand the relationship of our own riches to the starvation of those whose lands we ravaged. At the same time we were beginning to believe that the inability of the United States to solve its own social problems, problems such as poverty in the ghettoes, was an inevitable result of its political/ economic system. And finally, we began to believe the dictum that "if you're not a part of the solution, then you are part of the problem."

Toward the end of the sixties the rise of ecological consciousness was making many of us aware that not only was our luxurious living a result

69

of exploiting other people, but it also depended upon our systematic exploitation of the earth. We saw that we were quickly exhausting the fuel reserves that had taken millions of years to form. Furthermore, we were using those fuels and other resources in ways that were ruining our soil, water, and atmosphere. Here, too, our own life styles were "part of the problem."

Not all of our attention was focused outward, however. We were also learning hard lessons about our own psychological makeup. We were learning how difficult it was really to live the hippie philosophy of being open, loving, peaceful, and unattached to jealousies and material possessions. Anger and resentments, though we tried to bury them, would manifest themselves in strange ways. In our political activities, especially, it sometimes became difficult to discern how our "loving natures" really made us different from those in power.

The Human Potential Movement (T-groups, encounters, marathons) began equipping some of us with the tools to help each other grow. We were learning both to recognize our own patterns of self-deception and to express our emotions to each other in nonthreatening ways. The emotional changes we often went through merely as a result of trying to give and take accurate feedback within group settings were marvelous and exciting. It seemed that we were really learning better how to be loving and caring toward others.

The Spiritual Movement was giving others of us different tools toward many of the same ends. Ram Dass (formerly Richard Alpert of Alpert and Leary fame) and other teachers, both Eastern and Western, were helping us look inward to find personal happiness. Learning to experience bliss both in meditation and in surrender to God, made our attachments to material and nonmaterial possessions just so much ego-baggage. It seemed that with a cosmic perspective it would be possible to choose whether or not to pay attention to envy, angry feelings, or other stumbling blocks to interpersonal peace.

We left the sixties, then, with a firmer understanding of the nature of the U.S. political/economic system (as well as the futility of trying to change it through direct political action), with the beginnings of an understanding of our place in the world ecology, and with psychological and spiritual tools for growing in our ability to love one another. In addition, our experiences in demonstrations and sit-ins had taught us how exhilarating it could be to act in concert with others. There was both the sense of self-transcendence that came from marching with thousands who shared a single purpose, and the sense of community that developed among those who sat-in together and among those who were jailed together.

What was common to all these learnings, I believe, was that they all related in one way or another to the concept of sharing. In taking more than an equal per-capita portion of the world's resources, the U.S. had to devise elaborate strategies (including covert CIA activities and wars as well as the more subtle "development" of the exploited nations) to keep the world's deprived from demanding what many were beginning to see as their just share. Within the U.S.'s own political boundaries, those who profited from the tremendous disparities in wealth were faced with similar problems in appeasing the poor. And by refusing to share the earth both with existing animals and plants and with future generations of people, animals, and plants, we were already experiencing degradation in the quality of our lives.

On the positive side, we learned how sharing our emotions and sharing truthful feedback in groups could help to generate loving feelings. We learned the exhilaration of sharing and acting together upon common ideological beliefs, be they spiritual or political. And finally, we learned how peacefully secure it could feel to share with others a sense of community.

This was heady learning indeed for the sons and daughters of an increasingly fragmented middle class. Most of us had grown up in nuclear families almost entirely removed from extended-family ties. We'd lived in suburbs where both the design of the environment and the transience of the residents mitigated against the development of any real sense of community. And we, ourselves, were on the road to careers which would insure that our own lives would be similarly unconnected to the lives of others.

Given then both our despair over the social injustices endemic to our political/economic systems, and our optimism about our own ability to come together and create better environments in which to live, it now seems inevitable that so many of us would try to form communes in the late sixties and early seventies. These communes were radical attempts to restructure our own lives around the principles of sharing which we had learned. They were attempts to implement our ideas about social justice and ecological consciousness and to incorporate into our daily lives the loving feelings of the encounter group and the exciting feelings of acting together with ideological fervor.

Most of the communes that resulted, I will argue, emphasized one of those aspects of sharing over the others. The different events and movements outlined above touched the lives of different people in varying degrees. Out of those various experiences there arose at least four distinct visions of the communal alternative. Having a sense of what these visions were will help us to understand the present state of the movement and where it is going.

Communal Alternatives

The first vision is that of the commune as a small (i.e., 50–1000 member) communistic society, an egalitarian solution to the problems of social injustice. The dominant motif in this dream is the idea of economic sharing. This sharing is to be done within a group small enough to allow the generation of a sense of community. The vision is often accompanied by ideas of eventually building an integrated but decentralized network of communities. The Israeli kibbutzim and the kibbutz federations come closest to being models for this communal idea.[1]

The second vision recalls the early pioneer spirit of our forebears; it is of the commune as a relatively self-sufficient agrarian community in which independent individuals or families live close to nature, steeped in ecological consciousness. Members of these communes try to stay continually aware both of their interdependence with each other and of their relationship with the land. They want to develop and use a level of technology appropriate to maintaining their own, and the earth's health.[2]

Third is the vision of the warm, voluntary, extended-family, with all members sharing a common house and caring for each other's emotional needs. This vision is that of the commune as a nest, a nurturant environment within which to raise healthy children. It may or may not extend the idea of emotional sharing to include sexual sharing.[3]

Finally, there are those communes in which the sharing of a common ideology is all important. These take two different forms–the political and the spiritual. The former center around some theory of political action ranging from Ghandian nonviolence to Maoist revolutionary thinking. The vision is that of the support-group performing together significant political activities.[4]

For the spiritual groups the vision is that of the peaceful, centered life in a spiritual community. Under the guidance of a benevolent and wise guru, or a firmly established and widely shared set of spiritual teachings, such a commune's members hope to create an oasis of peace.[5] The sense of self-transcendence that comes from these extreme forms of ideological sharing often serves as a source of sustenance from which members can gather strength for active service in the world.

Thus far I have identified four different ideal types of communes, each with a particular mode of sharing as its dominant motif. For each type of commune there is, however, a wide variation in the amount of commitment to the three other modes of sharing. The amount of economic sharing, for example, that occurs in the spiritual, pioneer, and extended-family communes varies greatly from complete income sharing to the minimal economic bond of holding land in common. Similarly, the amount of emotional sharing varies from the extreme of complete sexual sharing and constant encountering to the other of the work-oriented, rationalistic, or spiritual communes that barely recognize the existence of emotions. One of the reasons that many communities appear unique is that each has its own peculiar blend of commitment to the four types of sharing. In looking at the data that follows, however, it will simplify things to pay attention primarily to the four main types, ignoring the differences among communes on the nondominant variables.

The Present State of the Movement

An accurate appraisal of the communal movement is nearly impossible to make, for there is no hard data available. Because Twin Oaks, in its early years, sought and gained a lot of publicity, and because we help publish the major communication tools in the movement,[6] a lot of information filters through us. We have on file about 650 communities, 320 of which write us occasionally. In addition, we correspond with a number of communal clearinghouses as well as the social scientists interested in the movement, and we hold discussions with college and high-school classes at schools in the eastern U.S. What follows are impressions based on that input.

It appears that the initial euphoric wave of enthusiasm for group living, an enthusiasm that saw communes as a panacea for loneliness and alienation, crested a couple of years ago, and by now has all but passed completely. High school and college-age people especially seem to be relatively uninterested. When we give lectures and hold discussions at colleges we often find that enthusiastic associate professors have fared rather poorly in communicating their excitement about communal living to the students. A number of observers on college campuses have said that they hear very little spontaneous talk about communal living. New Community Projects, a communal clearing-house in Boston, reports that not only has the number of people using its facilities declined over the past few years, but the people who do come are older (twenty-eight years plus), many with children.

Communities magazine's roving reporter, Allan Solares, observed recently (private communication) that few people in the Ithaca, New York area, once a promising center of communal activity, seem to be intentionally starting new communities. (Though the communes that have made it up to now seem much more stable than they were during the earlier period.) When he visited communes in the New Hampshire/Vermont area he saw the same thing happening there, an observation that agrees with Bob Houriet's report in a letter last Spring.[7] Both Hy Levy of Family Synergy[8] and Dennis Jaffe (a therapist who works with communal groups)[9] report very little activity in the Los Angeles area. We hear similar observations from people in northern California; Eugene, Oregon; Cinninnati, Ohio; and the Ozarks. All these reports, as well as the relative stability of our files now compared to previous years, seem to indicate that few people, especially younger people, are now starting communes.

Why Did It Happen?

What seems to have happened is that many people rushed into communal living in the late sixties and early seventies with a combina-tion of high expectations and little preparation, hoping that good intentions and a lot of enthusiasm would allow them to form warm, intentional families and/or return to the land with a group of pioneers. The dashed expectations that resulted from these experiments formed the basis of cautionary tales that have been circulated among would-be communards for the last few years. The inevitable dreamers no longer find audiences willing to feed upon and feed back their fantasies. Instead they hear horror stories about communes that have become emotional snake-pits or economic disasters.

It will be helpful, I think, to look at the reasons for all those dashed expectations within the ideal-typical framework developed earlier. Many of the difficulties we encounter in trying to adjust to communal life are related to just which aspects of sharing are emphasized and which are neglected.

In the kibbutz-like communistic societies, with their emphasis on the egalitarian distribution of economic resources, many members find it difficult to give up the freedoms that individual ownership and individual incomes can give. Within a community it becomes quite evident that if I drive away with a car, others may not be able to make the trip they've been planning. Or, on a different scale, if we as a community decide to buy enough cars so that we all have access to our own vehicles, then we can't spend that money on new housing. In the larger society we don't have to see the connections between our own ability to drive away in an automobile and the inability of some to even afford the subway. Similarly, we are rarely forced to realize that our society's choosing to provide most of us with automobiles was directly related to its neglect of mass transportation and indirectly related to its failure to provide adequate housing for the poor. The kibbutz-like communities, however, refuse to allow the development of economic freedoms for some at the expense of others. This is almost inevitably experienced by the sons and daughters of the privileged middle class as a loss in personal freedom.

Now, those pioneers who ventured back to the land often encountered a related but slightly different set of problems. Their ecological consciousness predisposed them both to try to make do with the minimum use of material resources, as well as to believe that if the individuals in a group use only that which they really need, then the group will function well. All members, they thought, would find their niches in the group ecology. Such communes, therefore, put little energy into making agreements that would insure equal access to economic resources. Many of the problems that arose did so primarily because so many of these groups found mere economic survival very difficult. They found both their desires to do with very little, and their determination to share what they did have, severely tested.

What they learned was that when people's basic needs are being satisfied, it is possible to share freely without resentment if they are determined to do so. It becomes very difficult, however, when the resources are so meager that even basic need satisfaction is in jeopardy. At that point, differences in how individuals define their basic needs (e.g., some see drug use as a basic need), and differences in access to economic resources (as when some receive money from parents or the State) become very volatile issues. At times when such resentments are really flaring, the prospect of individual homesteads becomes very appealing.

It will be worthwhile, I think, to make a few points about why these groups have had such difficult times economically. The most obvious reason is that many of them settled where land prices were cheapest, that is, in the most economically depressed areas. In those places jobs were scarce, and the market for any goods produced was nearly nonexistent. In addition, such groups were often not acceptable to the local people, so they were initially denied access to the equipment-, skill- and labor-sharing that made survival possible for the native populace. Most important, however, is the fact that many of the back-to-the-land pioneers wanted to do things in an energy-conserving, labor-intensive way. Because, from an ecological point of view, fossil-fuel energy is vastly underpriced,[10] the pioneer communities found it difficult to compete within the larger system for even the few economic resources they needed.

Turning now to the extended-family communes, we encounter problems of an entirely different nature. Operating on the idea that a warm feeling of family would arise from honestly confronting their feelings about each other, members of these groups tried to abandon the larger society's norms of (1) saying only that which others want to hear, and/or (2) veiling feelings in rational talk about ideas and issues. They were often confident that in such a way they would be able to handle even the potentially explosive issues involved in sexual sharing.

What actually happened was that many extended-family groups found that the energy required continually to "work things through," when added to the energy drain of their jobs and other involvements outside the commune, was just too much. Many members discovered, too, that their own progress in becoming open and truthful was not as great as they'd thought. The demons of jealousy and defensiveness were still firmly entrenched in many of their lives (tied as they are to feelings of self-esteem, feelings that are often independent of the immediate environment.) For many, these group experiences were times of intense growth. Though the communes may no longer be in existence, many of their former members would never consider the communal experiments failures. Nonetheless, the illusion of instant utopia was shattered.

About the fourth type of communal group, that type which has a high degree of ideological sharing as its primary focus, I must confess ignorance. We have some contact with a few of the spiritual groups and almost none at all with political groups. What we do know about the spiritual groups seems to suggest that they, like their nineteenth-century counterparts, are quite stable and are still growing in popularity. Some people seem to wander from group to group and discipline to discipline, but the little we've heard suggests that, overall, the turnover rates for these groups are quite low. Previous experiences with members of my generation would suggest, however, that many will go

through further intellectual and emotional changes. To the extent that
the ideologies of the groups are not flexible enough to incorporate such
changes, then I would expect members to move on.

Finally, one overarching reason why people become dissatisfied with
any of the above types of communes, including the spiritual groups, is
that members begin taking for granted the progress that has been made
in the dominant sharing area, and the focus shifts to the group's failure
to share in the other areas. At Twin Oaks, for example (the seventy-
five-member kibbutz-like group in which I live), we have no private
possessions other than those we keep in our rooms and we spend about
$3.00/person/week of private income, most of that while on vacation off
the farm. The remainder of our $300,000 gross income is spent accord-
ing to community priorities. In addition, we've broken almost completely the correlation between work and privileges. Doing one type of
work does not gain one more rights and privileges than doing another.

After awhile, though, we tend to lose sight of these accomplishments
and focus instead on the extent to which we do not approach our other
ideals. We notice the ways we are not being ecologically conscious, or
developing family-like feelings, and we lament our not having a firm
ideological sense of what we're doing. Furthermore, because we do not
have a widely shared ideology, we disagree among ourselves as to how
important each of the areas of sharing is.

Now, with the exception of my quite unknowledgeable speculations
about the ideological communities, all of this sounds pretty dismal for
the community movement. It is, however, only one side of the story. It
is the side that highlights many of the reasons why so many approach
the idea of communal living with extreme caution, why it's not fash-
ionable to daydream in public about the bliss awaiting us in some rural
utopia. The other side of the story is that most of the pressures that
drove so many of us to try communal alternatives in the late sixties are
still present: fragmented nuclear families, impersonal bureaucratic
relationships, meaningless jobs which often require moving from
place to place, a felt lack of any sense of community, a political/
economic system that renders us powerless to solve basic social problems, the deterioration of the cities, services, material goods, and food.
All of these are still causing many people, once they leave the haven of
school and begin discovering the patterns their lives are taking, to
begin questioning.

The New England Conference on Communities, sponsored by an
intergroup network centered at Another Place Community, apparently
generated a lot of interest, as have the annual Twin Oaks Conferences

and the New Haven conferences sponsored by Training in Urban Alternatives.[11] These events are attended, for the most part, by people who are out of school and are becoming disillusioned with what they're finding in the world.

What's missing, though, is the apocalyptic sense of urgency that prevailed in the late sixties. With the passing of the horrors of the Vietnam War, police and race riots, and with the illusory demise of the Nixon administration, a semblance of order and stability can now be maintained. Since the established order now seems likely to go on for some time, people are naturally less willing to take the kinds of risks that many of us took three to six years ago. I would maintain, though, that many are moving, but they are moving in directions that entail less risk. Many people are taking partial steps toward the kinds of sharing which take place in communal groups. Rather than plunging headlong into some vision of utopia, they test their capacity to share, they learn new methods of sharing, in various less drastic ways.

Partial Steps

It appears that many whose longing for justice and community would formerly have attracted them to kibbutz-like communistic groups are attempting instead to push "worker-control" projects. They hope that by building work places controlled democratically by the workers, they will be bringing some of their egalitarian ideals into their own and other's lives.[12] The same could be said about those who work to establish food co-ops, housing co-ops, and neighborhood governments.[13]

Instead of forming pioneer communities, many move to the land separately, and then slowly begin sharing equipment, food, and whatever with others whom they often persuade to move nearby. They may even share the purchase of land, but they are careful to keep their own land-use legally separate. (Interestingly enough, both Houriet and Solares have written us that commune members are themselves reaching out more and more to the surrounding community, seeking to situate themselves more securely in the local communities by participating in local affairs. This same development is occurring at Twin Oaks.[14])

Instead of forming extended-family-like communes, many are participating in programs like the Unitarian sponsored extended-family programs, where members try to care for each other without actually moving in together.[15] Others try to organize their neighborhoods into a caring community; still others move to small towns in search of a sense of community stability, or they participate again and again in encounter groups and other group methods of personal growth.

There are those for whom the sexual aspect of the emotional mode of sharing is the most important avenue toward significant involvement with others. I'll leave it to the other authors in this collection to talk about the various networks and organizations that are trying to facilitate people meeting those needs.

Finally, those who would otherwise seek the peace of spiritual communities immerse themselves in yoga classes, fellowships, and other spiritual activities, often engaging in economic sharing to the extent of paying substantial tithes.[16]

The Future

What does the future hold? My personal belief is that only an extensive federation of communal workplaces, a federation characterized by a moderate to high amount of emotional, ecological, and ideological sharing, constitutes an adequate solution to the injustice, alienation, impersonality, and lack of transcendent meaning that is a natural part of living in present day society. The ideal communal group would be, I think, a spiritually coherent, communistic, ecologically sound, relatively self-sufficient commune, one that allows for family-like groupings. Anything short of that, including Twin Oaks, is only a partial solution, a reform of sorts. And reforms, many would argue, are palliatives which merely serve to delay truly revolutionary change.

It is quite probable that the sexual sharing of Family Synergy members, the economic sharing of the worker in a worker-controlled factory, or the emotional sharing of a Unitarian extended-family would satisfy some of the longing for connectedness and social justice. I think, though, that it is equally probable that after some time, the successes that people have in one area will begin to throw into relief the other aspects of their lives that remain unconnected to those more integrated parts. A rewarding emotional and sexual life punctuated by stultifying hours in a traditional work place might eventually make one long to change the work place also. The probability of such a chain reaction occurring will be enhanced to the extent that we who are now experimenting, are able to build models of coherent life styles, and to the extent that we make our successes and failures known.

Sharing, I think, is the key. And many of us are working on ways to increase the amount of sharing in our lives. I hope that we can keep each other informed of the ways in which we are making progress.

NOTES

1. See Shimon Shur's *Kibbutz Bibliography* for an extensively indexed listing of some 1288 publications about the kibbutzim (revised 1972). It is available for $2.50 for the Higher Education and Research Authority of the Federation of Kibbutz Movements, P.O.B. 303, Tel Aviv, 62-098, Israel. For information on U.S. groups of this type, see articles on Twin Oaks, East Wind, Julian Woods, Dandelion, Aloe, North Mountain, and Shannon Farm in various issues of *Communities* magazine, especially issues 16 and 18, available for $1.25 each from *Communities*, Box 426, Louisa, Va., 23093. The newsletters of three of the groups can be quite informative: *Leaves of Twin Oaks*, Rt. 6, Box 17, Louisa, Va., 23093; *Dandelion Newsletter*, RR1, Enterprise, Ontario, KOK 1Z0; *North Mountain Community Newsletter*, Rt. 2, Box 207, Lexington, Va., 24450. Each is available for $3/yr. In addition, Kat Kinkade's *A Walden Two Experiment* (N.Y.: Morrow, 1972) gives a detailed picture of Twin Oaks' early years.
2. I have seen no good studies of serious back-to-the-land groups. Robert Whitehurst's 1971 reports of groups in Ontario were a good start, but no follow-up studies were done. Whitehurst's "Back to the Land: The Search for Freedom and Utopia in Ontario" and "Return to the Land in Ontario" are mimeographed papers, available while the supply lasts from Robert N. Whitehurst, Dept. of Sociology, University of Windsor, Windsor, Ontario, Canada N9B 3P4.
3. There is a good deal of literature on both urban and rural groups of this type. For information on the rural groups see: Jud Jerome's *Families of Eden* (N.Y.: Seabury, 1974); Elaine Sundancer's *Celery Wine* (Yellow Springs, Oh.: Community Publications Cooperative, 1973); *January Thaw* by the people at Blue Mountain Ranch (N.Y.: Times Change Press, 1974). On urban groups, see: Michael Weiss's *Living Together: A Year in the Life of a City Community* (N.Y.: McGraw-Hill, 1974); Andrew Kopkind's review of Weiss's book in *Ramparts*, October, 1974; Kanter, Jaffe, and Weisberg's "Coupling, Parenting and the Presence of Others: Intimate Relationships in Communal Households" in *The Family Coordinator* 24(4), October 1975; and Dennis Jaffe's "The First Four Long Years of a Family Commune," a thirty-six page unpublished paper available for $1.00 from Dennis at 11967 Walnut Lane, Los Angeles, Ca. 90025.
4. The work of the more peaceful groups are exemplified by *Win* magazine (Box 547, Rifton, N.Y. 12471); *WorkForce* (Vocations for Social Change, 5951 Canning St., Oakland, Ca. 94609); and *Fellowship* (Box 271, Nyack, N.Y. 10960). I don't know of the work of the more militant groups.

5. For a fairly complete listing of material available on spiritual communities, see the "Resources" section of *Communities* 13 and the Social Science Column in *Communities* 18. ($1.25 each from Box 426, Louisa, Va., 23093).

6. *Communities* magazine, *News from Communities* (an occasional newsletter sent free to some 350 groups), the *Intercommunities Newsletter* (circulated among the 40 or so groups in the Virginia area), the *Leaves of Twin Oaks*, and *Openings* (a pamphlet describing groups who are looking for members.)

7. Robert Houriet is the author of one of the most popular of the communal "travel" books. In *Getting Back Together* (N.Y.: Coward, McCann and Geoghegan, 1971), Houriet tells about his commune-hopping trip across the continent. He has since been living in a group in Vermont and editing the *New England Food Co-op Newsletter*. He's presently working on a book about the alternate culture in New England.

8. Family Synergy seems to be one of the most successful of the groups intended to help sexually open people come together in meaningful ways. For information write them at P.O. Box 30103, Terminal Annex, Los Angeles, Ca. 90030.

9. In addition to the articles listed in footnote 3, Dennis is working on a book about *Couples in Communes*.

10. The pioneers were trying to live now as they imagine all of us will have to live when gas, oil, and coal become very scarce. At that time, unless nuclear fusion becomes an economic reality, it will be very costly to fuel a tractor—even to build a tractor in the first place. At the present time, however, the fossil fuels are priced according to their present supply, so food and other goods produced with a high petroleum input can undersell food and goods produced by the pioneers. See my article, "Visions and Re-Visions" in *Communities* 16 for a more detailed development of this argument.

11. For information on these conferences, write: Another Place Farm, Merriam Hill Rd., Greenville, N.H. 03048; Twin Oaks Conference, Rt. 4, Box 169, Louisa, Va. 23093; and T.U.A., c/o Paul Frennolich, 2 Chapel St., Milford Ct. 06460.

12. A number of good articles on worker-controlled industries can be found in various issues of *Working Papers for a New Society* (123 Mt. Auburn St., Cambridge, Ma. 02138). See especially Michael Maccoby's account of the Bolivar Project in *Tennessee* (Summer 1975), David Tornquist's *Strikes in Yugoslavia* (Spring 1975) and David Jenkins's *Workplace Democracy in Europe* (Winter 1975).

13. I found Morris and Hess's book on their efforts to organize the Adams-Morgan neighborhood in Washington, D.C., to be very inspiring. *Neighborhood Power: the New Localism* (Boston: Beacon Press, 1975).

14. See Will Merion's "Making a Contribution to the County" in the October 1975 issue of the *Leaves of Twin Oaks*.

15. See *Developing an Extended Family Program*, available for $1.00 from the
    Unitarian Church, 1535 Santa Barbara St., Santa Barbara, Ca. 93101.
16. See *Awakening: Ways to Psycho-Spiritual Growth* (Englewood Cliffs, N.J.:
    Prentice-Hall, 1975) for an extensive listing of programs, including
    their costs.

Middle-Class Communes: The New Surrogate Extended Family

STERLING E. ALAM

S EVERAL COUPLES who are friends decide to live together and share
their finances, meals, child rearing and recreation. They are
neither rebelling against society, nor retreating to a rural area to live off
the land. They continue to hold and be committed to professional
positions. The mass media may not call this a commune. More than
likely, the participants themselves will not use this term because of its
countercultural connotations. This group may not even be found by a
sociologist or become notorious in the neighborhood because they are
unlikely to advertise their existence. They may or may not have a name
for their group. Probably they would simply say that they are living
with some other people. The quieter they can keep about it, the better.

In the broadest sense of the term, I would call this group living a
commune. In fact, the number of such quiet experiments may well
outnumber the better-known rural retreatist groups. Actually the
societal implications of such quiet experiments may be just as profound. Yet they have gone largely unrecognized by sociologists possibly because they are less sensational, but I would guess mostly because
they are quiet, harder to research, and nearly impossible to sample by
the usual survey research methods.

Middle-Class Communes and Other Communes

The word "commune" is no longer a popular one among those who reside in them. This may be due to the fact that the mass media has burned out the term by linking it primarily to spectacular countercul- ture and retreatist groups. If so, I feel this is unfortunate, for it is in fact a venerable term incorporating both old and new group living experi- ments of fantastic variety. Some may fit the popular media stereotype. Probably most do not. Some well-known groups are very large, but most have only a few members. They may call themselves a commune, a community, a collective, a tribe, a family, or merely a house. Many are organized around some cause. The pacifist Committee for Non-Violent Action is a good example. That cause may be a religious one, but the religion may vary from the so-called "Jesus freak" groups to Eastern meditation centers. Some support themselves by running businesses. For example, an Ashram at Bloomington, Indiana, at one time had five business ventures, including one of the best vegetarian restaurants anywhere. Others, such as the Year One Trading Company in Missouri have found arts and crafts a ready source of income. Some, like Stephen Gaskin's Farm are organized around a single charismatic leader. In other smaller groups it would take a sociometric study to uncover their leadership patterns and they would differ little from any other organi- zation in our society. Some communes resist anything that resembles organization, giving vehement allegiance to the principle of "do your own thing." These tend to be short-lived. A group such as Twin Oaks, on the other hand, is highly organized. For me, their organization combined with a tolerant pragmatism resulted in an atmosphere of considerable comfort and security. On an ideological level some com- munes would seem to have almost nothing in common with most others. For instance the notorious Manson Family must be counted as communal, but few other communes would approve their behavior or wish to be identified with them.

Yet, with all of their variety, there are certain characteristics common to all. I have been impressed many times by the fact that vastly differ- ing groups face amazingly similar problems in terms of personal rela- tionships and everyday survival. It is in these areas that I think we should search for the definitional characteristics of the broad phenomenon we call a commune. The two things all communes have in common are: 1) Some degree of economic and functional cooperation going beyond what is routinely expected in the modern family, and 2) A degree of interpersonal intimacy and commitment, which sets it apart from primarily business arrangements such as boardinghouses. I would like to preserve the word "commune" as a broad term within which one can distinguish a wide spectrum of subtypes.

What I am here calling the middle-class commune is a subtype of communal living arrangement, which is specifically not rejecting the larger society, but rather using the communal form to achieve society's normative goals. The hallmark of the middle-class commune is the fact that the members hold jobs in the larger society, and these are central to their lives. Thus my use of the term "middle class" is not meant to have the precise meaning found in stratification research. It rather refers to the life style of the broad majority of Americans in contrast to the so-called counterculture. What I am calling the "middle class commune" resembles in most respects what Ramey (1972a) calls an "evolutionary commune" and Kanter (1974) calls an "urban commune."

Because the middle-class commune differs both in its structure and in its goals from other communes, it is necessary to specify some of the models of communal systems which are either appropriate or inappropriate for understanding this form. First, and most obviously, one will misunderstand the middle-class commune completely if his only communal model is a counterculture one. Students have often said to me that they want to start a commune as soon as they can get some land. In the city, the neighbors are often suspicious even of the middle-class commune because of the free sex and drug orgies that they assume are taking place there. Those who assume this model of commune are quite likely to dismiss the middle-class commune, and say, "This is not really a commune at all," even though it meets the criteria of our broad definition above. Those whose only contact with the term "commune" is the mass media are most likely to react this way. Sociologists too, though, sometimes operate from this model and as a result ask quite inappropriate questions about the members' goals and practices.

Similarly, the Utopian model is inappropriate for understanding the middle-class commune. Unlike the members of many larger intentional communities and nineteenth-century experimental settlements, the middle-class communards are not out to save the world. Some of them may have a bit of the Utopian streak in that they feel they are inventing a new family form of wider applicability, but more than likely most of them are content merely to live their own lives in a more satisfying manner.

Urban communes now have little in common with their rural or spiritual counterparts. Their purpose is not a return to the land and a retreat from technology. Nor do they plan to build a new community or to further particular spiritual ideals. Urban communes exist to create a collective household, a shared home, an augmented family (Kanter, 1974, p. 36).

Probably the most subtly inappropriate model to avoid is the model of success based on longevity. Because this model is so pervasive in our society, it is very difficult for us to avoid the question of why a middle-class commune may last only two years. When asked why it failed, the members would most likely reply that it did not fail. "We never intended it to be permanent, and it was a wonderful two years." This seldom satisfies those of us who have grown up with the assumption that family ought to be forever. Yet, it is a truism to say that that model may not even be appropriate for understanding modern nuclear families. David Olson says,

While a successful marriage has often been determined by its longevity (i.e., those having twenty-fifth anniversaries) or by how well it fulfills the traditional roles prescribed by society (husband being a good provider and wife being a good housekeeper and mother), there is an increasing awareness that these criteria are not necessarily associated with a successful marriage. Youth has begun to seriously question these criteria and they have become somewhat cynical about marriage because of the alienated, conflicted, and devitalized marriages they see their parents and other adults tolerate . . . . In recent years, there seems to be more change in the criteria used to evaluate the success of a marital relationship. Increasingly, individuals are seeking a relationship that will provide growth for them as individuals and as a couple . . . Ideally, the successful marriage is seen as a relationship context in which growth and development of both partners is facilitated to a greater extent than it could be for either of these individuals outside the relationship. (1972, p. 390)

I am personally very much convinced of Olson's view. In fact if I were to make just one safe prediction regarding the future of the family, it would be the continuation of this trend toward seeing the chief purpose of the family as meeting the needs of the partners for interpersonal relationships and growth. The family does serve other purposes — eg., economic, political, procreative — but, I think even today people get married not so much to have children or economic security as to find companionship, emotional gratification, and their own personal identity. Moreover, whenever they find that a relationship is no longer meeting these needs, people are less hesitant to end it and try again. Of course, whether any trend will continue will depend in large part on how the larger society changes. I feel that the foreseeable changes toward an increasingly mobile, impersonal, bureaucratized mass society will make the family still more important as the chief source of personal relationships.

One of the major reasons for concern about the family today is that people are increasingly evaluating the traditional nuclear family by this new criteria and they are finding that the nuclear system is falling short of their increased expectations. One of the major reasons for looking to alternative forms is to see if they can do better in this respect. It seems appropriate therefore to evaluate a new form by the relationship-growth criterion, rather than by the older standard of longevity. This newer criterion is really more appropriate to the goals of those who form middle-class communes, and judged by this standard a two-year commune may well be far more successful than most fifty-year marriages. Therefore, I would propose that a more appropriate model for the middle-class commune would be that of a growth facilitating milieu.

Undoubtedly the most appropriate model for understanding the middle-class commune is a model of the extended family. This theme is often explicitly stated by the members themselves. One might even label the middle-class commune a surrogate extended family. There is desire in our increasingly impersonal and isolated society to want to recapture some of the values of kinship that have been lost in the small nuclear family. The difference is that this new surrogate extended family is a voluntary institution. One can choose one's own relatives and can, if need be, change them. To the extent, though, that this surrogate extended family is an extended family, one can anticipate some of its advantages and problems. We would therefore expect to find the advantages of a wider peer fellowship, more varied role models for children, economic efficiency, security against illness and other crises, and enriched recreational and interpersonal opportunities. On the other hand, we might also anticipate problems concerning privacy, freedom for the individual, and a complexity of interpersonal tensions. Both the positive and negative aspects may be modified somewhat by the voluntary nature of the structure, but at the expense of some of its integration and continuity.

Finally, to what extent is it appropriate to consider the middle-class commune as an alternative family form? It obviously lies in between a total rejection and a total acceptance of our conventional family norms. I would characterize an ideal type of conventional American family as being:

	It is also:	
obligatory		emotional
nuclear		economic
patriarchal		sexual
permanent		monogamous
legalized		neolocal
role differentiated		exclusive
		procreative
		parental

The middle-class commune would accept all the characteristics listed in the second column, but would explicitly reject the characteristics set forth in the first column. Thus, it does not reject conventionality completely, but the modifications it accepts are critical enough to qualify it as a true alternative, perhaps an alternative consistent with the contemporary trends toward skepticism of our received family traditions.

The Case Study

The core membership of the commune described here consists of three couples and their seven children. They lived together for two years in a small midwestern university community. Three other persons lived with the group for shorter periods. Soon after the commune disbanded, the author was invited to interview the members in order to record their experience while the memory was still fresh. The three couples all remained in the same community and remained friends. The project was as much theirs as mine. We met together and formulated a methodology consisting of an unstructured interview schedule, the composition of which was a joint effort. All interviews with the six adults and their children were taped, transcribed, and duplicated. They were then shared among each other and a joint session was held to compare impressions and clarify facts. These interviews averaged about three hours each. Interviews were also held with friends, neighbors, temporary residents, clergymen, colleagues, students, businessmen, a schoolteacher of the children, and a babysitter. The interviews with neighbors intentionally included some who had strongly opposed having such a group in their midst. Also, some of the church people interviewed were antagonistic toward the commune. In these latter interviews, identities were kept in confidence, but the information was summarized for the group at the final sharing session. The following account is based on the total group of transcripts.

Formation

Typically, the ideas for the formation of the group arose out of the reading of literature on communes, in this case an article by Margaret Mead in a Catholic publication. Two couples on an out-of-town trip to see a play began discussing the article, at first abstractly, but before the trip was over, very personally. Still regarding it as a somewhat farfetched idea, they nevertheless agreed to continue this dialogue between themselves and also with other friends. Their mate selection for the group that was eventually formed consisted mainly of whoever responded enthusiastically to the idea and had the courage to follow through. Those who did eventually join together were only casually acquainted at first, yet they turned out to be a highly compatible group in spite of strong individual differences. All were young, attractive, and competent professional people. Although they came from different backgrounds, they shared a similar, relatively liberal outlook on life and sought many of the same goals. This group consisted of two professors, one former professor, a clergyman, a parochial school teacher, and an undergraduate student. Their professional involvements were central to their lives. Like many people, they assumed that communes necessitated a rural way of life far removed from middle-class society. They stated to each other that they were urban, professional people who saw many intriguing possibilities for themselves in communal living, but saw no reason for retreating to the country. One major benefit of the commune for them was that it freed them both financially and in terms of time to pursue their professional goals. Thus, like many people of their ages and occupations, they wanted to change and improve their world, but were not in outright rebellion against it. This is crucial for understanding the kind of commune they dreamed of and eventually established.

No small part of the motivation for entering a commune was the sheer adventuresomeness of the enterprise—"just a wild exciting trip!" In retrospect, to be able to look back and say, "We did it! We actually made it work for two years," was a considerable satisfaction, especially since they had no pattern to follow and thought their idea unique. Beyond that challenge, they did have a series of rather definite goals. As time went on, they discovered that some of these goals

were of differential saliance to different individuals. This was undoubtedly one of the most significant stresses in the group. The goal
most frequently mentioned was to recapture the values of the extended family. The majority of them had come from large families,
some from ethnic neighborhoods. None of them were natives of the
community where they were now residing. The women especially felt
the isolation of their nuclear units. A commune would have the
structure of a larger family but with the added advantage that they
would be able to choose its members. This was clearly one of the
outstanding reasons for the experiment. Another major reason was
one which had considerable appeal to young middle-class professionals. This was the potential efficiency of sharing goods and services. In fact, they were able to demonstrate that there could be
considerable savings in such sharing.

> . . . People were very generous in sharing their clothes and their dishes
> and their furniture and their records and their books and their cars . . .
> just about anything you could name, everybody shared sewing
> machines, hair dryers, etc., etc. So this was a goal that we definitely
> achieved. We found that you can get along with just one washing
> machine and one dryer for this many people. You can get along wi¹h one
> stove and one refrigerator and it's too bad that every house and every
> little nuclear family has all these things on their own.

This gave them a sense of having found a way to combat what many of
them saw as the excessive materialism and ecological profligacy of
our society while at the same time enjoying all the comforts. Closely
related to this was the goal stated as "to minimize the living hassle."
In practice they found that the hassle took on new shape. Although no
one member was tied down to a particular task, when it was his or her
turn it was now a much bigger task. Even so, this provided a degree of
freedom to organize time in new ways which did, in fact, release
individuals to pursue outside goals. This was an aspect of communal
living which this group did fairly well. For some members of the
group, their success in achieving the aforementioned goals was all
that was needed to justify the experiment. Others saw this as only the
first stage and wished to achieve also another goal; namely, to form
really close personal relationships. Continuing until the end of the
group's existence was some controversy as to the form that sharing
should take and even its desirability as a goal. For a minority, though,
it was their primary goal. Intertwined with this variance was another

issue. That same minority tended to value emotional above intellectual expression. One of them gave this example:

> . . . One time Bill came home and he was having conflict over—at work, about the question of abortion. And so he brought the subject up at dinner time and immediately we launched into an intellectual discussion of abortion; whereas what was really happening was Bill was saying, "Something is happening that's bothering me, you know, that's making me feel uneasy," and we were not able to be sensitive to that for whatever reason.

It is curious that few of them mentioned communal child rearing except late in the list of goals. Most of them did feel strongly that the communal experience would be good for the children. They were all conscientious parents. Had they had any real doubts about this, they would have probably never entered the group. Yet when the children were mentioned in terms of reasons for forming the commune, they were as likely to be mentioned under the heading of "the living hassle" as they were to be seen as positive motivation for the experience. Of course, it was partly for the children's benefit that they desired the advantages of the extended family. In actual practice the children were far from neglected. Yet one cannot escape the conclusion that this commune was primarily an adult institution. We would hasten to add, however, that at the comparable point in the formation of most nuclear families love between the couple is more likely the motivation for their union than is the desire to become parents. Finally, women's liberation seems not to have been a major motivation for the group as a whole, though it was for some. Sex-role modification was one of the striking consequences of the group experience. But for most of the members, this was an unintended consequence. Two of the women had been active in the women's movement. One man was vocally opposed to it and would remain so even while his own behavior was undergoing seemingly inevitable modification. In the nuclear family a woman often gives up not only her own name but her identity as well. Whatever she does or thinks, it is as Mrs. Somebody Else. But in the commune she must learn to relate closely to a number of men. Thus she is compelled to face the question of who she is as an individual, and others must learn to relate to the distinct self she now projects.

During the spring and summer prior to the formation of the commune, the three couples spent considerable time discussing their reasons for forming the group as well as some of the risks involved.

They tried to do further reading about communes, but felt that most of it was oriented toward rural countercultural communities and not particularly relevant to what they wanted to do. What seemed to them more important was finding out whether they were or were not a compatible combination of personalities. So they not only talked together; they played together, too.

> . . . So, after this good meal, we had some good wine and we started listening (to music) and talking—and it was real loud and it had a lot of heavy vibrations—it was captivating music. We sat around and we, they had a pew in their living room—it was part of their living room furniture—an old church pew, and we laid under this church pew altogether, side by side, and we pounded on the under side of the seat of this church pew with the music and it was sort of a childish thing to do but it was carefree and I think that it, that pew bottom experience had a great deal to do with fusing some very good bonds within the group; namely, we can play together.

They took a couple of camping trips. As camping, their trips were disastrous. They had bad weather, crowded conditions, and noisy children. In retrospect, they felt that the survival of these experiences was perhaps something of a test of the survival potential of their friendship.

The other big project during this period was the search for a house. Failing to find rental property, they decided to buy. They found a banker who would finance the project even though he had rather quickly surmised their intentions. At last, they found a nine-room older home which had recently been used for student housing. The latter fact proved to be a big plus, for it meant that the property already had the appropriate zoning variance. One of the couples had provided living quarters for students during the previous summer, so they had experienced neighbors' objections on the basis of zoning. In fact, the commune was challenged in the Zoning Commission during its first few months. The variance was adequate defense. This house was far from ideal, but it was already toward the end of the summer. Rather than give up the idea of living together that fall, they took it gladly.

The virtues and deficiencies of the house became clear only in retrospect. It was really a bit small for so many people, but it had a large yard, two bathrooms, and adequate living and dining room. They were able to remodel the kitchen quite satisfactorily. There were three children's sleeping rooms and a playroom. Each couple had its own bedroom, which served the dual function of sleeping room and their only private retreat. In addition to the fact that the bedrooms were a bit small to do both things well for two people, none of them was ideally located. One couple said their room would have been satisfactory, except that it was located upstairs with the children's rooms and thus amidst much noise. A second couple's room was next to the living room, which was often in use late into the night. The third couple's room was adjacent to the busy kitchen. Thus all of the adults, to some extent, despised the only space in the house which they could call their very own. Clearly this old house was not designed for communal living. It also left something to be desired in terms of general attractiveness.

Two of the women did not even see the house until after it was theirs. When they did see it, they were shocked. That was the first time that they realized the extent of their individual differences with respect to standards of neatness, order, and an attractive atmosphere. The two who had not been in on the purchase were among the most particular. They insisted right then on a major renovation project. This was not what the others intended, but they went along. With one of the wives taking a leadership role, the group plunged into remodeling efforts which actually proved to be very good for the esprit de corps of the new commune. Later they termed this crisis one of the happiest periods of being together. They also did very well in working out most of the other practical problems such as finances, cooking, and work schedules.

Pragmatics

If there was any problem with money, it was what to do with the surplus. This is hardly the problem in most nuclear families. In the beginning they estimated their predictable expenses for house payments, taxes, food, liquor, household expenses, and recreation. Toward these, everyone contributed one-third of his or her income, whatever that was. One couple earned less, but the percentage contribution was regarded as fair all around. They ate well on this; better in fact than before. Still there was money left over. So eventually the amount was reduced to one-fourth. This left the remaining two-thirds or three-fourths for personal clothing, insurance, medical expense, and automobiles. The latter is a curious phenomenon, which seems to be characteristic of such communes. The auto is apparently so valued that it is one of the last items to be owned communally. Another group I visited did try, but found that the cars were far better cared for when they weren't everyone's responsibility. Even so, it was common that the cars were relatively free for use by whomever had a need. This was also the case in Weiss's group (1974, pp. 99–100). For furniture, they selected various items already owned, storing or selling the remainder. This seems to have occasioned little or no jealousy, much to the surprise of outside observers. Cost for repairs and damages were taken out of the common treasury. The economist in the group noted that in spite of the obvious savings thus made by avoiding duplication of possessions, this group may not have in fact realized the potential benefits because they had already invested in three sets of things before they entered the experiment, and then returned to three nuclear units after only two years. For them it required a longer time in order to make it really pay. This may be a significant caution in view of the apparent short life of most small communes. On the other hand, they did not lose money, and if this cooperative way of life were to become widespread, the economic and ecological implications would be potentially considerable. Even the attitude toward accumulation and affluence fostered in this least radical of all types of communes could have significant repercussions for what we refer to as "the American way of life."

Another aspect of daily living which the group handled quite successfully was the scheduling of routine work. The system which they settled on was a simple sign-up chart on the refrigerator. This meant that both men and women shared in the cooking, the cleaning, and the child care. The least popular task was house cleaning, so eventually they decided to hire outside help. The most popular job was washing the dishes. This was a two-person job and provided an opportunity for companionship which the other jobs did not offer. Among the most difficult tasks were those centering around child care: getting the children to school, caring for them in the late afternoon hours, and putting them to bed. The neighbors observed that these adults paid a lot of attention to their children, always taking them places and playing with them. This was partly because they found rather soon that the care of seven children so close in age required considerably more planning than ordinary babysitting. It was shockingly noisier, too. The men learned to cook rather well, and since each adult cooked only one big meal a week each meal tended to be something rather special.

> It was exciting to come home and eat dinner with thirteen other people. I thought that was nice and I thought it was fun to cook great pots of stuff and see people come roaring in and eat it all. I find it really boring to cook for three people now. I just have a hard time getting into that.

They ate well and the role sharing that they started here lasted beyond the two years of the commune, as I observed by visiting in all three of the couples' homes. My first formal interview with one of the husbands ended about 5:30 P.M. His wife had already started the evening meal. In order to maximize the use of time, she then started taping her interview and he, without instructions, took over fixing and serving the meal. This might work in some other American homes, too, but these were not among them prior to the communal living. During the communal living period, the women mentioned the advantage that they had on the job and in school by the fact that only once a week was it necessary for them to get home in time to fix a meal.

The food they cooked was another indicator of middle-class culture. None of the permanent members were vegetarian and their menu seems to have had more in common with that of the middle-class neighbors than with the diet of a stereotypical rural commune. In fact, they reported a tendency to use their one night a week to do gourmet cooking.

This same middle-class tendency can be seen in the rituals they observed. They did develop some celebrations unique to the communal atmosphere such as Sunday morning brunch and the fellowship following the evening meal. But the rituals they mention most often were traditional days such as Thanksgiving, Christmas, and birthdays. They celebrated these by dressing up and setting a pretty table with flowers and candles. They recorded these occasions on color film. The characteristic that marked this group most clearly as middle class to their friends and neighbors was the appearance of the house itself. The group used this reaction to win over skeptical neighbors of the community as well as their own skeptical parents. Among both groups the generalization was made that those who actually visited the house went away favorably impressed. As one member said, one main reaction of those who actually did visit was:

"For a commune, it's so clean, like very straight looking, average middle-class house." I think that was a comment that most people made. Sometimes people thought that was good and some people thought that was disappointing.

On the other hand, one mother refused to come near the place:

I think it did make a lot of difference in how his mother felt about him and felt about us and our marriage and the whole thing. And I don't know that we'll ever be able to remake that thing very well . . . I think she would like to be proud and happy and — about him and his family and be able to talk to her coworkers and friends about it. And she feels unable to do that because we're doing this hippy commune thing, you see. And how can she talk to her friends about her son who's living in a commune?

I asked about their decision making. The answer was that this was informal and largely by consensus. A vote was taken on only one item, the color of some wallpaper. That vote was reversed the next day. There was a natural occasion for informal conversation after the evening meal. But this seems to have been largely an occasion for conviviality. They did set one night aside each week for planning activities. These meetings tended to be a rather unorganized makeshift of business and pleasure, as I observed on my last night with them, when some joint decisions were to be made about this research project:

It was sort of an unwritten thing that you didn't do anything until Sunday night. By the time that Sunday night would come the occasion was gone and the Sunday nights were around the livingroom, we'd sit on the carpet with a nice roaring fireplace and a couple of glasses of Pink Chablis and all that bad stuff would just kind of phase into the woodwork.

As a result there was a tendency for everyone to "dump conflicts" in the area of interpersonal relations on one's own spouse rather than confront the offender directly or save up the gripe for the weekly meeting. This improved with experience, however. Their pattern of informal consensus decision making worked well for the routine, pragmatic matters that caused a little trouble anyway. As we shall see, though, it was really not adequate for the basic issues upon which there was major division of philosophy or opinion.

Problems

Two of the bigger issues that were never really fully resolved were child-care standards and interpersonal relationships. This is not to say that the children were not well cared for; they were. The job rotation system saw to that. Also like other middle-class parents, these couples made deliberate efforts to provide them a variety of educational and recreational experiences. A teacher reports:

I really felt that the children were getting so much more from the adult relationship than you do in a normal home. For example, here is one mother who is an excellent knitter and she said anybody who wants to learn how to knit, just come on over here and I will teach you to knit. It seemed that one was quite a gymnast and he said if anybody wants to learn any more about gymnastics, come on and I'll teach you. It seemed to me that the fathers and mothers were not sitting around in the evenings watching the boob tube. They were really doing things with the children. I remember, Jim was sick and I took some things over to him and it was around Valentine's Day and they were all gathered around the dining room table making Valentines. I felt that there was more give and take and more interest in one another and more understanding of one another as a result of this.

The problems over child-rearing came at several points, the most serious of which was over standards of discipline. One of the couples took a very laissez-faire attitude toward child-rearing. One was rather strict, enforcing rules by scolding and physical punishment. The third was deliberate, guiding their child through reasoning. The first two sets of parents were rather shocked when they saw each other's methods. The third was just as amazed by both of the others. Very early they saw the need to solve the issue of which adult had the right to discipline which child when and how. The resolution of this was to agree that whatever adult was on the scene was in charge. There would be no appeal back to the natural parents from his or her decision. The feeling was that this worked pretty well. The children adjusted very quickly to it — the parents somewhat more painfully. In fact, the children proved to be far more flexible than the adults.

At first it looked like chaos to me because I wasn't used to that many people, but then I began to see that the kids at least were doing things and they knew exactly what they were doing. I mean, they knew each other very well and they knew how to relate to each other in such a way, they knew what to expect from each other. At first I thought that all of these kids are going to be lost . . . I noticed that after a while when everybody would be doing something together and the noise level would be just insane and then I would begin to feel like there would be one or two people doing something that would be totally separate like they would be off in a different room. One of the kids would be reading or painting or something like they did. They were all as a group, but they weren't getting lost like I thought they would in a group.

The children figured out right away how far they could go with which adult, and how to unite in a kind of children's society against the adults. The adults had a harder time developing the united front.

> The children had a great sense of the power of their group and they brought it to play against either single adults or adults en masse whenever they needed to. They—they just sensed intuitively how to play one adult against another. We had a, many, many problems to work out in this area. And from things I've said before I'm sure you could infer that they never were worked out in a satisfactory way.

From time to time the adults would agree on a set of rules only to have the rules soon broken, especially by the laissez-faire parents. It is reported that arguments about child care occupied so much of the time in meetings that they came to resent anyone even bringing up this topic. Also, since they had not devised good mechanisms for resolving interpersonal tensions between adults, the children sometimes got caught in the middle of a hidden agenda dispute. In all of these respects child-rearing was a serious problem for the group.

We would not want to imply, though, that there were no positive aspects to this experience for the children. In fact, on balance, the contrary seems to be the case. I interviewed not only the members of the group, but also a babysitter, a schoolteacher, and friends who observed the children before, during and after the communal experience. Everyone seems to have been watching especially to see the effects on the children. The overwhelming verdict is that the commune was good for them. Even the most severe critics granted this. The two outstanding conclusions were that the children developed a marked degree of independence, initiative, and self-assurance, and that they learned to relate well to all adults, not just their own parents. On both of these points, specific, illustrative incidents were noted.

> Well, one thing that I noticed that the kids became a lot more trusting of just people in general than I think most kids are. A specific example of this would be like one time we were, the adults and the children, we were all out walking in the park and we had to go across a stream. The little kids just held out their hands for anybody who came along to take it. I know when I was small, and most kids, you don't do that. You wait for Mommy to come. They were willing for anybody at all to help them. That's because so many people were caring for them at once. I think that gave them the ability to trust people more.

One boy who had been considered immature by the teachers at school, became a class leader by the end of the period. One of the family friends describes the effects on another child this way:

> Now he is a lot more affectionate, physically; when we come over to visit, he'll tell us some secret that he's been doing or show us something that he's been working on. He got involved in politics this year. He organized a Kids for McGovern Club and he never had many friends. Now he has friends.

On the other hand, another boy who was a behavior problem before the commune was a behavior problem after it was over as well. The parents observed some of the same things, but they also noticed marked differences in the effect of the commune according to the ages of the children and their ordinal positions. Those who fared best were those who gained a new sibling of their own age. Others found themselves more isolated or more in the middle. The children who seemed to really thrive from the communal experience were the two children who were two years old at the beginning of the experiment. To them the entire group was literally their family and their new age mate was a real sibling. They also found, though, somewhat greater problems than the others on reentry into the nuclear family situation when the commune disbanded. One child resisted being interviewed as adamantly as any adult nonrespondent could. He just didn't want "to talk about it." In fact, it would seem that most of the children adjusted readily to the formation of the commune, but less well to its breakup. All in all, the most common comments about the children were ones like, "She is one of the best adjusted little children I've ever met." An additional advantage to the parents was the built-in-baby-sitting feature, which allowed them freedom for much needed vacations from the kids and the commune.

Another problem area which was never fully resolved was that of interpersonal relations between the adults. We've already noted what the group itself took considerable time to realize; namely, that there was no agreement on the degree of intimacy considered desirable. Although one man realized this very early, and made his own adjustments, it became clear to everyone only late in the experience when they decided to call on an outside facilitator to help them with interpersonal problems. Several of them were very enthusiastic, feeling that at last they were about to do what they should have been doing all along, i.e., work on better communication of inner feelings. One man especially had academic reservations about the whole process and did not really want to enter into it. He saw this as a false manufactured intimacy, a poor substitute for the real thing, which could only develop spontaneously. Another of the men, on the other hand, described the group at this point as becoming little more than a boardinghouse. In fact, at this stage several members report that their jobs and community activities occupied an increasingly larger place in their lives. Also at this point, the predictable myriad of little irritations mounted into major headaches. They had fairly well worked out the routines of living together. They had put long hours into remodeling a building. Now this was done. They were living together and were beginning to wonder why.

One form the question of intimacy took was the issue of sexual intimacy. By their initial agreement this was to be a group of monogamous couples. Of course, one of the most common suspicions of the community was that the free sharing of sex was the group's main motivation. It was not, and no orgy ever occurred. They were fairly free about nonsexual intimacies and mild demonstrations of affection but that was as far as it went. Some extramarital affairs were revealed during this period, but none of these incidents were in any way due to the fact of living in a commune. Yet the very idea that people could be having problems like this so unobtrusively, occasioned a crisis and concern over the lack of interpersonal sensitivity. Even so, the group support available in the commune was seen as highly beneficial.

> I don't know how I would have survived without them. I probably would have had to have gone home to my parents or something. But they were a help in every way. I think they were a help to both of us because they didn't take sides and they were there to listen and they made extra efforts with the children so that, well, I just don't quite know what to say, but I don't think we would have gotten along without them. Anyway, then we all stayed up all night that night. That was quite a night! It would take a whole tape to tell the whole story of that night.

Comarital sex became an issue of general discussion when one of the women reported enthusiastically on her reading of Robert Rimmer's utopian novel *Proposition 31*, in which a bill advocating marriage reform and legalizing group marriage is put on the California state ballot. At her instigation, they scheduled discussions of whether they should open the group to consensual sexual relations between nonspouses.

Immediately they revealed an entire spectrum of reactions to the suggestion ranging from enthusiasm to willingness to reluctance to outright disdain. The biggest surprise was the extent of one woman's enthusiasm. The most surprised person was her husband, who, himself, held the most conservative views in the group on this issue. After this initial impasse, there were several attempts to bring up the topic again, but most people were reluctant to discuss it further. Two quotations show that some members thought this impasse critical to the survival of the commune:

> It was probably a mistake to talk about deepening friendships in a sexual context. 'Cause that — was so threatening for them — and it was for me, too, but I wanted to explore that with myself. I wanted to know how I felt about that, and if I could handle that. But because of their reaction, and because of our own feeling that if everybody in the group was not in this direction, the rest of us drew back from pursuing personal relationships fully even without sexual contact. I think that that really sort of colored the whole rest of the year. That — because of those meetings, the whole thing blew up on us.
>
> We never really recovered from that . . . and we kind of settled into what seemed to be a pretty long winter. We just became a boardinghouse again. We talked about some other things, and we tried to bring back up some other topics . . . but for the most part at that point, I think that the thing died that evening with the discussion of sex.

There was another irritation nowhere nearly as significant as the last two, but nevertheless a problem that most such groups face. This was how to relate to visitors and friends. Communes are a curiosity, especially in the midwest, where they are rare. Even if this were not the case, each couple had their own set of previous friends. The combined total number made for a steady stream of company, which sometimes interfered with the need of the group to work on their own internal relationships. One of the couples and their friends were accustomed to rather informal drop-in visits which bothered some of the others. On the other hand, some friends who were mutual acquaintances of several members in the group reported that the commune was a hard place to visit because you were never sure just who you were visiting. The members of the commune found it impossible to drop everything they were doing every time any one person in the group had company, leaving some of the guests with the impression that they were unwelcome. More seriously both friends and members reported that so much time and energy was being spent by the communal members on the new relationships within the group that they tended to lose track of old friends. Their visitors were a concern to the neighborhood, too.

> They seemed to be, all the people that lived there as far as I know, were pretty nice people, but I think they got into a few things that they didn't expect when they started this. I mean, they had a lot of visitors coming through . . . That was really our main objection and the neighborhood's because we got to wondering if they weren't on national hook-up over there, because you would see these old hippy vans pull in with these out-of-state licenses and . . . there were an awful lot of what we would call trash that we wouldn't want in our home, let alone in our neighborhood, really; I hate to see that and we couldn't understand why those people would want them in their homes.

A special sort of visitor were college classes and sociology students. Some members of the group had considerable interest in sharing what they regarded as a significant experience and welcomed these opportunities. One man emphatically rejected this as "missionary work" in which he had no interest. I am grateful, though, that this man was one of my best informants, even though he felt frankly less interested in this project than did the other people. There was an interesting objection to the home economics researchers, too.

> One that was a little different though — was when some people from the Home Economics department came over to the house and did interviews on all kinds of things. But, that was pretty near the beginning, and the thing about that that I might have objected to later on was that what they wanted to do was they wanted to talk with the women about the practicalities of, you know, more of the home management aspect. That assumed, you know, that the men were not involved in that. And that was not the case.

Friends and visitors were perceived by members of the commune as both a nuisance and an opportunity. But how, then, did the outsiders perceive the commune? We collected considerable information on this.

Reactions

In reality, the reaction of the community was far less negative than the members of the commune thought at the time. In fact, among their friends, the most common reactions were admiration and envy. Most of them accepted at face value the group's own explanation of their motivation and achievement. They viewed the experience as generally beneficial to all concerned, especially the children. Those who were initially opposed to the commune were far fewer in numbers than expected. When interviewed, they tended to speak indirectly of why "people" were skeptical rather than owning up to these objections themselves. The most common reaction among the neighbors was to confuse commune with communism. Some were fearful of the example being set before their own offspring. About as frequent was the fear of free sex, drug parties, and police raids.

> Mostly because there are different types of communes, no doubt, and we have all read of the different types in all the magazines. There will be pictures and stories in regards to the ones in California and Oregon, on across and I think in most of them, they just don't sound like anything you would want in your own neighborhood. I think that is what we all had in mind.
> Then there were incidences of like parents asking some other source was it okay for their children to play with these children from the commune. I'm sure it stemmed from the mystery again, well, these children involved in orgies and whose mommy and daddy sleeps with what and what language do they learn and what these poor little kids stuck up in the attic while mommys and daddys are on drugs, what effect would it have on the kids.

When they saw no evidence of these things, most of them were eventually converted, especially after the group held an open house for the community. Thus, even among the "enemies" there were favorable comments about their cleanliness, their respectability as professionals, and especially about the children. Favorable comment about the effect on the children came even from one neighbor who never met the people personally, yet "observed" enough out her window to recognize the individuals and analyze accurately their personal relationships. While the local business people seemed to accept the group as good customers without much further question, the insurance and telephone companies were unprepared to deal with this alternative family:

> The insurance people simply couldn't handle three different non-blood-related families in one house without classifying it a three apart-

ment house. So we had to pay a commercial rate for a three apartment house for the insurance. And with the telphone company — Ohhh — we had all sorts of problems! Trying to get three different family names listed with one telephone number — You know we wanted a listing for each couple . . . and they simply would not do that. And so the telephone number the first year went into the telephone under one man's name, so . . . we didn't have our name in there at all. So essentially we had no telephone number. The second year, when it came time to list our telephone in the telephone book, I called them. I called the telephone company in September, and went through a whole long rigamarole of talking to one person and then that person's superior and then finally got the district supervisor . . . and everything and got them to agree that since they listed — in places where students were living together, they listed the telephone, one telephone number under different students' names, this was the same situation, and that they should list our telephone number under three different names in the telephone book. We even offered to pay for it — pay for extra listings and all that . . . and got them to agree that yes, they would list the number under three different family names. Unfortunately, after we got all this agreement, and yes, they would do that, it turned out that they had already sent the telephone book to the printer.

One serious tension point was within the local church. As a result of this controversy, one man nearly lost his job as a clergyman. One dispute centered around the fact that by joining the commune he would no longer be living in the parsonage furnished to him by the church. Initially he compromised by spending most of his time at the commune, but moving back to the parsonage each night. Eventually he moved into the commune full time, and lost his parsonage rights even after the commune ended. In fact what was at issue was much deeper than that, since his style of ministry was controversial even before the commune. The details of this controversy themselves could make a fascinating study in sociology of religion, involving as they do considerable debate about the role of the minister, the mission of the church, and the place for difference of opinion. Among my informants, there was considerable disagreement whether the result was beneficial or harmful to that church. One's answer, I suspect, depends mainly upon whether one values tranquility or challenge, tradition or change. Even nonmembers made remarks like, "That's kind of strange, isn't it, that the church should be the only one objecting? Isn't it terrible?" The communal clergyman did survive, but is not a clergyman today.

Termination

After the group ended, a common question was "Why did it fail?" The group's only answer is that it did not fail. It was a good two years together and it was never intended to be permanent. I agree, especially by the relationship-growth criterion. Nevertheless, there were reasons why they decided to continue at the end of the first year and to dissolve at the end of the second. I am sure that the realization of the lack of consensus about the group goals was a subtle but a major factor here. A lack of agreement on child-care standards certainly ranked high. Probably most important of all, however, was lack of consensus on the kind and degree of intimacy desired.

In any case, it is important to note that the process of this dissolution was a highly amiable one, even fun at times. The practical details were handled with a minimum of disagreement or regret.

> The tactical error we made was that we decided who would buy the house before we decided what the price was. That certainly changes your view of what the proper price is. . . But we did resolve the price of the house anyway without any hard feelings. I think that shows in effect that we do have a lot of respect for each other and that we are still friends . . . But we settled all the financial details and that was another major project. It was funny that once that we had a project of that sort the good feelings were better, but we had one session where we started passing checks to one another. It was funny: O.K., I'll write a check to you and then you write a check to me. But we got through that in relatively good condition.

They remain friends and worked together well on this research project. All of them insisted that overall the outstanding result of the experience was considerable personal growth.

Personal growth in this context has at least as many meanings as there are informants. To an outsider the most obvious change was in terms of sex roles and sex-role identity. About as frequently mentioned, though, was learning to face and to live with jealousy — no easy task, especially for those who had previously seen themselves as quite liberal. Then there was the ubiquitous problem of the neat versus the messy, and the growth of learning to tolerate each other, and also to understand one's own most extreme tendencies. Finally, as parents, they learned from each other, and saw themselves better as they saw how they each differed. Immediately after the experience most of the adults claimed that their own nuclear marriages had been strengthened. They had been forced to think through their own values with respect to virtually all aspects of their lives together. They developed at least some sharper understanding of their meaning to each other.

> Looking back, I think I've covered those things I thought I liked best about the whole thing — the enhanced relationships, even those I was not entirely satisfied with, really were far deeper and a greater of degree of friendship than would have been possible under any other circumstances. And just the experience of knowing, really knowing different kinds of people and appreciating different viewpoints was a very good experience. It makes you, you know, this process of constant questioning one's own attitudes and one's own feelings was a very good experience. And that's probably the primary growing that I did. And I had to relearn and rethink a lot of things about my attitudes toward personal relationships, primarily toward my children, toward marriage, toward other women, toward other men. The whole growing experience is probably the best, you know, the best result for myself. If I had two years, I would do it all over again just to have had that experience . . . Another very good result is that I think our own marriage is more firm, more honest, more open and I'm very much happier about that. Especially the fact that I think we are communicating. I thought we were really pretty good before we moved in, and we're a lot better now. I think we are a lot more open with each other. Finally, we, it was much easier to take this business of the sharing of domestic duties and the blending of man/woman roles in regard to how we operate within our home. I think that that would have been very difficult if we had tried to undertake that on our own . . . I just don't think we'd ever be where we are now and it would not have been an easy growing process, the way it was in group living.

Conclusions

Overall, we must conclude that this commune was a success in its own terms and a viable alternative family form. Remember that longevity, Utopia, or rebellion were never its goals, but that it did strive for personal growth, intimacy, and the values of the extended family. As an extended family, it did provide a wider fellowship and an efficient mechanism for meeting pragmatic tasks of daily living. The children seem to have been major beneficiaries here. On the other hand, like the extended family, there were problems of privacy and individuality, particularly with respect to external relationships. Also, the complexity of interpersonal relationships was a problem never fully resolved. The most important consequence of life in the middle-class commune was personal growth, the goal that Olson (1972) set forth as the emergent major goal for families in our society. This fact alone, but especially combined with the congruence between the communards' goals and the criticisms of conventional family forms, would seem to be ample justification for regarding this as a viable alternative form for many persons in our contemporary society.

To this researcher, the middle-class commune seems to be like a mirror. Through it the individual communards came to see themselves as individuals, as women and as men. Quite clearly reflected in it in a new way were their various relationships as couples, as friends, and as parents. The middle-class commune may even be a mirror for the society of which it is a part, whose values it both incorporates yet ever so subtly challenges. The middle-class commune is not so spectacular, perhaps, as its country cousins, but its effects may be just as profound. In a quieter way, a way more acceptable to some people, it definitely calls into question our materialistic values, and the exclusivity of our personal relationships. It does provide for the children at least some of the advantages of multiple adult and peer relationships. It provides an opportunity for personal growth to those who are discontent with conformity, but not yet so alienated as to seek another society. To traditional marriage it is both a mirror and an alternative. In the words of one of the women:

(I feel) like sharing this experience because — mainly because it was done with what I perceive to be pretty average middle-class liberal people . . . not people who are on the fringes of society . . . It might be helpful for people who are interested in thinking about this, to know what happened to us . . . When we started into this, we had no model to go by. I think a lot of things we came up with were good. That doesn't mean everybody should do it that way — but, at least it gives one idea of the way to do it. I would never say that this is the best way for all people to live. But I think that it's a good way and that for some people it might be better than the nuclear family kind of experience. For me the notion of sharing is really an important one, and if you can do that at all, I think it's nice to do that on an everyday basis. I think it's good in terms of having people depending on people again rather than on things . . . So I don't have any universal things to say; you know — all people should live in communes! I can't say that! But I'm saying that maybe a lot of people who aren't doing it might like it.

REFERENCES

Johnston, C., and Deisher, R. "Contemporary Communal Child Rearing: A First Analysis." *Pediatrics*, 52 (1973): 319–26.

Kanter, R. M. *Commitment and Community: Communes and Utopias in Sociological Perspectives*. Cambridge, Mass.: Harvard University Press, 1972.

Kanter, R. M. "Communes in Cities." *Working Papers for a New Society* (Summer, 1974): 36–44.

LeBlanc, J. "Communes for the Middle Class." *Chicago Tribune Magazine* (April 21, 1974): 43–45, 48.

Olson, D. "Marriage of the Future: Revolutionary or Evolutionary Change? *The Family Coordinator* 21 (1972): 383–93.

Pat, Ed, and Duffy of New Communities Project. "It Isn't Just Me." *Communities* 2 (1973): 37–38.

Ramey. J. "Communes, Group Marriage, and the Upper-Middle Class." *Journal of Marriage and the Family* 34 (1972): 647–55. (a)

Ramey. J. "Emerging Patterns of Innovative Behavior in Marriage." *The Family Coordinator* 21 (1972): 435–56.

Weiss, M. *Living Together: A Year in the Life of a City Commune*. New York: McGraw-Hill, 1974.

SWINGING, OR COMARITAL SEX

[6]

I REFERRED earlier to the similarity in backgrounds between swingers and those in open marriages and group marriages regarding high needs for autonomy, poor parental relationships, and high sex drive. The mechanisms for handling these circumstances, however, may be somewhat different. For swingers, the key mechanism would seem to be *regulation*, and, to a somewhat lesser degree, *depersonalization.* *

The individuals involved in a swinging marriage may fear the effect of emotional entanglement so that it becomes necessary to keep the spouse under a sort of surveillance and to be assured that in the swinging session there will be a maximum amount of time allotted to sexual activity and a minimum to fraternization. The antecedent state pushing individuals toward attempting to regulate interpersonal interaction in this way is probably anxiety. It is necessary to avoid letting the spouse relate in an unsupervised fashion because it may be feared that someone else might be found to fill one's shoes permanently. Depersonalization is also understood as a defense against anxiety. Since the other may be treated as a body rather than a person, no emotional relationship and concomitant threat to the marriage may ensue. Moreover, for some persons intimacy, even with the spouse, may be threatening. For such persons, swinging should provide spice without the fear of getting too close.

---

*Some swingers claim to be very involved with their partners. If this were true, they would be more likely to fall under the rubric of "open marriage," according to the categorization used here.

Anxiety in interpersonal relationships may diminish with successful encounters. Individuals may, in time, crave something more profound than a passing sexual contact. For such individuals swinging may eventually pale and become wearisome as they long to be accepted as something more than a penis or a vagina. Thus swinging for some may be a transitional state as Ramey has also noted (Ramey, 1972); a developmental stage of growth along the route to richer interpersonal interactions. Just what proportion move on in this fashion, and what proportion desire to remain in swinging or lack the interpersonal resources to move on, is moot. Whatever the factors involved, the majority of individuals who swing do not remain in that category for any length of time as the following chapter documents.

REFERENCE

Ramey, J. W. "Emerging Patterns of Innovative Behavior in Marriage." *The Family Coordinator* 21 (1972): 435–56.

Swinging

BERNARD I. MURSTEIN

T O SWING or not to swing," is a decision that few couples have faced, primarily because only a bit more than half of the population have ever heard of it, with but a handful who knowingly have ever had contact with swingers. Despite its statistical paucity, swinging has received much publicity in the media, and its mixture of deviation and conformity with respect to the institution of marriage makes it unique as an innovative life style. In this paper I shall define swinging, explore just how extensive it is, and describe how swingers get together. At this point I shall describe the background and personality characteristics of swingers and the effect of swinging on the swingers' marriages. After analyzing these data, the causes of swinging will be determined followed by an assessment and summary of its advantages and disadvantages. The chapter will close with an estimate of the future of swinging.

Definition

Swinging first came into the public eye in the late 1950s though one can scarcely doubt its unofficial existence from the dawn of history. It was first called "wife swapping," a term which adhered to the idea, only relinquished lately, that the wife was a chattel whom the man could exchange for more delectable merchandise. The more egalitarian "spouse swapping" has been used and more recently "comarital" sex has gained favor (Smith and Smith, 1970, 1974). Although I can appreciate the aesthetic preferability of "comarital" to swinging, I shall retain the latter phrase only because it is fairly well understood by the populace, whereas comarital sex is open to a multitude of ambiguities. (It may be thought by laymen to be some form of open marriage). It is also much easier to write about "swinging" than "comaritalizing."

Swinging is defined as *a form of extramarital behavior involving legally married or pair-bonded couples sharing coitus or other sexual pleasures with one or more persons in a social context defined by all participants as a form of recreational-convivial play.*

How Many Do It?

The number of swingers who have engaged in swinging at least once has been estimated from 500,000 to 8,000,000, the latter figure being based on rather faulty reasoning (Breedlove and Breedlove, 1964). There are data available, however, which permit more accurate estimates.

Athanasiou (1973) conducted a survey of 20,000 *Psychology Today* readers as to incidence of mate-swapping with the results as shown in Table 1.

TABLE 1. Percent respondents, by sex, to a question concerning mate-swapping

Have you participated in wife-swapping?

	Males	*Females*
1. Frequently	1.3%	1.5%
2. Once or twice	4.2	3.1
3. Not ever, but I might	41.4	21.6
4. Never; would never consider it	53.1	73.8
	100.0%	100.0%

Hunt (1974) sampled approximately 2000 men and women and found the incidence of swinging to be 2 percent for men and less than 2 percent for women. Below the age of twenty-five, about 5 percent of the husbands and 2 percent of the wives had engaged in swinging, but some of this was premarital experience. Considerably less than 1 percent of each sex engaged in swinging regularly.

Spanier and Cole (1972) did an area sampling of a midwestern town of 40,000 and found that 1.7 percent had swung. Fifty-five percent had heard of "wife-swapping," but only 6.7 percent had friends or acquaintances who claimed to have indulged in this activity. Only 2.8 percent had themselves been approached and propositioned in this regard.

White and Wells (1973) did a random 5 percent sample of a northwestern state university and received only 14 percent refusals. Among the questions they asked was whether "mate-swapping" was of no interest or some interest to the students. Among men, 49 percent expressed no interest, with 51 percent expressing some interest. Among the women, 84 percent expressed no interest and 16 percent some interest.

None of these surveys is representative of the population of the United States. The *Psychology Today* readers, for example, were self-selective (they elected to fill out the questionnaires and mail them in). *Psychology Today* readers are also relatively young, of better than average income, and of liberal political persuasion. Hunt's sample resembled the United States population in most economic and background characteristics. However, 4 out of 5 subjects approached turned down the interviewer, so again a selective, volunteer, population resulted. Spanier and Cole, of course, sampled only one city, and the midwest is not necessarily typical of the entire country. Considering that the Athanasiou and Hunt samples because of selectivity probably overestimate the number of swingers, the best estimate would seem to be that in the early 1970s between 1 to 2 percent of the population had swung at least once.

Note the disparity in Table 1 between engaged in "once or twice" and engaged in "frequently." These figures accord with the Breedloves' earlier estimate that perhaps three-quarters of swingers had dropped out before a year was up. The best estimate, therefore, is that at most, no more than 0.5 percent are steady swingers and the percentage may well be smaller than that. Nevertheless, at least in professed attitudes, a considerable portion of the population shows some interest in swinging. It seems reasonable that the percentage of swingers would increase considerably if swinging were more out in the open and swingers more actively and openly sought recruits. Why they do not do so at present I think is obvious and requires no discussion. As long as very few have contact with acknowledged swingers on a personal basis, however, the spread of swinging will be inhibited.

How Do Swingers Start Swinging?

Most researchers have found that the man generally initiates the idea that the couple ought to swing. The wife's reaction is often one of shock. She may feel repulsed by the idea and wonder how she has failed her husband in bed, whether he is "sick," or if her marriage is now headed for the rocks (Varni, 1973). The husband usually seeks to allay the fears of the wife on all counts but stresses a variety of reasons depending on the circumstances: differences in sex-drive, sex and love can be separated, variety will enrich their desirability for each other, etc. Most women have been conditioned that sex without accompanying love is "dirty" and find it difficult to accept these arguments.

Even if the couple eventually become swingers, there is usually a gestation period of weeks to months in which the possibility is discussed, reviewed, and discussed some more. Finally, in a small number of cases, the couple decides to swing. The determinants of their decision are varied and subject to debate. I shall, therefore, defer dealing with this question until later when all of the data on swinging have been reviewed. In the meantime, there is the problem of how a pair of swingers meets other swingers.

How Swingers Meet

Getting to meet a fellow swinger is a problem for the novitiate couple: they fear disclosure and, in addition, there is a paucity of couples who actually swing. One way is to insert or answer an ad. One magazine ad read as follows:

> S–225: Married couple, middle thirties. Wife 37-25-36, husband muscular, Los Angeles area. Willing to try anything. Interested in French, Greek, and Arab culture. No single men (Bell, 1970).

Much of the ad is self-explanatory. The references to culture hardly indicate a hunger for international esthetics. They represent a code: French culture signifies that the couple likes oral sex, the Greek allusion means that they are amenable to anal intercourse, and the Arab features points to an appreciation of sado-masochistic practices. Ads, however, are risky. Photos may result in blackmail, or people may send doctored or old photos and misrepresent their age or "vital" statistics. And since there is also no control over the kind of mentality one may encounter on a blind date, many swingers prefer that initial contacts be made at "socials" sponsored by swingers magazines, at swinger bars, or through friends (Denfield, 1970). Once established, future arrangements are simple. There are extensive networks, and a couple moving to a different locale can usually be put in touch with others in the new area.

The Swinging Scene

Most swingers range from twenty-five to forty-one years of age (Symonds, 1968); the average number at a get-together is five to eight couples (O'Neill and O'Neill, 1970), with an average frequency of twice a month.

There is a great deal of variability in how swingers engage in swinging. Often the couples arrive at the home of the hosts and the evening starts out as a social one with light banter and drinks serving as ice-breakers. Sometimes the hosts may introduce risque games to get people in the mood, or show pornographic movies of the home grown or commercial kind. At a certain point in the evening the hosts may suggest that it is time to get going, or experienced couples may start pairing off by themselves and leaving for the bedrooms, or the hosts may simply start undressing — a signal no one can miss. If the hosts have children, these may have been sent off with relatives or friends to spend the night. A few swingers keep the children at home.

The man usually initiates the courting behavior. No one is obligated to swing with anyone or everyone, but rejection is of course rather ego-threatening and may be couched in palliative phrases "I'm too tired" (after an earlier episode) or "I'd like to rest just now." Any woman who rejects too many men is not apt to be asked back.

A couple may retire to a bedroom and close the door. In some circles this "closet swinging" is acceptable, whereas in other circles this is frowned upon. A door left open ("open swinging") signifies that anyone is welcome to come in and join the fun or just watch. A group of people may link up in any number of coital, oral, or anal positions in what is known in the vulgate parlance as "cluster fucking."

Not all swingers go to parties. Some prefer to swing with only one other couple. If the exchange relationship continues for any length of time with only two pairs, it generally indicates that an emotional closeness is developing concomitantly with the sexual relationship, and the definition of "satellite relationship" rather than swinging might be more appropriate.

Women swingers often become bisexual, a happening which is relatively rare among men. In one sample, 65 percent of the women *admitted* having sexual relations with other female swingers. In the swinging sessions which he personally observed, the anthropologist Gilbert Bartell (1971) recorded 92 percent of the women becoming sexually involved with one another.

Several factors account for female homosexual relationships among swingers: Most men are hardly matches for sexually aroused multiorgasmic women. While the men rest, they often experience sexual restimulation if they watch women make love to each other. Presumably the sight of another man making love to their spouse (while they are not similarly occupied) would be too ego-threatening to some men, but practically no men are threatened by the sight of two women making love.

Many women are esthetically disturbed by the concomitants of heterosexual love-making. They find semen messy, and the thought of fellating a stranger or even their own spouse is somewhat repulsive. With other women, they can at least avoid semen.

The effect of novelty can be highly motivating. Many women have wondered what it would be like to make love to a woman, but have never had a socially sanctioned opportunity. Homosexuality is often interpreted as an inferior activity in our need-achievement-oriented society, because it assumes that the individual cannot successfully "score" with the opposite sex. Because men occupy a higher status in society, they stand to lose more by such activity than women. As a result, there is rarely any male homosexual interaction at swinger parties, although younger swingers show more "flexibility" in this regard than older ones.

A large number of typologies of swinging have been offered (Denfield, 1971; Varni, 1974; Bell, 1971; Smith and Smith, 1974; Symonds, 1968). Undue publicity has been allotted to the "hard-core" or "recreational" swinger who is wholly absorbed in bodies and parts — not people. This type has been generalized by the cynic who advised Bartell (1971) that "People will tell you they do all sorts of things, but when it comes right down to it they're only interested in going off to another room and screwing your wife" (p. 13).

On the basis of published reports and interviews, I am inclined to conclude that such a generalization is patently unwarranted. There are, true enough, an unknown number of swingers who are focused exclusively on sex. Others appear to be searching for intimacy with others besides their spouses. Where people are conditioned to respond in highly stylized ways to others, with little involvement and emotional contact, sex may be regarded as the key to surmounting the barriers to a hoped-for emotional contact. For most people, sex is not an impersonal act. Although many individuals will pretend emotional interest in someone else in order to spirit a partner into bed, others may use sex to gain friends and intimacy. Extramarital sexual intimacy — the breaking of a taboo — may be used as a device for entering into friendship, particularly in the absence of kin-neighbor-friendship relational systems that reduce some of the demands on the marital bond (Ramey, 1972).

Many swingers may conclude that a person who can overcome the deep-seated inhibition against sex activity with a stranger will also be the kind of person who can rapidly cut through inhibitions to emotional interaction. There is no evidence of the validity of this assumption, but the literature does indicate that some swingers prefer swinging because it avoids problems of intimacy and involvement with others, (Bartell, 1971), whereas other swingers hope to enrich their coterie of friends as well as of their sex partners (Palson and Palson, 1972; Margolis and Rubenstein, 1971). The presence of a dichotomy is suggested by the responses to the above-cited questionnaire (Gilmartin, 1972). In response to the statement "expressing feeling of 'love' for a swinging partner is generally considered undesirable or unacceptable in the swinging world," 68 percent of the swinging men and 49 percent of the swinging women disagreed or were uncertain. Some 32 percent of the swinging men and 51 percent of the swinging women agreed with the statement.

Where swingers do develop friendships, their sexual interaction often decreases or is terminated (Margolis and Rubenstein, 1971). Why this should be has not been investigated. It may be that when a friendship develops, the vagaries attached to the sex act threaten the new relationship. For example, if one member of a foursome loses sexual interest in his extramarital partner, the friendship of all four might be threatened. Since, to a swinger, sex may be available almost anywhere — whereas friendship is not — he may decide to safeguard the new relationship by avoiding sex.

There is no question, however, that a swinger is very different from the run-of-the-mill adulterer. Most adulterers (who are usually men) do not wish their spouses to mimic their adulterous behavior. Swingers, on the other hand, espouse a single standard, and the swinging wife is accorded equal privileges. If the wife cannot participate in a "social" — for example, if she is menstruating — the husband usually is not allowed to participate.

Background and Personality Characteristics of Swingers

Swingers in some respects are described quite differently in different studies. In a Chicago survey (Bartell, 1971), swingers appeared to be quite conservative. The majority opposed drugs, and 40 percent admired George Wallace. Swingers have also been described as traditional and religious (Walshok, 1971).

On the other hand, the most thorough and controlled study to date (Gilmartin, 1972, 1974) presents another picture. In this study 80 swinging couples were obtained through sexual freedom groups, another 20 coming from other sources, making 100 couples in all. These were matched with 100 controls, who were legally married couples similar in age, neighborhood residence, annual income, level of education, and number of children. A major factor which could not be controlled was that the 200 couples were collected with almost no refusals from solicited swinging subjects, whereas a 60 percent rejection rate characterized the controls.

The data, obtained from a lengthy questionnaire, show some major differences between the swingers and controls. The swingers were much more liberal and antiestablishment. Their politics were liberal, they were antireligion, nonnationalistic, belonged to few community organizations, were more geographically mobile, and favored more freedom for women as well as liberal divorce laws. They were more tolerant of drug usage, drinking, long hair, civil rights, protestors, abortion, and nudity around the house.

Swingers believed much more in autonomy than did controls. They emphasized that rights were more important than duties, that conscientious objectors should not be punished, and that a military officer should be disobeyed if he ordered soldiers to fire on women and children. Obedience was not as important for children as the controls thought it was; kids should be allowed to date when they felt old enough, and their sexuality should not be suppressed by adults.

The childhood and adolescence of swingers was decidedly different from that of controls. They were more apt to be only children or to come from a small family. Male swingers perceived their parents as less happy, and reported more parental divorce than did controls. The males also reported a more laissez-faire attitude toward them including a liberal attitude toward sex and fewer parental rules. Both male and female swingers said they were less happy as adolescents, with female swingers currently finding themselves much less close to their mothers than control women. The better emotional relationship with parents by controls was also found in another study with a sexual freedom league group (Twichell, 1974).

The most outstanding difference between swingers and controls, a difference found in *every* study comparing swingers with controls whether the swinger was conservative, liberal, recreational swinger, or utopian, was in the area of sex. In a Chicago sample (Bartell, 1971) 99 percent of the men read *Playboy*. In a California sample (Smith and Smith, 1970) 90 percent acknowledged being nude in the presence of others, with 57 percent having engaged in intercourse in this situation.

Again, the most complete information comes from Gilmartin's data. It is apparent that the swingers' interest in sex was manifested at an extremely early age. Approximately one-third of the swingers experienced a romantic interest in the opposite sex from the period of kindergarten to third grade, compared to one-tenth of controls for that period. Swingers also dated earlier, had more dates, and commenced sex earlier than controls. In fact, despite the fact that they married early, they averaged better than a 90 percent premarital sex rate compared to the later marrying controls, whose premarital rate was slightly less than 70 percent.

Swingers had more premarital experience, many more premarital partners and fell in love with many more partners. Not surprisingly, the swinging women were more likely to have been premaritally pregnant. I am inclined to suspect that there is a biological predisposition to this sexuality in addition to the more permissive environment. In this connection, it is noteworthy that the swingers perceive themselves currently as in better health than the controls perceive themselves.

Does the involvement in swinging result in less marital sex so that swingers save themselves for swinging sessions? The facts flatly contradict this supposition. Although the average age of the swingers as well as of the controls was in the thirties, 55 percent of the swingers experienced four or more copulations per week with their spouse as compared to only 16 percent of the control group.

These are cold facts, but they do not do justice to the sexual intensity that permeates the swinger psyche. One male swinger describes his love of crowds, bodies pressing, squirming, breathing against him: "I love all kinds of groups, with everybody pressing me on all sides,

somebody's pussy in my face, somebody's finger in my behind, somebody's mouth on my penis — it's groovy!" (Hunt, 1974, p. 47).

A fifty-year old women described an experience this way: "It was one
after another, and really, after a point it didn't make any difference *who*
it was. It was just one great big prick after another. And I *never*
experienced anything like that in my whole life . . . I think in the course
of three hours I must have had eleven or twelve men, and one greater
than the next. I just kept on getting better every time. It snowballed"
(Palson and Palson, 1972, p. 30).

Finally, a free-lance swinging writer in much more sedate language
still manages to illustrate the sexual needs of swingers.

> Without going into the gory details of my divorce, it is necessary to
> mention that my husband and I always had a good physical relationship,
> and it nearly proved to be my undoing to have that cut off so sharply
> when we parted. I used to stand in the middle of the living room, tears
> streaming down my face, and with an ache of longing to reach out to
> someone, to be loved again and to return it with every ounce of my
> physical being (Stanton, 1974, p. 18).

A basic assumption of the average layman vis-à-vis swingers is that
they must be a very "sick" group to carry on such "shenanigans."
However, a study of swingers administered the Minnesota Multiphasic
Personaltiy Inventory revealed rather normal personality profiles. The
Rokeach Dogmatism scale, likewise, indicated that they were not
dogmatic (Twichell, 1974).

Gilmartin's questionnaire did not inquire very much into the mental
health of his subjects, but the few indirect questions pertaining to this
area show no indication of maladjustment. Job satisfaction was equally
satisfactory for swingers and controls. Swinging men, however, were
less often bored and less likely to suffer from anomie. Swinging
women described themselves as more warm and affectionate than
control women do. A study by Schupp (1970) also found no difference
in adjustment between swingers and controls.

One possible sign of maladjustment that does differentiate swingers
from controls is that the former are much more likely to have had
psychotherapy or counseling (Gilmartin, 1974; Smith and Smith, 1970).
Going into psychotherapy or counseling, nevertheless, can not be
taken as a direct indication of inadequate functioning any more than
can the fact that many more swingers than controls have been divorced.
Many swingers married young, often to nonswingers. The resulting

incompatibility must have led to difficult times, with divorce providing a means of rectifying this incompatibility. However, this may be a function of the mismatching of a deviant with a conformist rather than the basic inadequacy of the swinger. Supporting this interpretation is Gilmartin (1974), who reported that in his study *"none* of the divorces occurred *after* a man or woman had become active with either a present or a former spouse in comarital sexual behavior . . . divorce antedates the initial mutual involvement in mate sharing. It does not postdate it," (p. 316).

Pursuing the topic of adjustment further, we might inquire as to what effect swinging has on the marriage of swingers themselves. Here we find overwhelming testimonies by swingers that they believe the effect has been highly beneficial. Gilmartin (1974), for example, points out that swingers found their sex life greatly improved after they started swinging. Comparing swingers and controls, no differences were found in global indices such as subjective estimate of happiness and egality of decision making in marriage. Compared with controls, however, swinging women derived much more *emotional* satisfaction from sex. Swinging men were more satisfied with the affection shown them by their spouses compared to male controls. They also said that their wives seemed to have an easier time saying "I love you" to them. Last, both swinging men and women reported spending more time talking together informally than did their control counterparts. Many other measures of marital satisfaction which were statistically nonsignificant invariably showed a trend favoring swingers. In short, it appears that the swinging marriages studied were certainly no worse than and in some ways were better than the marriages of the controls.

There is a fly in the ointment, however. The swinging marriages studied were those of persons *actively committeed* to swinging who also *volunteered* to participate in a survey. These results, therefore, in no way imply that *anyone* taking up swinging would achieve comparable experiences. Indeed, from our earlier surveys, we inferred that for every long-term swinger there were three to four dropouts. Therefore, the typical reaction to swinging is to give it up soon, and it might be suspected that these cases often resulted in marital dissension among the swinging couples.

The only study on dropouts yet published involved canvassing 2,147 marriage counselors by mail (Denfield, 1974). About 45 percent replies were obtained and about half of the counselors had counseled swingers. The reasons for dropping out of swinging were catalogued as shown in Table 2.

TABLE 2.   Problems or reasons for dropping out of swinging

Problems	Number of Couples	Percentage
Jealousy	109	23%
Guilt	68	14
Threatening marriage	68	14
Development of emotional attachment with other partners	53	11
Boredom and loss of interest	49	11
Disappointment	33	7
Divorce or separation	29	7
Wife's inability to "take it"	29	7
Fear of discovery: community/children	15	3
Impotence of husband	14	3
	467	100%

Inspection of this table indicates that items involving marital complications of one sort or another constitute the vast majority of reasons for dropping out of swinging. In short, most couples probably don't adjust to swinging very well.

Moreover, the myth of swinging as an egalitarian relationship does not bear up under close inspection either. Henshel (1973) in an interview study of 25 swinging Toronto women found that 59 percent of the husbands made *all* the initial decisions about swinging, 28 percent were joint decisions, and 12 percent were made by the women. When dropout decisions were made, however, wives initiated these 54 percent of the time, husbands made 34 percent of the decisions, and the remaining 12 percent were mutual. In sum, husbands press for entrance into the swinging arena, wives somewhat reluctantly go along, perhaps because of an implied threat to the marriage by husbands. Eventually, most of the women decide that swinging is unsatisfactory, and the couples leave. This reaction, as we have seen, is quite different from swingers who stay in swinging.

Having concluded our review of the data, we can now speculate more freely about the origins of swinging.

Why Sex Outside of Marriage?

Let's start by positing some reason why individuals might desire sex outside of marriage in general and then see why they specifically pick swinging. These reasons may be categorized under Qualities of Perceived Partner, Qualities of Self, Context, and Societal Influences.

QUALITIES OF PERCEIVED PARTNER

The spouse may be perceived as sexually unattractive for a number of reasons: obesity, prudishness, physical deterioration, cleanliness, impotence, and lack of capability for satisfying one sexually (Johnson, 1970). Another enemy of marital sexuality is habituation. Even the most scintillating partner at last becomes predictable and loses his or her glamour. One's jokes may be new to the party — they are old hat to the spouse. Certainly, novelty in a partner has a facilitative effect on sex for a number of species. Kagan and Beach (1953) for example, were able to demonstrate that male rats who had copulated to satiation with females with whom they were raised, could be "revived" by introducing females into the cage with whom they were not raised. Also, the countless trivial resentments built up in the course of a relationship may become effective inhibitors of sexual response. Resentment and spontaneous sexual expression are often antagonistic to each other.

Another difficulty is the declining reinforcement value of the spouse. As habituation takes place, his or her approval is taken for granted. It is after all one's *role* to support the spouse and to suppress destructive feelings. The husband, for example, then may lose his power to reward his wife by complimenting her though he retains the power of punishing her by unkind remarks (Aronson, 1969). Conversely, the stranger's compliments may be highly flattering. It is not the stranger's *role* to pay compliments, and depending on the stranger's status and turn of phrase, his or her compliments may carry more weight than those of the spouse.

QUALITIES OF SELF

The individual may be highly "sold" on himself and believe that more fitting rewards will be provided by novel or more exciting partners. There may be doubts about one's own sexuality, and the individual may seek to assuage them with a new partner. He or she may be attracted to behaviors which seem immoral or risky, but also thereby exciting and adventurous. There may be fear of too much dependency on one person and attempts, therefore, to dilute interpersonal needs among many persons. The individual may be alienated from people and believe that he is powerless to control his own life. Extramarital sex may be at once a means of demonstrating to the participant that he has control over his life, and that he can establish a relationship which will terminate his sense of alienation and isolation.

Another possibility is that the individual may be geared to a life style which ignores traditional norms and enjoys iconoclasm. The taboo of extramarital sexuality becomes one which is therefore enjoyable to break. Last, the person may possess poor social controls. To want something may be the sole necessary stimulus to obtain it no matter what the cost. Guilt feelings may accompany extramaritability in such a case, but they manifest themselves after rather than before the extramarital sexuality.

CONTEXT

Some people do not engage in extramarital relationships only because they do not perceive the opportunity to do so. The anticipated pleasures of extramarital sex are more than compensated by the fear of being discovered by others and their anticipated disapproval. Johnson (1970) was able to show that for his sample, twice as many men as women engaged in adultery. However, when the ratio of adultery to perceived opportunity was computed, slightly more women than men engaged in adultery per perceived opportunity.

With increasing mobility, an increasing number of women workers, and urban anonymity, the opportunities to remain undetected in extramarital activities are greater than ever before. However, if one can engage in extramarital sex concomitantly with the spouse, a major potential source of criticism may be averted.

SOCIETY

One of the primary indirect supports for extramarital sex is the changing societal ideal of "how to live." The Puritan ideal of supervision, hard work, and time perspective for eventual goals has been attacked by those forwarding a countercultural ideal of another ilk. The most treasured aspect of living in Charles Reich's *Consciousness III* (1970) is "personal experience" which now replaces achievement-oriented goals and preoccupation with occupational status. Traditional monogamy, which limits the extent of and depth of interpersonal relationships outside of marriage, thus seems incompatible with this style. Moreover the focus on honesty in the "new" life style seems to preclude the traditional means of handling extramarital desire — clandestine adultery.

The traditional mores looked askance at sensualists who sought to pleasure the body in myriad ways. Only when traditional educational and occupational goals had been achieved could the individual permit himself a bit of "self-indulgence," and then only in a conjugal way. Philip Slater, however, enunciates the new calling which argues "that instead of throwing away one's body so that one can accumulate material artifacts, one should throw away the artifacts and enjoy one's body" (Slater, 1970, p. 106).

Solutions to Dissatisfaction

What then does the individual do who finds that ennui has permeated his or her marriage, who is dissatisfied with the marital sexual relationship, or who has many other complaints? Some of the alternatives open to such individuals are as follows:

1. sequential polygamy (divorce and remarriage)
2. clandestine adultery
3. bachelorhood
4. swinging
5. "grin and bear it"
6. extramarital heterosexual emotional attachments without sex
7. multiple egalitarian attachments with emotional intimacy and sex
8. open marriage (freedom to indulge in varying kinds of extramarital relationships whose limits are agreed upon by the participants of the marriage) (Murstein, 1974).

The singularly clearest finding that has evolved from swinging studies is that swingers for the most part possess very high sex drives and also a craving for variety in sexual partners. The need for novelty was apparent even in swingers who had good marital relationships prior to swinging. It seems logical that when otherwise normal individuals find that their goal satisfactions are not met by traditional conforming behaviors, they select alternate means. The tendency of these alternate means to depart radically from normatively prescribed behavior is probably a function of the intensity of the need as well as the probability of achieving it through traditional channels. Deviant behavior such as swinging, therefore, may tell us more about the failures of conformity to satisfy essential needs than it does about exotic, perverse personalities.

Although swinging does not involve equal motivation on the part of both wife and husband, as we have seen, it does make for more open communication than does the traditional clandestine adultery, and is thus more in keeping with the increasing emphasis on honesty between marital partners.

Aiding and abetting sex as a motive for swinging is the lack of socialization toward conformist ideals. Swingers, by and large, unlike most married couples, are able to separate sex and love.

The seeds of this inadequate socialization lay in the lesser probability of swingers finding stable pillars of conformity in their parents (more parental divorces) — especially true in the case of the male swinger. As only children or as siblings in small families, they have had less need to inhibit expression of their needs. The parents' laissez-faire attitude and failure to apply sanctions when they were out of line may also have furthered their insistence on self-gratification. Their lack of organizational, religious, and community bonds made it difficult for society to exercise social controls over them. Their peers replaced parents and relatives as guiding normative influences, and the fact that peer norms, especially among the young, usually reinforce autonomy made a decision to violate traditional sexual norms all the more likely. Swinging thus resembles a compromise between radicalism and conformity in which the swinger violates a norm but limits the violation to carefully limited and prescribed conditions. There is no full acceptance of the spouse's independence in interpersonal relationships. Instead a bargain is struck in which only limited extramarital sex is permitted to both partners. By retaining the measure of control over each other, the participants are in effect saying that they fear complete autonomy and think that the spouse might leave if he or she were free to interact in any spontaneous manner with another.

Some swingers move on from this phase to more person-oriented relationships. The majority, however, retreat when they learn that anxiety, jealousy, and insecurity make even swinging threatening to them, let alone open marriage. In sum, the causes of swinging are myriad, but a high sex drive, inadequate socialization to conventional societal norms, and a fear of too great trust in the spouse are predominant.

Before closing this section on causes of swinging I would like to offer an additional purely speculatory hypothesis. No one has yet studied the probability of swinging as a function of the discrepancy in physical attractiveness between husband and wife. In a still male-dominated culture, such as the United States, it may well be that the case in which the husband is more physically attractive than the wife may result in a greater dissatisfaction with marital sex on his part and a greater willingness to push his wife into swinging. He may believe that, from the exchange point of view, he risks little and may gain much. Even if the other's wife he interacts with is not a raving beauty, since the focus is on sex, it may not matter so much. On the other hand, the husband with an attractive wife may be less willing to risk damaging his valuable "goods" when his return is unknown or marginal. This hypothesis should hold only for male-initiated encounters, relying as it does on a male-centered marriage. Hopefully, the role of physical attractiveness, seemingly so intrinsically a part of swinging, will be investigated in future research.

At this point let us summarize the advantages and disadvantages of swinging to the participants involved, using earlier published works (Denfield, 1971; Denfield and Gordon, 1970; Nemy, 1971) as well as common sense. First, the advantages:

It is less time-consuming and emotionally demanding than an affair.

It is less expensive than an affair.

It offers sexual variety for couples bored with each other.

There is less danger of losing one's spouse as compared to discovered infidelity.

If often rejuvenates sexual interest in the spouse.

It is educative sexually.

It offers a chance for a couple to share the thrill of the risque as they plan for and attend swingers' affairs. It affords a camaraderie that others cannot share.

It is democratic and honest.

It is ideal for those who fear intimacy with their own spouse.

It allows complete satisfaction for both partners despite a difference in strength of sex drive.

It offers opportunities for acquiring social contacts.

In sum, it is in the best American tradition: "to be popular, to have friends, to be busy" (Bartell, 1971, p. 282).

On the other hand, swinging is not without drawbacks:

There is often a lack of emotional closeness between sexual partners, which robs some individuals of sexual enjoyment and/or the ability to perform adequately.

There is little ego satisfaction when the "other" can be won, not by dint of one's charm and attractiveness but merely by being available.

Fantasy often gives way to disappointed reality as one becomes aware that the "other" is rarely a Venus de Milo incarnate, but is flabbier than he or she appeared with clothes on, or has bad breath or is addicted to unacceptable sexual techniques.

There is a competitive air that inhibits performance. From the woman's point of view, there is always a woman who is sexier, bigger bosomed, more curvaceous, and more attractive. From the man's point of view, there is always a handsomer fellow, "better hung," and more potent. Not surprisingly, therefore, Bartell reported that 12 percent of the women never experienced orgasm except with their husbands, while less than 25 percent of the men were fully adequate at all swinger sessions (Bartell, 1971).

There is a cult of youth, and everyone becomes less desirable with age.

Many individuals find that they cannot overcome their jealousy and fear that someone else will appeal more to their spouse.

Some individuals cannot shed their feeling of guilt and lowered self-esteem after engaging in what they believe is basically immoral.

For those who adhere to the dictum of swinging only once with another person, or for those who collect new sexual experiences like trophies, there is a never-ending search for new, beautiful partners. Many fatiguing hours are spent on the phone, in writing letters and driving hundreds of miles for interviews, and then perhaps feeling embarrassed at vetoing unattractive prospects or, even worse, experiencing the ignomy of being rejected.

There is a subliminal fear that swingers may introduce veneral disease.

In sum, swinging is neither a sexual paradise nor the road to perdition. It is, in fact, not even a unitary phenomenon. There are male swingers who become impotent with a women unless they can talk for hours before attempting intercourse. These are swingers who probably "can't make it" with people after they become too intimate with them.

The swingers who have been studied appear more content than the controls or the average man on the street. Moreover, their marriages seem no worse than others, perhaps even slightly better. The difficulty is that no one yet knows much about the attitudes and experiences of those people who try swinging and drop out. How large a number do they constitute, and what is the effect of swinging on their personality and marital adjustment? Rectification of this omission through research will be a major contribution to our ability to predict the viability of swinging marriages.

The Future of Swinging

In predicting the future of swinging it is helpful to understand why swinging did not arise much earlier, say in 1910. The answer would be that at that time there was insufficient acceptance in the population of sex as recreation, of women as sexual creatures, of enough leisure time to indulge in extracurricular sex, of media for rapid communication of interest in swinging. There was also acceptance neither of extramarital sexual behavior as subject to negotiation between spouses, nor of the importance of honesty of communication between spouses regarding sexual needs and desires. Extramarital sex then meant clandestine sex. By 1978 the requisite conditions for swinging were strongly entrenched. I do not foresee an immediate change from these conditions.

Not everyone is relationship-oriented. There will still be people who will want to limit their intimacy or who will be simply incapable of being intimate. Yet they will sometimes have strong sex drives which demand expression. If they are not strongly socialized to conventional norms or are in fact socialized to unconventional swinging norms, if they are sufficiently insecure about allowing their spouse to develop their own relationships, if they need to have exchange-rules to avoid threatening their marriage, if they need to act autonomously to achieve self-worth, then they may be drawn to swinging.

Most will recoil from it after brief experimentation. It will seem too impersonal, arouse jealousy feelings and feelings of inadequacy, rejection, and guilt. The minority who survive and graduate into regular swinging will find it a titilating spice to life which may support their marriage. The dropouts will find it a threat to their marriage. In time many will graduate from it to more person-involved relationships, but not all will be capable or motivated to do that. In sum, swinging provides a solution to rather specific needs and thus should survive and even expand somewhat though it is doubtful that it will be adopted by any extensive segment of the population. Sometime in the future it may come into conflict with the concept of an individualism which respects the right of the individual to sexual independence even though he or she is married. At some future point in time there may be sufficient alleviation of sexual jealousy so that a larger number of married persons than currently may operate within the more flexible arrangements of open marriage and other, nonmonogamous arrangements. I don't foresee the millenium just quite yet. Instead, the Marlowian swinger may for years to come chant, "Come swing with me and be my [temporary 9 P.M.-2 A.M.] love, and we will all the pleasure prove."

REFERENCES

Aronson, E. "Some Antecedents of Interpersonal Attraction. Edited By W. J. Arnold and D. Levine. *Nebraska symposium of motivation 1969.* Lincoln, Neb.: University of Nebraska Press, 1970. p. 143–73.

Athanasiou. R. "A Review of Public Attitudes on Sexual Issues." In *Contemporary Sexual Behavior: Critical Issues in the 1970's,* edited by J. Zubin and J. Morey. Baltimore: Johns Hopkins University Press, 1973, p. 361–90.

Bartell, G. D. *Group Sex: A Scientist's Eyewitness Report on the American Way of Swinging.* New York: Peter H. Wyden, 1971.

Bell, R. R. *Social deviance.* Homewood, Ill.: Dorsey, 1971.

Bell, R. R. "Swinging — The Sexual Exchange of Marriage Partners." Paper presented at the Society of the Study of Social Problems, Washington, D.C., 1970.

Breedlove, W., and Breedlove, J. *Swap clubs.* Los Angeles: Sherbourne Press, 1964.

Denfield, D. "Dropouts from Swinging: The Marriage Counselor as Informant." In *Beyond Monogamy,* edited by J. R. Smith and L. R. Smith. Baltimore: Johns Hopkins University Press, 1974, p. 260–67.

Denfield, D. "How Swingers Make Contact." *Sexual Behavior* 2 April, 1972: 60–63.

Denfield, D. "Toward a Typology of Swinging." Paper presented at Groves Conference on Marriage and the Family, San Juan, Puerto Rico, May 8, 1971.

Denfield, D., and Gordon, M. "The Sociology of Mate Swapping: Or the Family that Swings Together Clings Together." *Journal of Sex Research* 6 (1970): 85–100.

Gilmartin, B. G. "Sexual Deviance and Social Networks: A Study of Social, Family, and Marital Interaction Patterns among Co-marital Sex Participants." In *Beyond Monogamy* edited by J. R. Smith and L. R. Smith. Baltimore: Johns Hopkins University Press, 1974, p. 291–322.

Gilmartin, B. G. Unpublished tables on a sample of swingers and controls, 1972.

Henshel, A. M. "Swinging: A Study of Decision Making in Marriage." *American Journal of Sociology* 78 (1973): 885–91.

Hunt, M. *Sexual Behavior in the 1970s.* Chicago: Playboy Press, 1974.

Johnson, R. E. "Some Correlates of Extramarital Coitus." *Journal of Marriage and the Family* 32 (1970): 449–56.

Kagan, J., and Beach, F. "Effect of Early Experience on Mating Behavior in Male Rats. *Journal of Comp. Physiology and Psychology* 46 (1953): 204–8.

Margolis, H. F., and Rubenstein, P. M. *The Group Sex Tapes* New York: McKay, 1971.

Murstein, B. I. *Love, Sex and Marriage through the Ages,* New York: Springer, 1974.

Nemy, E. "Group Sex: Is it 'Life Art' or a Sign that Something Is Wrong?" *The New York Times,* May 10, 1971, p. 38.

O'Neill, G. C., and O'Neill, N. "Patterns in Group Sex Activity." *Journal of Sex Research* 6 (1970): 101–12.

Palson, C. "Swingers and Non-Swingers: Conceptions of Sex." *Sociological Abstracts* 18 (1970): 971.

Palson, C. and Palson, R. "Swinging in Wedlock." *Society* 9 (1972): 28–37.

Ramey, J. W. "Emerging Patterns of Behavior in Marriage: Deviations or Innovations?" *Journal of Sex Research* 8 (1972): 6–30.

Reich, C. A. *The Greening of America.* New York: Random House, 1970.

Schupp, C. E. "An Analysis of Some Social-Psychological Factors which Operate in the Functioning of Married Couples who Exchange Mates for the Purpose of Sexual Experience." *Dissertation Abstracts International* 31 (5-A) (Nov. 5, 1970): 25–24.

Slater, P. L. *The Pursuit of Loneliness.* Boston: Beacon Press, 1970.

Smith, J. R., and Smith L. G. "Co-Marital Sex and the Sexual Freedom Movement." *Journal of Sex Research* 6 (1970): 131–42.

Smith, L. G., and Smith, J. R. "Co-Marital Sex: The Incorporation of Extramarital Sex into the Marriage Relationship." In *Beyond Monogamy* edited by J. R. Smith and L. R. Smith. Baltimore: Johns Hopkins University Press, 1974 pp. 84–102.

Spanier, G. B., and Cole, C. L. "Mate Swapping: Participation, Knowledge, and Values in a Midwestern Community." Annual Meeting of the Midwest Sociological Society, April 21, 1972, Kansas City, Missouri.

Stanton, E. "Swinging as a Way of Life." *The Humanist* 34 (1974): 18–20.

Stephenson, R. M. "Involvement in Deviance: An Example and Some Theoretical Implications." *Social Problems* 21 (1973): 173–90.

Symonds, C. "A Pilot Study of the Peripheral Behavior of Sexual Mate Swappers." Unpublished master's thesis, University of California at Riverside, 1968.

Twichell, J. "Sexual Liberality and Personality: A Pilot Study." In *Beyond Monogamy*, edited by J. R. Smith and L. G. Smith. Baltimore: Johns Hopkins University Press, 1974, pp. 230–45.

Varni, C. A. "An Exploratory Study of Spouse Swapping." In *Beyond Monogamy* edited by J. R. Smith and L. R. Smith. Baltimore: Johns Hopkins University Press, 1974, pp. 246–59.

Walshok, M. L. "The Emergence of Middle-Class Deviant Subcultures: The Case of Swingers." *Social Problems* 18 (1971): 488–95.

White, M., and Wells, C. "Student Attitudes toward Alternate Marriage Forms." In *Renovating Marriage*, edited by R. Libby and R. N. Whitehurst. Danville, Calif.: Consensus Publishers, 1973, pp. 280–95.

GROUP MARRIAGE
& MULTILATERAL
RELATIONS

[7]

AS CONSTANTINE points out in his article on group marriage, little research has been forthcoming beyond that considered in his book. The evidence on group marriage, as I read it, suggests a communality with other deviant groups: "swingers," "open marriage." Like them individuals in group marriages show, compared to traditional married couples, poorer relationships with their parents, more liberal nonreligious backgrounds, and an extremely high sex interest (see their Edwards Personal Preference Schedule scores for n Sex in Constantine and Constantine, 1973). They also tend to be unconventional in their behavior, with a goodly number with extramarital sexual experiences prior to entering into group marriage. The Constantines also found that members of group marriages were high on the need for change and autonomy and low on the needs for endurance, abasement, deference, and order. Men and women differed radically on two needs. Compared to traditional women, group-marriage women were low on nurturance, whereas group-marriage men were high on nurturance compared to traditional men. Group-women were high on aggression but group-men were low on it. Thus, group marriage seemed to have some appeal for assertive women and nonaggressive, nurturant men.

The advantages of successful group marriage are that it satisfies a need for variety and results in a variety of different needs being satisfied, which would be less likely to occur with any one given partner. If the group lasts, there is greater economic and emotional security. It is cheaper to live as a group than as a couple; a lost job is not a calamity, a fight with a spouse does not lead to emotional isolation.

The potentialities for interpersonal growth are substantial, and children thrive in the variety of adults and peer contact.

Alas, there are also substantial costs. Over half of the groups studied by the Constantines survived less than a year. Some people are simply overcome by interpersonal overload. In a six-person group there are nine possible heterosexual pairings for the night and fifty-seven different relationships of from two to six people. Problems of sexual jealousy may arise, but competition for time with a desired person may be a bigger problem. Moreover, it is becoming increasingly rare these days for a couple to be sufficiently compatible to stay married for a lifetime. The difficulty in matching a group for compatibility rises geometrically with each member added.

Careers, which often require mobility, may have to be sacrificed to remain in the group, and in any event, the emotional demands of relating to several people in an intimate fashion may leave little energy left for careers. Last, the hostility of outsiders toward something "different" like the group, expressed by legal problems of property transference, zoning ordinances and the like, are further hindrances to the survival of the group. In sum, group marriages do not seem likely to increase to any great extent in the near future. There just aren't that many people who at the same time have great interpersonal and sexual needs and capacity, and the opportunity to meet sympathetic, like-minded persons who also are unafraid to violate societal norms. Thus, the number of group marriages should increase somewhat in the near future, but I would not foresee a rapid or extensive growth rate.

REFERENCE

Constantine, L.L., and Constantine, J. M. *Group Marriage: A Study of Contemporary Multilateral Marriage*. New York: Macmillan, 1973.

Multilateral Relations Revisited: Group Marriage In Extended Perspective

LARRY L. CONSTANTINE

I N 1972, as we completed the manuscripts for our book on group marriage (Constantine and Constantine, 1973), Joan Constantine and I made some private predictions about the groups in our study. Of the eleven groups in the core study (fifteen others had been studied less intensively), only three remained intact. One of these appeared to us to be unstable and we predicted its imminent demise. The group split before we finished proofing the galleys. The remaining two groups presented an interesting contrast.

The Wyeths (not their real names, of course), two young couples with a preschool son, lived in the small town in which they had grown up. Their group marriage had evolved out of Joe and Mark's close friendship, with ideology provided by *The Harrad Experiment* (Rimmer, 1966), a novel they discovered and passed around only after the two couples had already become quite intimate. After nearly five years of group marriage, they had developed good communications and problem-solving skills, an easy comradeship between them, comfort, closeness, and communicativeness as a group, and they were clearly committed to their life style. After living in two separate houses for a time, an accommodation to relatives in town, they moved in together again just before our book was published.

The Trebles were a triad with two school-age children living in The Fellowship, a small hilltop commune in the Pacific Northwest. The five-year group marriage had evolved from Bill's affair with Cindy. Though they worked hard at it, the strain in the relationship between Cindy and Bill's legal wife, Judy, was often much in evidence. On our last visit to this group, a community member who was not part of the group marriage took us aside. Under the assumption that we only had a surface view of the group, he cautioned us at length about assuming that all was "sweetness and light" among the three principals. Actually, in our view, their relationship had many of the features of a conflict-habituated marriage (Cuber and Harroff, 1969). They were sincere, committed, likable people, but conflict was a definite component of the bond among them. As often happens in ordinary families, their stress had a tendency to be manifest in the behavior of their children, particularly their youngest, a boy who, though in no way seriously disturbed, was among those children in our study who had the lowest self-esteem and poorest family and social adjustment.

In reviewing the structure and dynamics of these two groups, we identified a number of factors contributing to their continued existence. At the time, the Wyeths appeared to have a better working internal system. When they disagreed, they tended to discuss or fight constructively. There were seeds of potential trouble in the fact that Mark was somewhat of a secret holdout who exercised control in part by withholding and that Carol and Ann, though good friends, had yet to develop a deep emotional bond with each other. With four adults and only one child, this group had ample resources available for working on improving the adult relationships. The Trebles had the advantage of a more supportive community and a less complicated, though more openly troubled, internal system. In general, smaller groups like theirs had proved to be more stable than larger ones. In the final analysis, these two group marriages differed from others in our study primarily in the degree of "fit" between members in terms of their basic personal styles and in their realism in acknowledging and confronting areas of conflict. Without putting a number on it, we predicted that both these groups would be together for many years, very possibly for the rest of their lives.

Since then we have continued to correspond with both groups. In 1975 we received the first of a series of letters from each of the four Wyeths: letters filled with pain, frustration, and long neglected anger. The group was falling apart and was appealing to us for help or at least for understanding. The incipient problems we had identified earlier had erupted into a crisis. Before we could finalize plans for some sort of long-distance intervention, we learned that the crisis was past, that once again the problem solving we had seen in action so many times had carried them though to a new basis for their relationship.

We received a note for Christmas 1975 from Cindy of the Trebles. Linda was doing well in a public junior high school, having "graduated" from the community's own school. Cindy and Judy had joined a women's group and their relationship was much improved. All in all, the scene at The Fellowship appeared to be relaxed and comfortable.

That the Wyeths and the Trebles remain together after ten and eleven years respectively seems to be a positive thing. That others continue despite unremitting stress, denial of the realities of their relationships, and the evident scapegoating of some family members is unfortunate. These disabled groups survive because they are frozen into their dysfunctional patterns of interaction. If anything, we had underestimated the power of open communication and conflict management to sustain and develop good relationships. The open fighting among the Trebles, though appearing at times to be symptomatic and excessive, was in fact one of the real strengths of their group marriage and a major mechanism for their continued growth.

We would regard a few group breakups as unnecessary. Insufficient commitment to each other and to working difficulties through to resolution appears to be at the root of the dissolution of group marriages that were otherwise sound.

It should be apparent that staying together is no more today than ever a reliable indicator of success in relationships. In group marriages, as elsewhere, where the mechanisms that maintain family structure, the so-called *morphostatic processes,* are consensually determined and validated, stability tends to be a healthy sign; where morphostasis is forced and the result pseudomutual processes, longevity is a negative outcome (Wertheim, 1973).

Multilateral Marriage: Origins

We originally coined the term *multilateral marriage* not as an impressive new substitute for *group marriage,* but as a single term to cover both triads (three-partner marriages) and group marriages (four or more partners) in which every person had, at least, a dual commitment. Although not bound by any legally recognized relationship, members of multilateral marriages regard themselves as really married to more than one other person. For the most part they have the same sense of commitment, the same expectations of intimacy and permanence that conventionally married couples have.

Our information about contemporary multilateral marriages comes from a handful of sources. Journalists have provided a few reports (Buckley, 1970; Claiborne, 1970; Houriet, 1971; Hutchinson, 1973; Stein, 1970; Walley, 1969). First-hand reports by participants (Gourley, 1968; Harrad West, 1970) and other close observers (Fairfield, 1971; Henricksen, 1969; Smith and Rose, 1970) provide a few more glimpses. We have been disappointed that more research has not followed our book. Insights from family professionals have not, for the most part, been based on research, though this has not restrained many from commenting (Bernard, 1972; Ellis, 1970; McKern and McKern, 1970; Neubeck, 1970). The research has been quite limited. Ramey (1972) analyzed a survey taken among the membership of an upper-middle-class organization of people interested in expanded families and conducted a few informal interviews. Kilgo (1972) based her conclusions on student group marriage participants who came to her for counseling help. Seal (1974) also draws on experience in therapeutic work with group marriages, in this case from Los Angeles. Some group marriages found in communes were included in studies of communal families by Berger and associates (1972), and Johnston and Deisher (1973). Only Salsberg (1973) conducted first-hand research exclusively on group marriage. The bulk of what is known of group marriage today is still from the three years of research by the author and Joan Constantine. The data below generally integrates the Salsberg and Seal reports with that study.

Who participates in group marriage and what are they like? The typical female participant is twenty-eight years old; the typical male, thirty-one. The average age in urban groups may be somewhat higher than in rural groups (Salsberg, 1973). Most are couples who have been legally married for six or eight years and have one or two children. Nearly half of both men and women are employed in professional or managerial work and have a college education. Almost all of them formed groups of four with another couple or triads with a single man or woman. On the average the groups that have split up lasted about twelve to sixteen months. About half of all groups studied had broken up by completion of the research.

Although most group marriages are found in ordinary urban and suburban communities, many participants have an interest in intentional communities and a third of them had some prior communal living experience. Their original family backgrounds were unexceptional. They described their parents as having been typically American — strict, authoritarian, but inconsistent. They did tend to come from liberal religious backgrounds, and had become more liberal with time. Almost three out of five now consider themselves to be humanists or agnostics.

To the surprise of many conservative family professionals, the majority of them turned out to be mentally healthy, in-touch, flexible individuals with better-than-average marriages. Instead of people incapable of or fleeing from intimacy, they proved to be distinguished by an exceptional capacity for intimacy.

They got into group marriages for many of the same reasons any *two* people get married: for companionship, sexual intimacy, growth as persons, because of love, and to create a good environment in which to raise children. Women were more likely than men to be seeking something missing from their prior relationship, trying to strengthen their marriage, looking for more freedom, easier childrearing, and to avoid having to choose between two people. This is consistent with our own view and that of Bernard (1972) that conventional marriage is more restrictive for women than for men. Although both men and women regarded multiple sexual partners as an advantage of group marriage, women were less likely than men to be strongly motivated by sexual variety.

Their problems within the group marriages were equally unexceptional. The biggest ones usually reported were communication and value or personality conflicts. Jealousy, especially jealousy over time spent with other partners, and commitment came next, followed closely by such "tremendous trifles" of daily living as housework and utilization of living space. Women found the use of leisure time and issues of mutual caring and concern to be more trouble than did men. Most reports, ours included, have concluded that sex in group marriages is not much of a problem *per se*, but that jealousy and related issues, such as the primacy of some relationships and exclusion, can be.

Although we still feel justified in regarding triads as variations of the same essential phenomenon as group marriages, some definite differences emerged from the research which have been confirmed in clinical observations since.

Triads have tended to evolve more "naturally" with less intention and design than groups of four or more. This may give them a substantial advantage over those groups whose structures are less spontaneous and fitted to the participants. Seal (1974) even sees triads as the dominant form of group marriage. Triads in our study were significantly more likely than other types to have been motivated by existing love or friendships. As a rule, members of a triad seemed more strongly committed to each other and to the group and had a greater investment in personal growth within and through the marriage. The family systems they formed were distinctly "tighter"; they were more likely than foursomes to see their group marriage as a "fortress or protection from the outside world." Though often an advantage, this cohesion and closeness could also pose problems. Triad members were more likely than others to list among their problems "dysfunctional cycles of behavior," "personality friction," and "neuroticism." The imbalance created by one established, legal relationship as against the newcomer "third party" led to more problems associated with existing marriages than in foursomes. That Seal reports "exclusion of the mate" as one of the biggest problems in groups he has counseled may reflect the predominance of triads among those groups.

Since

There is little that we would change or retract since completing *Group Marriage*. Were we to rewrite the book, it might differ in emphasis or focus but very little in content. Salsberg's research, conducted about the same time but unavailable to us before publication, generally corroborates our own, though more of his informants were in group marriages within communes, more in a rural setting. We were more hopeful than Salsberg in our conclusions, however, and would have to be even more positive now.

From correspondence, our own therapy work with a number of group marriages, and from many informal contacts, we find that interest and involvement in group marriages continues unabated but more quietly. The situation appears to be similar to that reported by David of Twin Oaks concerning communal families.

Popular media interest in group marriage peaked in 1970; three-quarters of all recent articles on the subject appeared in that single year. By 1974 the media had declared alternative life styles a dead issue. After the initial flourish of hurried and unplanned experiments spurred by dissatisfaction, excitement about new frontiers, and countercultural ideology, the scene changed. Today's groups appear to be better motivated, more committed, and longer lived. People are getting into group marriages because they have become involved with and grown to love more than one person.

JEALOUSY

On that ever recurrent issue of jealousy, the outlook is very good. The basic model of jealousy we assembled to explain our findings has been expanded into a comprehensive theory of jealous behavior (Constantine, 1976). The view has been successfully used as the basis of workshops by the author, Joan Constantine, and others.

Basically, jealous behavior emerges as the result of specific transformations of cues in a particular context. The context always involves two people in a pair relationship and an "agent" that threatens the boundary of that relationship. The perception of actual or theatened loss in that relationship leads to discomfort (hurt or anxiety), hence to jealous behavior of any of a variety of forms directed toward either the partner or the agent.

The detailed model is useful not only for furnishing insight to individuals about their jealous behavior but highlighting specific points of intervention through which the likelihood and seriousness of jealousy can be reduced. Since the insecure person in an uncertain relationship is more likely to see a triangular situation as threatening, jealousy can be reduced by building personal security and confidence in a relationship. To the extent that one sees one's own satisfaction and fulfillment as intertwined with one's partner's, jealousy becomes less likely. The availability of alternative feeling responses to the jealousy situation makes hurt and anxiety less probable. Attempts at communication and problem resolution can become means of expressing jealous feelings in behavior.

Jealousy is, of course, not unique to group marriages. In a group marriage, however, the "outside agent" is an "insider." There are both more opportunities for jealous behavior and more options available for dealing with it. Many possibilities open up when the person triggering the jealousy participates in the attempts to resolve the situation to the satisfaction of all. It seems that jealousy *is* more likely to surface and become plainly visible in the group marriage than in the conventional closed marriage, though the incipient causes — personal and relational insecurity — may exist in either case. Where the conventional marriage can survive intact with high levels of insecurity and fairly easily triggered jealousy, the group marriage depends for its continuance on steady progress in its members' ability to cope with jealousy. Fortunately the problem has proved to be far from intractable, and we find many individuals and groups who are almost totally free of dysfunctional jealous responses, not because they do not feel or care, but because they feel secure and care as much for their partners' pleasure as their own, which for them is integrally linked with that of their partners.

CHILDREN

Our original study reached a "not proven" verdict about the effect of group marriages on children. It seemed to us, from extensive observations and interviews of the kids and their parents as well as from psychological testing, that multiple parents were neither a clear advantage nor disadvantage to kids. We concluded that women were the main benefactors of the group marriage experience, whether it endured or not.

In 1974 we presented to the Child Welfare League of America our invited review of the literature on children in alternative families. Somewhat to the surprise of all, we reversed our earlier opinion. On the basis of 7 separate studies of children and child-rearing in over 150 group marriages and communes (Smith and Sternfield, 1969; Berger, et al., 1972; Johnston and Deisher, 1973; Salsberg, 1973; Hunt, 1972; Constantine and Constantine, 1973; and Eiduson, et al., 1973), it is now clear that children of multiple parents do indeed enjoy some advantages over those in two-parent families.

The findings of these studies were strikingly consistent in certain respects, despite marked variation of method and intent. Children were reported to be self-reliant and exceptionally competent interpersonally, well integrated into their families, and making valued contributions to them. They were above average in sense of self-worth, happy, and confident. In our final report (Constantine and Constantine, 1976) we use a family systems model to relate these results to features of the child-rearing setting — the enlarged family, parenting by many adults, family boundaries that permit easy interaction with still other parent figures, and nonrestrictive, nonpunitive child-rearing that integrates children as full-fledged, valued, contributing partners in the family unit. Children were generally treated as the equals of adults, having the same rights of self-determination and the same responsibility to contribute according to their abilities. Norms of high flexibility in male-female and adult-child roles prevailed. All these contribute to a greatly enriched environment in which to grow up. Not that growing up counterculturally is an unmixed bag. There have been casualties, a very small number of children whose disturbed behavior and emotional upsets were tied up with their parents' attempted group marriages. But more often, the open, flexible family with numbers of parents available has made difficulties, even divorce, easier for children to manage. Rothchild and Wolf (1976) present a particularly rich, even if somewhat unoriented, journalistic portrait of children in counterculture families. Autonomy can take its toll where it drifts from what Ginott would call "benign neglect" into simply neglect. But neglect is uncommon and abuse almost unheard of in the communal and group marriage families studied thus far.

In some religiously dogmatic settings described by Rothchild and Wolf (the Krishna Consciousness school, the Synanon community, and Gaskin's "The Farm") children are by contrast rigidly programmed into fixed value structures. Elsewhere the values themselves are flexible, and similar to those of young, counterculture couples in two-person relationships (Eiduson, *et al.*, 1973; Rath and McDowell, 1971). All seem to favor actualization of each child's innate potential, development of self-confidence, high self-esteem, early independence, and personal responsibility. Most value openness to change, open interpersonal communication and emotional expression, tolerance, cooperation, sharing, and nonviolence. The group marriage or communal family simply provides a context in which success in applying these values is more likely than in conventional marriages. The key in all cases remains the quality of relating, not the family structure. Emergent values place the highest premium on quality of open, honest, congruent communication; a committment to these values and to acquiring the requisite skills may be the best basis for better parenting in group marriages and others.

OPEN FAMILIES

The possible benefits of group parenting show up as a trend in the summaries, but the basic value structure in which they are grounded can be extracted to become the central focus of an emerging family life style called "open family" (Constantine, 1977). The open family extends the voluntary mutual committment of group marriage to embrace all members, minors included. It can be thought of as an extension of open marriage. Its ideological base is to be found in Farson (1973) and other literature advocating "childrens' rights." It is open in the sense of being (1) highly open in its boundaries, inside between members and externally with regard to free association, access to information, and the right to leave; (2) open in role definitions, with no fixed roles associated with either age or sex; (3) open to change, continuously monitoring, discussing, and revising its own rules and structure.

In varying degrees, most of the group marriages studied have been open in these ways, but in the open family the mutual commitment to a single standard of roles, rights, and responsibilities regardless of age or sex is paramount. *Open-type* families have been contrasted with two more traditional type of families by Kantor and Lehr (1975) and McInnis and Ayres (1975). The traditional or *closed-type* family is rigid, closed, authoritarian, and emphasizes stability, unity, and fidelity. The modern permissive *random-type* family that McInnis calls "disordered" is chaotic and anarchic, stressing as functional values spontaneity, individuality, and creativity. The *open-type* family is evolutionary, emphasing flexibility, interdependence, and authenticity. Roles are flexible and functional rather than either blurred or rigid. Everyone is free to parent or be parented. Individual differences are respected, not denied or suppressed.

"Every family has its problems," it is said. Actually, Kantor and Lehr (1975) found that each of the three types of families is most prone to its own specific class of problems. All families that value open communications have some tendency at times to respond too rapidly to changing demands. And the authentic and immediate sharing of feelings which is the hallmark of open process can lead to emotions being amplified and reverberated through the family. Consequently, open-type families are often subject to very pronounced swings in collective mood. The demand for authentic involvement can also sometimes make it more difficult for a family member to stay out of what is happening than would be the case in the other types. But most of these potential pitfalls of the open family are mitigated by the family's close monitoring of its own processes and flexible restructuring of itself to correct problematic situations.

Though it might seem that children, especially very young ones, could have difficulty handling the freedom and responsibility of living in an open family, even among pre-schoolers this is not often the case. As in the "synergic societies" described by Ruth Benedict (1956), nothing is expected of a child (or any other member) which they are incapable of, but all are expected to do what they can. It is the sensitivity with which they accommodate to individual differences that frequently distinguishes open families from closed-authoritarian and random-permissive families, both of which may tend to disregard individual and developmental differences, either within strict rules about what children of a certain age should or should not do or within a more indifferent laissez-faire approach.

Next

In our original study of group marriages, we found that they formed in one of two basic ways: by design and serendipitously. Many of the earlier groups, and certainly most of the less stable ones, had been constituted as part of deliberate personal programs of social experimentation, strong personal interest in the *idea* of group marriage, or a conscious attempt to improve a marriage relationship. Serendipitous groups, by contrast, grew more or less spontaneously out of other relationships — established friendships, joint living arrangements, mutual support networks, church groups, and other groups. With the rise in publicity on group marriage during the late 1960s and early 1970s came a loss of innocence, or at least of ignorance, and an increase in the number of people who set out to "try a group marriage" first and then looked for people to fit the dream. The people seldom fitted the dream or each other, especially when the dream was a fantasy borrowed from popular fiction.

But there has been somewhat of a return to a certain kind of innocence in recent years, and we find that recently formed group marriages again conform more to the picture of serendipitous groups. The constituent relationships have most often grown out of "open marriages" with a general openness to intimate friendships, the group marriage resulting as commitments deepened and some grouping developed intrinsic stability. The group marriage seen within this perspective was simply one of many potential outcomes, one which in certain cases seemed to be a natural outgrowth of the fit among those people.

It is legitimate to wonder why more people do not end up in intimate, committed relationships with more than one partner, why so many have difficulty with the notion of sharing an intimate partner with others. Elsewhere (Constantine and Constantine, 1977) we have argued that innate human sexual propensities are shaped simultaneously by two factors, one favoring novelty, the other favoring secure familiarity. Basically, everyone is a candidate for some sort of multiple relationship. People who do not actualize this potential undoubtedly fail to do so for a multiplicity of reasons. Beside the declared reasons like religious and moral values, or social, legal, and other practical considerations, we have noted some common background elements in strongly negative responses to multiple relationships. Prominent among these are unpleasant and unsuccessful prior experiences in situations — such as competition over a girlfriend, sibling rivalry, or a spouse's affair — that serve as a reference model for adult multiple relationships. Some people's responses to potential multilateral relationships are so rapid and automatic as to preclude serious consideration of such options. Others are too insecure personally and in their relationships to manage the risk of following through on any alternate relationship. Furthermore, societal disapproval and lack of recognition of open, multiple relationships may make the costs excessive for many who might otherwise become involved in them. Certainly the extent of secret affairs indicates a sizable pool of possible participants in more open multiple relationships if these had social sanction. While the foregoing list oversimplifies, it identifies some of the most salient factors in nonparticipation in multilateral relations.

A key factor in the acceptance of group marriage by the parents of adult participants in our study was a prior positive experience within a context which could be generalized to cover group marriage. A happy, close mutual friendship with another couple, for example, was mentioned by several parents as a related experience that made their offspring's life style seem more plausible and acceptable. But most common social contexts that might be considered related to group marriage are socially shaped to be competitive and conflict-ridden. Most people almost automatically assume that, on finding themselves in a triangular situation, they would be in a competition to decide the winner and the loser of someone as object. The socially approved responses of jealous behavior promote unpleasant outcomes in these situations.

Generally, men appear to have had somewhat greater difficulty in adapting to multilateral relationships than women have had. If the "men's movement" with its emphasis on noncompetitive male-male relationships succeeds as the women's movement has, fewer potential multiple relationships will founder on competitiveness and insecurity.

A pool of experienced potential partners is growing, not only from among the graduates of earlier group marriage attempts, but also including members of communal families and participants in various kinds of cooperative group living arrangements that favor openness and sharing, even if balking at multiple sexual relationships. More young people have experience in cohabitation, a widespread nonlegal relationship, and many have lived with several different partners, though rarely with more than one at a time. Nevertheless, for many people their multiple experiences in intimate living make multilateral relations seem more plausible.

A fraction of cohabiting couples attempt to have an open relationship permitting outside friendships and intimacy with other partners, although often they have encountered difficulty in combining the open-relationship ethic with the kind of indeterminate commitment common to cohabitation. In the sexual area, some experience with group sexual encounters, especially in threesomes, is becoming quite common, though usually only a single incident is involved (Hunt, 1975).

In general, then, a case can be made that group marriages should be expected to be on the increase, albeit slowly. For the same reasons outlined above, a growing portion of those groups that form can be expected to remain together over long periods. Group marriage has never been a widespread life style, not during the peak of interest in alternatives nor even in cultures that did validate it, as among the Kaingang of South America (Henry, 1964). That a small minority can and do effect a lasting commitment to loving and living with more than one partner may be seen as a commentary on human potential. Certainly, group marriage should be among the legitimate options which people can structure personally enriching life styles, in turn enriching and contributing to the viability of our society.

Open family represents for children the kind of life style option that group marriage is for adults. After the relationships between men and women, the next frontier for revolution is certain to be that between parents and children.

REFERENCES

Benedict, R. "Continuities and Discontinuities in Cultural Conditioning." In *Personality in Nature, Society, and Culture,* edited by Kluckholm, C. and H. A. Murray. New York: Knopf, 1956.

Berger, B., Hackett, B., and Millar, R. M. "The Communal Family." *Family Coordinator* 21 (1972): 419–28.

Bernard, J. *The Future of Marriage.* New York: World Publishing, 1972.

Buckley, T. "Oh Copenhagen." *New York Times Magazine,* February 8, 1970.

Claiborne, W. "Monday Night Class." *Washington Post,* December 24, 1970.

Constantine, L. "Jealousy: From Theory to Treatment." In D. Olson, *Treating Relationships,* Lake Mills, Iowa: Graphic Publishing Co., 1976.

Constantine, L. "Open Family: A Lifestyle for Kids and Other People." *The Family Coordinator* 26 (1977): 113–21.

Constantine, L., and Constantine, J. *Group Marriage: A Study of Contemporary Multilateral Relations.* New York: Macmillan, 1973.

Constantine, L., and Constantine, J. "Sexual Aspects of Group Marriage." In *Marriage and Alternatives: Exploring Intimate Relationships,* edited by R. Libby and R. Whitehurst. Glenview, Ill.: Scott, Foresman, 1977.

Constanine, L., and Constantine, J. *Treasures of the Island: Children in Alternative Families.* Beverly Hills, Ca.: Sage/NCFR Monographs, 1976.

Cuber, J., and Harroff, P. *Sex and the Significant Americans.* Baltimore: Penguin, 1969.

Eiduson, B., Cohen, J., and Alexander, J. "Alternatives in Childbearing in the 1970's." *American Journal of Orthopsychiatry* 43 (1973): 720–31.

Ellis, A. "Group Marriage — A Possible Alternative." In *The Family in Search of a Future,* edited by H. Otto. New York: Appleton-Century-Crofts, 1970.

Fairfield, R. *Communes U.S.A.* Baltimore: Penguin, 1971.

Gourley, W. "Group Marriage: Utopian Ethics." *The Modern Utopian* 2 (1968): 25–27.

"Harrad West." *The Modern Utopian* 4 (1970): 13–14.

Henricksen, A. J. N. "An Alternative to Monogamous Marriage." In *Harrad Letters to Robert H. Rimmer,* edited by R. Rimmer. New York: Signet, 1969.

Henry, J. *Jungle People: A Kaingang Tribe of the Highlands of Brazil.* New York: Vintage/Random House, 1964.

Houriet, R. *Getting Back Together.* New York: Coward, McCann, and Geoghegan, 1971.

Hunt, A. "Multilateral Marriage from the Child's Perspective." Unpublished, Multilateral Relations Study Project, February 1972. [Excerpted in Constantine and Constantine (1973) and Constantine and Constantine (1976)].

Hunt, M. "Sexual Behavior in the 1970's: Part I–VI." *Playboy* 20 (10,11,12), 1973, and 21 (1,2,3).

Hutchinson, W. "Group Marriage: Three Is a Crowd." *Detroit Free Press,* August 12, 1973.

Johnston, C. M., and Deisher, R. W. "Contemporary Communal Child Rearing." *Pediatrics* 52 (1973): 319-26.

Kantor, D., and Lehr, W. *Inside the Family.* San Francisco: Jossey-Bass, 1975.

Kilgo, R. "Can Group Marriage Work?" *Sexual Behavior* 2 (1972). (Reprinted in L. Gross, Ed., *Sexual Issues in Marriage.* Holliswood, N.Y.: Spectrum Publications, 1975.)

McInnis, T., and Ayre, J. *Open Family Living.* New York: Doubleday, 1976.

McKern, S. S., and McKern, J. W. "Will Group Marriage Catch On? *Sexology* (June, 1970): 31–34.

Neubeck, G. "Polyandry and Polygyny — Viable Today?" In *The Family in Search of a Future: Alternate Models for Moderns,* edited by H. Otto. New York: Appleton-Century-Crofts, 1970.

Ramey, J. W. "Communes, Group Marriage and the Upper-Middle Class." *Journal of Marriage and the Family* 34 (1972): 647-55.

Rath, R. A., and McDowell, D. J. "Coming Up Hip: Child Rearing Perspectives and Life Style Values among Counter Culture Families." *Sociological Symposium* 7 (Fall 1971).

Rimmer, R. *The Harrad Experiment*. New York: Signet, 1966.

Rothchild, J., and Wolf., S. *Children of the Counterculture*. New York: Doubleday, 1976.

Salsberg, S. "Is Group Marriage Viable?" *Journal of Sex Research* 9 (1973): 325–33.

Seal, H. *Alternative Life Styles*. Dulwich, South Australia: SA Growth Press, 1974.

Smith, D. E., and Rose, A. J. "A Case Study of the Charles Manson Group Marriage Commune." *Journal of Psychosomatic Medicine and Dentistry* 17 (1970): 99–106.

Smith, D., and Sternfield, J. "Natural Childbirth and Cooperative Childbearing in Psychedelic Communes." *Excerpta Medica*, International Congress Series, No. 207, April 1969, 88–93.

Stein, R. "Not Just an Ordinary Family." *San Francisco Chronicle*, August 28, 1970.

Walley, D. "Getting it Together." *Scenes* 2 (1969): 39–41+.

Wertheim, R. "Family Unit Therapy and the Science and Typology of Family Systems." *Family Process* 12 (1973): 361–76.

A Triadic Relationship*

ROGER H. RUBIN
WITH CAROL, DUANE, AND CHARLOTTE

Introduction

C AROL, DUANE, and Charlotte have lived in what they term an "open triadic relationship" for three years. I have been fortunate enough to observe and interview them over this period of time.

*Gratitude is extended to Mark and Kathy Nerenberg for their assistance on this project.

The following are excerpts from several audio tapings that have been edited and categorized to improve readability, grammar, and diction. The narrative deals with the formation and development of this relationship and conveys information in several areas of general interest.

Background and Formation

CAROL: Duane and I are legally married. We will be celebrating our eleventh wedding anniversary. We were college freshmen together and after six months of his pursuit for a date I finally succumbed to his advances. Then we made the fatal mistake of becoming absolutely exclusive. We had no other types of relationships for the next eight years. Within the first three years of marriage we had our first child. In between the first and second child we started talking about things that had never occurred to us before because of our exclusivity. Neither of us had ever had any kind of deep or intimate relationship with any other person. Now here we are twenty-five years of age and you look at the other person and you say, "My God till death do us part?" You're talking about the next FIFTY YEARS and so we went through a whole intellectual process at that point of trying to decide whether or not we wanted to do that. It was all an intellectual trip about how we would feel about certain situations.

A few times I considered divorce. I had my bags packed once, but I never got out the door. I would have walked out if we couldn't have talked about it. Most people walk out the door because they can't talk about it. We did talk. There's a song that Roger Miller wrote about husbands and wives, and the theme is that pride is the downfall of husbands and wives. A lot of times, when I find that I'm really mad at Duane, I sit down and really think about it, and say, "Goddamn it. That's all it is. It's my own stubborn pride." Big deal. To go that far out for something as stupid as pride and nothing else of real substance is ridiculous.

Eventually, we found Bob Rimmer's book, *Proposition 31*, and that was our saviour. Because we were searching in the wilderness, we felt like total pioneers. There were no road maps, no landmarks, no directions, nothing. We felt really freaky because nobody felt the way we felt, which was an extremely isolating experience. We read the book and felt secure that at least somebody else out there was thinking like we were. So that gave us enough fuel to continue our search. One of the things that we decided we did not want was a casual one-night-stand-type affair. We felt that we wanted to have something significant in a relationship because if you're going to spend the time to find another person to relate to, it seemed kind of silly just to do it for one night.

We had hoped eventually to expand our family beyond just husband and wife. I was the first to develop a relationship outside the house, and it was a very typical American affair. This man was extremely hassled over the fact that Duane knew about the relationship. He had visions that one night Duane was going to pop up from the back seat with a shot gun, and it would be all over. It was very difficult, but then again it was good because this was the first relationship. It was a nice way to get a feel for the temperature of the water. I wasn't hurt. So the first experience was nice. Subsequent to that, Duane had his first relationship, which was a little bit different because his relationship was much heavier and more intimate. When that broke off it wasn't casual, but rather painful. Eventually, Duane had several relationships with other women. Charlotte was one of them. I had a few relationships with other men including the present one with Steve.

Later on we met somebody who said, "Haven't you heard about Future Families of the World (FFW)?" We said, "No." We went to our first meeting and we had at last found a peer group in the people we met. They thought our ideas were almost conservative. The purpose of the organization is simply to support people who are thinking about changing their life style. You talk to people who have experimented, and whether it's succeeded or failed they still have learned something. It's really nice to know there are people that you can talk to and socialize with.

Today we choose to call ourselves an "open triad." We are not closed. We are not exclusive. Should the situation arise when all members are in agreement, we would open up the family to other members, but that's probably some time in the future. Steve has had a relationship with me for two years but he doesn't want to be involved in the triad.

We think it would probably be easier in terms of everybody's head if the next person were male. That isn't an absolute requirement. It's just that it would make things a hell of a lot easier. Managing with three women and one man I think would really begin to start to play on a lot of time requirements because all three females would have to relate to only one male. Incidentally, when I was a little girl my father said, "Listen, it's all right to shack up with a guy if you're fifty years old, because society doesn't care when you're fifty. But don't do it when you're fifteen, because then you're gonna have a lot of trouble." I agree. There are different things that you are allowed to do, that you want to do, that you're capable of doing at different times in your life that at other times you're not. If we were in this situation ten years ago, we couldn't handle it. We didn't have the living experience that we have gained the last ten years. I couldn't have done it two years ago.

Basically, it's like we just started our marriage all over again, but now there are three instead of two. You don't know somebody until you live with them. I don't care what anybody says, that's true. You've got to see them twenty-four hours a day, in the middle of the night, and the first thing in the morning with no makeup, and unshaven. Then you begin to get some kind of real picture of what the person is like.

DUANE: I went to a private military school for six years. I wanted to go. It was a boarding military school and I started at ten and graduated high school at sixteen. So a lot of my growing up was with 250–300 other men.

My parents thought I had to fulfill all of society's expectations about being a male. I was loosely what would be termed a redneck and I was bigoted. I was very straight. I came to college during the early sixties and took senior Air Force ROTC in order to go into a career as an officer in the Air Force. Carol and I got married when we were twenty-one. We were looking very much for the standard monogamous relationship because that's all we knew. I thought it was my role to go out and find a wife in college as well as get an education. I would have at least two children. I would live in the suburbs and have dogs and drive a station wagon. By the age of twenty-five I had fulfilled a great deal of society's roles.

Basically, it sounds pretty easy. Actually it's boredom and that's it. Two kids, a house in the suburbs, a car, good job, and you've got it made. You have everything. Now, what do you do with your time? I found myself wasting an awful lot of time. I wasn't reading. I was plopping myself down in front of the TV set. I was going out and drinking with the guys on Friday and getting drunk, which I didn't like to do. You just look around you and say, "Now what?" I think that's where a lot of this comes from. It's getting to the point where sheer boredom gets you. You become a "blah" and you stop growing. You shouldn't ever stop growing. There are a lot of important things to do. Triads and FFW's aren't the only answer to boredom. This is our answer, and it works for us. There are lots of people who join Common Cause, or they go to a Boys' Club or they start hobbies. FFW was something that we did.

At the start of this process I lacked an identity as to who Duane was. I always had the feeling that I was never Duane, I was always Carol's husband. It was like I married my mother, and at the time I knew I needed someone to take care of me. It took me two and one-half years of courting to make sure that I was going to get the right mother. Now I wanted my own identity along with maintaining the identity that we had as a couple. So we essentially started into what is now being termed an open marriage. The way I went about establishing an identity was by opening up the marriage and trying to form my own relationships. There are a lot of problems involved in all of this. There's been a lot of hard hate, pain, and growth experience. I felt people couldn't look at me as Duane. They were labeling me. Someplace in the back of their head you're a married man. You're untouchable.

After that first relationship that Carol referred to broke up, I got into a very bad place again in my own self-identity. I wanted a divorce because people were still labeling me a married man. I thought the only way for me to live was to be single. One of the reasons that that relationship broke up was because of societal pressure. The woman I was going with was married.

Then there was another woman for about three or four months. Then I met Caroline. That's where a lot of our history starts. During this third relationship, Carol and I found out about FFW. For the first time in the two and one-half or three years we'd been experimenting, we finally met with a bunch of other people who didn't consider us freaks. It was very good to have that support, and to find that there are other people out there who are doing the same thing we are doing. We brought Caroline into FFW a month or so later. This is where we met Charlotte, who was married to Joe. Caroline began a relationship with Joe in addition to me. I subsequently started a relationship with Charlotte. We spent most of that summer toying with the idea of the five of us living together, and if Steve wanted to, we'd make it six. However, Caroline and Joe decided to go into a dyadic relationship. Steve did not want to join, so Charlotte, Carol, and I were left.

Steve doesn't threaten me as much as my attitude in growing up as an American male does. I was raised believing men didn't have relationships with other men. I grew up to be very heterosexual, so it's much easier for me to have a relationship with more than one woman. I look on society as having created a situation in which a woman has always been able to form a closer bond with another woman than two men could form with one another. Any threat is really in my own head. I am realizing that sometime I may have to try to form a relationship with another man.

Today, we don't have many friends basically because FFW provides most of our social activities, and most of our generated friends come from there. All three of us worked in the organization.

I find it's a hassle constantly to defend my life style. Most of the people who are threatened by us are people who know that we consider ourselves very committed and that we live together. They are people who are in a dyadic relationship. Once they know that three of us are living together, it automatically brings up a whole lot of questions those two people are going to have to deal with between themselves.

CHARLOTTE: I came pretty much from a very traditional background. The idea was that you find the right man and you marry him and that's it for life. I got married when I was twenty. After two years, however, my husband and I started thinking about how we were totally limiting ourselves to each other. We had both had several relationships before we were married. Thus, we weren't one-person oriented. We met some people who had an idea to form an organization that would support and promote changing the attitude that monogamy is the only way for two people to live. It would question the idea that you have to get married and restrict yourselves for the rest of your life to one person, or else continually get divorced and find somebody else.

My husband and I began having relationships with other people, partly because my attitude toward something new has always been that if I've never tried it before, why not try it now? One of the things that I didn't like about myself was that I was extremely introverted. I was afraid of people, which was something that I consciously wanted to change. Through meeting different people the first few years of our marriage, Joe and I decided that it wouldn't be such a bad idea to try opening up our marriage. The people I was meeting and relating to began to make me feel better about who Charlotte was.

At first I was thrown in with people who were interested in almost a courting-type relationship. I began to see that people really did like me. Once I started dating Joe I really didn't date too many people. Yet the feeling persisted that people just didn't find me a worthwhile person, not just sexually, but as a total person. I really just didn't think that there was very much that people knew about me. I began to express myself. I found out that people did respect my feelings. Sometimes they shot me down, but I learned that I could handle that too. It was just really more a matter of forcing myself to do something. If you know where your strengths are and where you're at at the moment, you kind of judge how many little risks you can take and still be safe enough so that if it hurts, you can drop back and reevaluate.

Therefore, the initial relationship that Joe and I had was changing drastically. Because of these changes and both our insecurities, the marriage was pretty much on the rocks about four years ago. It was at this point that Joe and I became involved with the other people who were thinking of getting together and had this idea of FFW. After it had been in existence a year, I met Carol and Duane. Joe and I throughout that period had been trying to get our heads together on what the problem was and why we weren't relating satisfactorily to each other. We weren't just saying that opening up our marriage was going to solve our problems. Now I think today we both realize that opening up our marriage had created problems. If we hadn't opened it, we might have been married twelve years instead of six. It would have ended eventually because I didn't like who I was. After I met Duane we started a really good relationship. Then I started a relationship with Carol and the kids because I was down in the house so much. Joe and I decided that the only sensible thing to do before we absolutely hated each other's guts was to split. At that point my feelings toward both Carol and Duane were such that they were the people I wanted to go to get the support I needed. I needed emotional and financial support, because I was still in school and they felt it was very important for me to finish. The triad was accidental. None of us realized that we were going to be in a triad in less than a year. It wasn't that kind of thing. It was a very gradual process and eventually we became a triad. I don't ever remember a point at which we said we're a triad now.

The problems in forming the triad aren't really monstrous. My moving in was very slow. I spent weekends there for six months and often one or two nights a week, so that my moving in was no real traumatic thing. I knew the house. I was really doing things around it. Carol and I had developed a relationship although initially my relationship started with Duane. It wasn't the kind of thing that when I was in the house I was there for Duane. Nor did they say come live with us so we can label ourselves. You can't say I want to go into a group marriage or open up my marriage and bam there it is. Somewhere along the line you go through a head trip and intellectualize how far you can go. Somewhere in between you get that head and stomach together.

Another thing that I ran into was that the man that I married was definitely a father-type person. He was extremely supportive. He really helped me along because he wanted to take care of me and see me happy. It did help that I had the support of someone behind me. It doesn't make any difference where the support comes from either. It's nice to know that there is somebody there who'll sit down and listen to you. A person who can reinforce your feelings that you're worthwhile. It's very important for you to feel that way. You learn to say I'm lovable because you are. Man, it really does go a long way in helping you start to feel good about yourself again and that's important.

Relationship to Family of Orientation

DUANE: My parents don't know about the triad at all. There's been an emotional divorce between my parents and myself probably ever since I was one year old. They've never known how to be a friend to me or to rap with me on an intellectual level. At the age of thirty-two I'm supposedly a fine, upstanding family man and all that kind of stuff. However, my mother still gives me advice. They were always telling me what I wanted to do. I went around completely dazed for years. I have nothing that even comes close to an intimate relationship with my parents. So I don't even bother trying to tell them about the triad.

CHARLOTTE: My mother knows, doesn't like it, and just wishes it would go away. She's going to have to face the fact that it's not going away. My aunt and grandmother live with my mother, and they don't know. I've left that up to my mother. Let her tell them when she feels it is necessary. She's the one that lives with them. I don't have to feel the flack from that. My sister knows and she accepts it and probably thinks it's strange because she's monogamous. But she accepts Carol and Duane and the kids. I assume my brother knows. I don't have that much contact with him because he lives so far away.

CAROL: My parents are divorced. My father lives in the metropolitan area, but my father and I have not exchanged words in twelve years, at his choice. So he has no idea what I'm doing, except he does know he has grandchildren, whom he has never seen. We consider him a functioning psychotic. My mother knows and she's unhappy. She was unhappy about it for a long time because she was trying to accept it in the context of her own life style, which of course she couldn't do. One day last year I said to her, "I'm not expecting you to live my life style." I said, "I want you to do *your* thing. Just accept my thing." I guess since then she's become much more relaxed toward my life style. She isn't overjoyed by it. I think she was hassled by it. The man she is married to knows about it, and I suppose has known about it from the very beginning. However, only recently has he started opening up to me in terms of wanting to know more about me. He's been very, very slow to find out anything about who I am other than that I'm Grace's daughter. I assume he accepts it.

Economic Factors

CAROL: I'm a computer programmer, Duane is in data management, and Charlotte is a student and works part time. Thus we have an adequate income.

We're living in a house we bought so we don't have a landlord problem. It's a very large old house and everybody around us is in a town house. It's very much in the city. You have an awful lot of privacy.

We don't have financial problems like, "I think I want to go out and buy a new car or I think I want this cashmere sweater." The kind of problems that we encountered before Charlotte came were basically ones of how do you support another person. In other words, if a person is having a financial problem, how do you help them solve it? That's the kind of problem we have now as a triad.

The three of us have separate checking accounts mainly because we work in three different places. We just deposit the money in separate checking accounts, and when we need money for the bills there's usually more money in one account than there is in another. So whichever account has the money, the bills get paid out of that one. Another reason why we have different checking accounts is it's hell to balance a checkbook when more than one person writes checks.

It's taken us a long time to become affluent enough to even take a vacation. Of course, along with everything else now, we plan a vacation with the three of us. We have to work around our schedules to make sure we're all off at the same time.

DUANE: The people we work with know little about our personal lives. Many of the people I work with or have worked with over the past few years have a hard time accepting my beard and my hair. I don't go around saying, "Hey, man, you know, I've got two wives," — that's just not cool. Selected people do know or suspect, but I haven't really gotten into it. I've gotten more hassles over my hair and not wearing a tie.

Decisions and Chores

CAROL: Decisions are basically a group thing. It's possible that more than one person would have the same attitude, therefore you try to give a convincing argument. But there's no coercion, and no ganging up.

CHARLOTTE: Carol's the cook, I'm the laundress, and Duane's the housecleaner.

One of the nice things about it is that there's only a certain amount of housework you can do. If one person does it, it's dreadful. But the more people you have doing it, the more fun it becomes because then you can mostly do the things you enjoy. Our problems as a triad are basically the same as a dyad, because we still have three individuals relating to each other as most people have two. Some of it is alleviated in terms of just physical work. There's a lot less physical work to be done. Carol doesn't have to do as much work as she used to, I don't, and neither does Duane, because it's split. There are more demands on me now, because all of a sudden I have two children that I am responsible for. Child rearing is lessened on Carol and Duane, because they don't have to be just two people with children to relate to. If Carol and Duane are in a bad place, they've still got somebody else who could possibly be in a good place and be willing to give the children the attention they need.

Time, Jealousy, and Sex

CHARLOTTE: We don't have a jealousy problem with the three of us. We're all very conscious of feelings of exclusion. When the three of us are in the house we sleep together. When Carol's other male relationship is in the house, then Duane and I sleep together. At times we all sleep alone. At other times one of us will request to sleep alone. So we pretty much have things under control, and we're really sensitive to each other's feelings.

DUANE: Often, all three of us will sleep together. It isn't a group thing though. The three of us have slept together, and I've had sex with Carol or Charlotte. The other one's not really involved. Plus, there are other places to sleep. It's a big house.

CAROL: When I am very tired I have to sleep alone, because it's the only way I can get needed sleep. I just can't hassle having everybody else around me. Charlotte and I are not bisexual at this point. We haven't really talked about it. It's either we're really not into that or we aren't each other's type, which is possible. It's just something we're not out looking for. Neither of us feels frustrated by the fact that there is no sexual relationship.

I think in terms of jealousy, aside from the exclusion, there is the problem of time. There are only twenty-four precious hours in every day, and you can do just so much in twenty-four hours. I want time. That is something that is really critical. Being jealous of another person often has to do with feelings inside. Other moments, however, there is a time jealousy which is easier to correct. Sometimes I'll feel that Duane hasn't been spending time with me, that most of his time has been spent with Charlotte. It's not that I'm jealous of the fact that Charlotte is getting his time. It's just that I want a piece of that time.

Rarely has there ever been conflict over two of us simultaneously wanting a piece of time. Usually, we can perceive our mutual needs and the neediest person prevails. Sometimes, for example, if Duane is in a bad place he'll reject both of us. Occasionally he hasn't responded to the person most in need. However, it's not been a problem.

CHARLOTTE: Time to me is elastic. It can start here and you can stretch it. There's a limit to how far it can be stretched, but you *can* stretch time. It's to make the time that you have together as important as possible, and so the amount of time that you need is, therefore, much less in terms of absolute time. Also, because of the fact that the three of us are committed to each other, there's no splitting, okay? We spend the time together when we are in the house. The time hassle is when there are relationships outside. That is a hassle, and it is just basically a matter of priorities.

DUANE: Jealousy is just something that you deal with in terms of why you're feeling it and what the basis of it is. Generally, the basis of jealousy is some bad feeling about yourself. You may be feeling helpless or worthless. Then you may depend on someone else to make you feel better. You become jealous when the person you're dependent on shows interest in someone else.

What is called "time jealousy" is not that you're jealous of the other person, but at that particular moment you have a need that's not being met because the person is not around.

CAROL: Jealousy has not been a problem in any of the relationships Duane has had, except for one. It was a new experience for me. It was the first time I've ever had to deal with it. The woman he was dating had never been married and wanted him all to herself. Duane stopped dating her because she threatened his life style so in the end, I didn't have to handle the situation.

DUANE: I went through jealousy on Carol's first relationship. Putting your intellectual ideas into behavioral patterns is difficult. So I had to sit down and deal for a while with jealousy. A lot of the jealousy wasn't over Carol and the relationship. My jealousy was not feeling good about myself. I resented that I wasn't having a relationship. That's where a lot of the jealousy was coming from. If Carol had found a relationship with another man and I didn't have one, and she wanted him to move in, then I would have attempted it, but I would've had a lot of difficulty dealing with it. After Charlotte moved in it was easier.

CAROL: My feeling is that love is the most unselfish thing you can do, in terms of another human being. If you love someone enough you also love them enough to let them go. Love is not a possession. You cannot hold on to something like that. Love is complete freedom. If you are capable of truly loving someone, then you know what perfect freedom is, because there aren't any doubts between you. If there aren't any doubts, then you're not going to feel threatened by this. I'm not saying what we have is perfect, but we're working on it.

CHARLOTTE: Most of your doubts come from within yourself, and because of the past few years I've experienced an awful lot of personal growth. I just feel so much better about myself. I am more sure of who I am as a person, secure in the fact that I need people, but not needing any one specific person. I enjoy being with people, but if something happens, I can make it on my own. I discovered I could make it on my own when my marital relationship weakened. I wasn't going to spend the rest of my life being dependent upon my husband. It's very much a personal thing. Your jealousies and your doubts all go right back to yourself, not to the other person.

CAROL: I think basically you have to be a self-sufficient person, capable of standing on your own, but that doesn't mean being rigidly on your own. It's awfully nice to lean. But you can't depend on leaning.

Never have the idea that you own someone. You can never own another human being. I think our society runs counter to that. Many men, particularly, think this is my wife to have and to hold, literally. The idea of sharing is easier for women. Polygamy has been around a long time. I think it's probably a little bit easier for women to accept another woman, than it would be for a man to accept another male into a triad. However, it still takes an awful lot of thinking about what you are, what you're willing to put up with, what you feel, and what would threaten you. For my husband to have a sexual affair with another woman doesn't threaten me at all.

DUANE: One thing is you can't confuse being secure with not having problems. We are very secure among all of us. Carol and I got to the point in our marriage where we were just very secure with each other. We knew that whatever we were attempting to experiment with on the outside would not destroy that relationship. That's security. We had a lot of problems, a lot of personal growth, a lot of pain, a lot of hurt, but that original bond wasn't broken. There was the security that we always knew what we had. We're now getting to the point where we have that security about the three of us.

Legal Issues

CAROL: There are a lot of legal problems or situations like wills and various things that we're going to have to consider. We haven't gotten into them because in the past there hasn't been a need to. Eventually, we are going to cover Charlotte in wills, custody of the children, and so forth.

We have an old will that's going to have to be redone. Every time we go away on a long trip we say we should have done the will.

The most immediate legal hassle we want to deal with is to make sure that none of the children's grandparents get the kids, nor the state. I think that we can cover that legally in a will and make Charlotte the guardian.

CHARLOTTE: I would just like to do away with the marriage laws instead of trying to liberalize them. I would prefer the three of us just going through a church ceremony without any piece of paper.

We would eventually like to see FFW involved in getting tax laws rewritten to where you could have a legal three adult group. Some people also want to get legally married to more than one person of their choice.

CAROL: What if something should happen to Duane? That's something we have to live with realistically since Duane drives a motorcycle. I think Charlotte's and my reaction would be that there is no reason for her to leave or for me to want to leave. There is a very intimate relationship between the three of us. Intimate not being the same as sexual. It's very, very close and, therefore, the lines of intensity within the relationship are the same. For example, I don't have quite as intimate a relationship with Steve. It's because of the nature of the kind of person Steve is.

CHARLOTTE: I feel spiritually that the children are mine even if something happened to Duane and Carol.

I'm also interested in becoming a mother. We plan sometime in the foreseeable future for me to try and get pregnant. The children are protected if I have any. Duane is going to claim paternity. His name is going to be on the birth certificate.

Parenthood

CAROL: I have two children who are six and eight years old. I'm not a possessive person. I don't look upon my children as MY children. My feeling toward children is anybody can be a parent. It's where their heads are at, not where the baby was originally produced from. The fact that Charlotte is there as an adjunct is fantastic for me because my kids are able to interact with somebody who really cares about them. It's not that she's taking anything away from me as a person or any love away from me that I am not giving them. You know there's just so much you can give. Kids are like parasites. They need tremendous amounts of attention. Charlotte will take them upstairs and sit with them or watch TV or maybe find out what they want to do. She'll give them attention at a time when I can't give it to them. It's better than saying go away totally. Sometimes that happens too. There's always a grownup around, somebody to at least listen to them.

Raising children is a lot of work, it's a lot of fun, but it's work. You've got a twenty-year commitment with kids. You can say I'm going to marry you one day, but I can always divorce you. That's not so with kids. You know that's a long-time commitment, and it's nice to share the burden.

The kids, I think, are totally aware of our arrangement. We decided a long time ago that kids learn much more by observation than they do by what we tell them. Our kids really are cool. In our house there's no place that's secret or off limits. The only exception to that is when a person wants quiet time or alone time, which is very important to everybody.

It seems that I haven't seen anything that I would consider negative as a result of this. Sometimes we would have family pow-wows among the adults. We recently had a problem with Derek, one of the children, in terms of discipline. He can't think he can play one of us off against the other.

The children go to a private day care center. Kirsten's in second grade and Derek's in kindergarten. So they're there all day long. Most of the school children come from single-parent homes so the fact that Kirsten and Derek have two natural parents still living together makes them unique to begin with. The fact that there's another adult around really is superfluous.

The neighborhood we live in is a very diversified neighborhood where there are communes and expanded families through relatives.

CHARLOTTE: As to my relationship with the children I would describe it as very much on the same level as the one I had with my aunt and grandmother. I was brought up by three women. You can get the care or love you need from that other person. You know that there is another adult who cares about you, and I know that the kids feel that way. My bedroom adjoins their bedroom, and that is generally the first bedroom they check. When either one wakes up with a nightmare or is sick they go to the closest person. They know that I care and I will give them the support they need. Carol and Duane are definitely Mommy and Daddy. I get them up in the morning sometimes. There's no scheduling. Someone gets them up. Someone gives them a bath. Someone feeds them. Carol and I both take them to school on and off, depending on who it's more convenient for.

I have stopped referring to Duane as "Daddy" when I'm talking to them or Carol as "Mommy" and they don't either. They pretty much refer to them by their first names. We haven't said, "Don't call me 'Mommy.' " It's just something that was started before we got into the triad. And pretty much started by Duane himself. So that very often they're referred to as Carol and Duane. When someone asks who I am, I'm their friend.

Epilogue

What has been written is like a composite snapshot in time. The triadic relationship of Carol, Duane, and Charlotte is a constantly evolving one. However, it is the oddity of the arrangement that is intriguing. Are these people deviants and individuals who have intellectually suppressed their emotions? Or are they pioneers representing a vanguard of future multiple relationships adapting to new realities? Ultimately, it is not the success or failure of this triad that really matters. Rather, the questions it raises concerning such issues as exclusivity, personal identity, cooperation, management, and child-rearing may be its most significant contribution.

SINGLEHOOD

[8]

IN THE PAST, singlehood for men often suggested social reprobation, personality inadequacy, homosexuality, alcoholism,
psychopathology, or other insalubrious states. Indeed, in Puritan New
England a bachelor was sometimes not permitted to move to a new
town without a letter from a responsible official of his old town attesting
to his good character. Single women, on the other hand, bore little
semblance to their single brothers. They were independent, courageous, nonphobic, and achievers. The difference lay in the fact that
marriage was oriented toward the satisfaction of men. Thus, men who
did not want to enjoy the benefits of marriage often had a quirk or two.
Some women saw marriage as unfair to them and instead chose
spinsterhood. Even those who opted for marriage had to follow Milton's
motto, "They also serve who only stand and wait," because society
frowned on the idea of women playing an active role in courtship. Men
set the standards for what they wanted in women, and beauty, or at least
reasonable attractiveness, was an important criterion. Those women
who failed this criterion often had to make do as singles; consequently,
single women were not selected out for interpersonal inadequacy as
were men, and were much better adjusted.

Today society places less value on marriage. Marriage as a duty to
populate the earth is hardly the motivational force it was formerly. Most
individuals needn't marry to enjoy sex, and society is becoming increasingly tolerant of and oriented toward the single person. Will
singlehood become a goal for many in the future, or is there some
emotional need for pairing, whether within matrimony or outside it? It
is my guess that the latter alternative will prevail. But this doesn't mean
that people will jump into matrimony or pairing with the traditional

163

haste of the female senior in college. Indeed, the percentage of single women aged twenty-two (typical age of the college senior) increased 12.5 percent between 1960 and 1975. Although observation indicates that young adults are still pairing with some frequency, this pairing seems to be on a more temporary basis more than previously. Thus they are spending more time in singlehood, and Roger W. Libby offers some challenging ideas about this important but hitherto neglected state.

Creative Singlehood as a Sexual Life Style: Beyond Marriage as a Rite of Passage*

ROGER W. LIBBY

S INGLE PEOPLE have received little attention in research, theories, and scholarly analysis of social scientists. Family sociologists have either ignored singles or relegated them to boring, out-of-date discussions of dating, courtship, and mate selection as steps toward marriage and parenthood. The neglect is blatant in that the number of adults between twenty-five and thirty-four who have never been married increased by 50 percent between 1960 and 1975 (U.S. Bureau of the Census, 1960, 1975). About half of those aged eighteen to thirty-nine are unmarried, and typically about a third of a woman's adult life is spent as a single person (U.S. Bureau of the Census, 1970). There are more

*"Creative Singlehood as a Sexual Life Style: Beyond Marriage as A Rite of Passage," Copyright© 1977 by Roger W. Libby. From *Marriage and Alternatives: Exploring Intimate Relationships* by Roger W. Libby and Robert N. Whitehurst, published by Scott, Foresman and Company. Reprinted by permission of the author.

The theoretical models were created with Molly Laird, who was also a valuable resource person for many of the ideas. The author also wishes to acknowledge the following for their comments on various drafts of this article: Judith Long Laws, Bernard Murstein, Gilbert Nass, Kathy Everly, Donna Dempster, Ronald Mazur, Sharon Rucker, Bob Thamm, Gordon Clanton, Bob Whitehurst, Elizabeth Havelock, Sterling Alam, Carolynne Kieffer, Shirley Nuss, and Norman Bell.

women than men who are single at any given time, but as will be seen in this chapter, single men appear to be less happy as a group than single women. Since most writing on singles has been journalistic or descriptive social science unrelated to any well-developed theory, little is understood about singlehood as a sexual life style.

The stereotype of the Joe Namath kind of swinging single and the opposing stereotype of the frustrated and miserable single person (as in George Gilder's *Sexual Suicide* and *Naked Nomads*) obscure the realities of singlehood. These polarized images which surface in the mass media and in everyday interaction blind social scientists and others to the range of life styles being lived or contemplated by singles. Furthermore, the bulk of descriptive research on premarital sex and on cohabitation among college students has not informed social theory concerning singlehood. This is because the college years are too early to identify singlehood as an active choice rather than a premarital stage in the monogamous model. The same may be true of the post-college singles subculture which has received attention in the mass media.

Computer dating, singles' bars, career orientations in urban areas, and even a singles' church (*Newsweek,* June 12, 1972) offer opportunities for single people to socialize and work together; but in many if not most singles' social functions, the end goal is still to find a partner to live with or to marry. We are socialized in a couple-oriented society where at least 90 percent are expected to (and in fact do) marry.

However, at any one time about a third or more Americans are unmarried, separated, or in some way "unattached." Census figures do not allow for a precise delineation of living arrangements such as cohabitation, but the high divorce rate, the rise in the average age of first marriage, and the apparent longer period between divorce and remarriage (when remarriage occurs) provide a demographic basis for speculation about the dissolution of couples and emergence of singlehood as a life style. It is also important to take into account divorced, separated, and widowed people when discussing singlehood as a sexual life style. It may be significant, for example, that widowhood is increasing more for women than for men. This is because men are older when they marry than are women, and women tend to live longer; this creates stiffer competition among women for marital partners (Glick, 1976, personal discussion).

Singlehood is beginning to emerge as a positive option to marriage and other couple images. Social and ideological support for singlehood as a choice, rather than as a residual category for the unchosen and lonely, has come from the women's liberation movement, from the alternative life styles and human potential movements, and from such groups as Zero Population Growth (ZPG), Planned Parenthood, and the National Organization for Non-Parents (NON). In addition, discrimination against singles in the tax structure has lessened (1972 Tax Reform Act, Dullea, 1975).

Ira Reiss (1973) has noted a trend toward increased legitimacy of choice of sexual life styles and toward greater permissiveness in attitudes and behavior in heterosexual relationships prior to and after marriage. Murray Straus (letter to author, November 1975) has proposed the hypothesis that the more sexually restrictive a society, the more singleness will be defined in negative ways (because marriage is necessary to make sex legitimate). And yet, family sociology has not investigated singlehood as an important life style or satisfactorily analyzed various social sanctions for and against singlehood.

This chapter will attempt to bring us one step nearer to a clear conceptualization of the costs and rewards of choosing singlehood as a sexual life style. The focus will be on the roles and position of single people over their sexual lives or "careers." I will discuss definitional issues first; then review the available literature; present some theoretical models; and finally suggest questions for future research.

Definitions: Who Is Single?

In both the professional and popular literature, single people have been inconsistently defined. While some researchers would simply limit singles to never marrieds, others include divorced, separated, and widowed people who are not cohabiting with a sexual partner. Others incorporate legal, social, and personal dimensions into the definition, such as age, intention to remain single or to marry, acceptance or nonacceptance of multiple sexual and emotional relationships, living arrangement, means of financial support, involvement in primary (even if not exclusive) sexual relationships, and the budgeting of time between one or more people and other obligations. Some distinguish between the labels *unmarried*, *single*, and *unattached*. Others simply state that singlehood, like marriage, is a state of mind rather than a legal status or a label conferred by others. Some define singlehood in terms of marriage (thus the stages "premarital" and "postmarital"), while others view singlehood as a choice rather than a stage. Although the definition of "single" may seem obvious to some, the definitional issues are complex.

Rather than defining singlehood in any narrow way, I will consider the whole range of sexual life styles that potentially fall within the single category. In this context, singlehood might be a choice for some, or a stage leading to marriage or remarriage for others. It might also be a stage leading to cohabitation, which could in turn lead to marriage. On the other hand, marriage may be seen as an interim stage, with divorce and singlehood emerging as choices at later stages. My emphasis is on the *process* and on the concept of a sexual career involving different choices made at different stages in the life cycle. *Yesterday's choice could be today's stage in transition to tomorrow's new choice.*

To go further with this conceptualization of sexual career choices, there are costs and rewards involved with any choice. Those who *choose* to be single do so after evaluating the relative costs and rewards of other life styles which are realistic options. The existence of a theoretical choice is not the same as having the option to make that choice, or to openly act on one's preferences. For example, one may want to have multiple sexual partners, and one may visualize this as a choice, but unless there are partners available and willing, along with a network of people and social institutions to support such a life style, the option does not actually exist.

Before continuing to define singlehood, perhaps it would help to say what a single person *is not. For the purposes of this paper, "creative singlehood" is not legal marriage or cohabitation. A creatively single person is not emotionally, sexually, or financially dependent on one person; psychological and social autonomy are necessary to be defined as single* (Margaret Adams, 1971). If one person allows another to monopolize the majority of his or her time to the near exclusion of others as sexual partners, that person would not be considered single. A single person is committed to various leisure and occupational relationships, but does not make an exclusive commitment which precludes other emotional and sexual experiences.

Singlehood is a state of availability. This definition rules out those who are totally or mostly dependent on a relationship which demands conformity to the monogamous model, but it could include separated and divorced people, regardless of whether they are parents. This definition, then, goes beyond legal categories to focus on self-definitions and on the social identities acquired through labeling.

Although a person may be single either by choice or from the lack of opportunity to find a suitable partner, I will stress those creative singles who choose to remain single, and who choose not to cohabit or limit sexual behavior to one person. A single person may be eighteen or seventy-five, but this paper will emphasize the upper-middle-class college graduates in urban areas who are involved in professional careers and have a rather open opportunity structure for relating sexually with multiple partners. Although single people may change their life styles at any point after reevaluating their particular situations, I will emphasize those who have chosen creative singlehood instead of cohabitation, sexual celibacy, marriage, or communal living. Being single need not mean being alone, but some time alone is assumed here. Furthermore, having primary and/or coprimary (equally primary) intimate relationships, as well as secondary and transitory relationships, would not necessarily conflict with singlehood.

There are *degrees* of singlehood, as I will illustrate later. One may be more single one month than another but still not move outside the single status. Or, one may be single, choose to cohabit or marry, and perhaps choose to later divorce and become single again. In this sense singlehood and other choices are *reclaimable* statuses or identities. One has the option of repudiating a current identity or reclaiming an earlier status. [1]

The strong emphasis on marriage as the final outcome of the dating-courtship script has essentially made singlehood a "deviant" choice. In spite of increased acceptance of premarital and nonmarital intercourse, for many *marriage is a rite of passage to legitimize sexual expression.* The emerging legitimization of singlehood as a sexual life style flies in the face of the traditional view of premarital relationships leading to marriage. Roy and Roy (1977) identify reasons for the emphasis on marriage and offer a suggestion for social policy. They state:

> It is principally because of the fear of sexual involvement that the singles are excluded from married society. In the new dispensation, a much more active and aggressive policy should be encouraged to incorporate single persons within the total life of a family and a community (p. 31).

The fear of intimate or sexual relationships with married people is an underlying factor which contributes to the isolation of many singles from community life. A single person's availability to others is a critical factor affecting his or her identity.

Singlehood can change along various dimensions as one moves through the life cycle. A single person's role responsibilities and rights depend on familial, economic, and other considerations; commitment may shift from singlehood to some form of coupling and back again in response to other factors in one's life (Gilbert Nass, letter to author, October 1975). Roles shift in that they are defined by the self and by

---

1. The concept of reclaimable identities was arrived at with Ronald Mazur (letter to author, October 1975).

various reference groups and significant others. As social acceptance of singles increases and a social support system evolves, the roles attached to the single position will multiply. Institutionalized support for the sexual conduct of available single people may be minimal currently, but it is growing, particularly in large cities where the proportion of singles is high.

This brings me to some basic concepts which underlie creative singlehood and other multiple relationship life styles. The social scripting of sexual and sex role behavior (or alternative sexual life styles) is based on the following assumptions:

1. There is an eternal, erotic, emotional attraction between people, and a permanent availability of people to each other for emotional and sexual expression regardless of marital or living arrangements or sex. Bernard Farber (1964) predicted a trend away from the orderly replacement of marriage partners (lifetime monogamy) toward a more free-floating permanent availability. He stated: "Permanent availability implies that the basic needs of the individual may change . . . and that meeting personality needs at an early age may not suffice to maintain the marriage" (1964, p. 168).

2. There is an emerging autonomy of sexual expression apart from marriage, the family, and reproduction, so that the individual, not the couple or a larger entitiy, is the lowest common denominator when considering the meaning of sexual conduct (Jetse Sprey, 1969).

3. There is increasing visibility and viability of sexual life styles (called the legitimacy of sexual choice by Ira Reiss, 1973); the full range of choices is receiving increased social support so that realistic options are increased.

4. We live in a secretive society where people can do as they wish without negative social sanctions if they are relatively discreet (open opportunity structure).

5. Change in one aspect of a culture or in one stage of a sexual career (such as increased sexual intercourse before marriage) affects change in other institutional arrangements or stages (such as the ground rules for sexual behavior for married partners). New definitions of coupling (such as sexual friendships outside a primary relationship as in sexually open marriage) force a new look at singlehood.

6. Sexual behavior cannot be isolated or compartmentalized from the

rest of a relationship. Nonsexual motives for sexual behavior and sexual motives for nonsexual behavior make compartmentalization of sex from various emotions, desires, expectations, and fantasies impossible.

The above assumptions give support to creative singlehood, and they encourage multiple sexual and emotional relationships for all categories of single and coupled people. The assumptions also feed into the social scripts for two contrasting sexual life styles described in Table 1 (Libby, 1976). After looking at these two social scripts, I will comment on the relevant empirical, theoretical, and journalistic literature on singles.

A Selective Review of the Literature on Singles

The purpose of this review is to present the essence of what is now known or suspected about singles. Demographic data on age trends for first marriage, divorce rates, and similar descriptive information will be briefly covered. Then the few relevant empirical studies of singlehood as a chosen life style will be described, and some journalistic literature will be discussed.

DEMOGRAPHIC DATA

Paul Glick (1975) and Jessie Bernard (1975) have presented some of the most current statistics on the delay in marriage and the increase in divorce, single parenthood, and various living arrangements for never married and other unattached people. It is difficult to predict whether marriage rates will continue to decline. We do know, though, that the average age of first marriage for women increased from twenty to twenty-one between 1960 and 1974, and the age increase for men during that period was from about twenty-two plus to twenty-three. Single men and women are delaying marriage and choosing to remain single longer. The proportion of women aged twenty to twenty-four remaining single has increased from 28 percent in 1960 to 40 percent in 1974 (U.S. Bureau of the Census, 1974). The figures for men are obscured by the movement of men in the armed forces.

Glick notes several reasons for the increase in age at marriage for women. About three times more women were enrolled in college in 1972 compared to in 1960, and the increase in employment for that period was greater for women than for men. Also, women at their peak marrying age (twenty-one) have outnumbered men at their peak marrying age (twenty-three) in any given year. Because the peak is about two years earlier for women than for men born the same year, there is a younger but larger group of women competing for partners from the smaller and older group of men. This situation, which Glick calls the "marriage squeeze," will probably exist until the average age of marriage for men and women equalizes.

As Margaret Adams (1971) explained, the economic autonomy that college degrees and employment provide is critical to the emergence of singlehood as a life style for women.[2] Both Glick (1975) and Adams (1971) consider the women's liberation movement to be a contributing social force supporting singlehood for women. Glick concludes that the postponement of marriage and childbearing by women appears to be part of a trend toward choosing alternatives to marriage, and he feels women may both try and like alternatives, including singlehood (Glick, 1975, p. 4).

The census data make it difficult to reflect on singlehood as a sexual life style because living arrangements are not precisely delineated. "Living alone" and "living with nonrelatives" does not distinguish singlehood beyond a legal status; one might be cohabiting, monogamous, or creatively single. Since a sexual career may include frequent changes in living arrangements, more frequent data collection and/or accurate biographical information on individuals is necessary to chart role transitions. Although Jessie Bernard (1975) used census data to describe changing life styles from 1970 to 1974, she admittedly could only speculate about their meaning and trends in sexual and living arrangements. Nevertheless, Bernard's and Glick's data tentatively indicate that marriage is becoming less popular.

The decreasing popularity of marriage appears dramatic when one observes the linear increase in divorce rates. There were over one million divorces in 1975 in the U.S. — 6 percent more than in 1974. In contrast, the marriage rate dropped 4 percent that year, to roughly 2.1 million (U.S. Bureau of the Census, 1976). Glick and Norton (1973) estimate that one in three marriages for women thirty years old has ended or would end in divorce. After comparing marriage and divorce rates over a seven-year span, Ivan Nye (personal discussion with author, February 1976) predicted that national statistics on divorce will soon reach the levels of such states as California and Washington, where about 50 percent of first marriages, and even more remarriages, end in

---

2. Also, as Gordon Clanton has suggested to the author (letter, January 1976), we may find that with greater affluence more people will choose to remain single. There may be an economic threshold operating; as a society we can only sustain single people to the extent that we have the housing, jobs, and social support for singlehood.

TABLE 1.   Two social scripts for sexual relationships

	"Primrose Path" of Dating	Branching Paths of "Getting Together"
Fifth to Sixth Grade	Structured heterosexual activities, spin the bottle type of activity; having one boyfriend or girlfriend.	Unstructured activities, with no emphasis on marriage or relating to one member of the opposite sex. Interest-orientation rather than obsession with one opposite sex person.
Seventh to Ninth Grade	Group dating and dating with parents as chaperone figures. Parents drive car, etc. Sneaking around with opposite sex. Emphasis on meeting personal needs and acceptance from peers by conforming to their expectations.	No parental imposition of monogamous expectations. Nonpossessive, equalitarian relationships with no emphasis on dichotomy of sexual and nonsexual relationships.
High School	Double dating and single dating in cars with exclusive expectation once one dates a person a few times (going with one person, or "going steady").	"Getting together" *rather than* dating, with female initiating relationships as much as male and paying and driving car as much as male does.
After High School	• Work and continue monogamous dating, or date more than one person, or go to college and do same, or marry monogamously. Static, rigid role expectations for female and male. • Stress physical levels of intimacy as a basis for sexual morality. Sex viewed as economic ownership, meeting one's personal security needs, and as exclusive. If live together, it is sexually exclusive. • Divorce, tolerate unhappy "marriage," or for a minority, live happily ever after in a sexually and emotionally exclusive monogamous marriage.	• Stress qualities and common interest in relationships as a basis for decision making about sex and other relationship concerns. • Touching and sensuality encouraged. Sex only in mutually appropriate and mutually discussed situations. Sex as one language in some relationships with a range of symbolic meanings — from mutual pleasure (or horniness), to friendship, to love (love not seen as exclusive but as multiple following Robert Rimmer in *The Harrad Experiment,* and other novels).

TABLE 1.   Continued

"*Primrose Path" of Dating*	*Branching Paths of "Getting Together"*
After High School *(cont.)* • Remarriage and divorce, or a repeat of the above (serial monogamy with "cheating" on the side by both spouses). • Emphasis on the weakness of the participants in marriage when unhappiness or divorce occurs, rather than questioning the monolithic image of marriage as "the answer" for anyone who chooses to marry. • Disillusionment with marriage for many. Searching for the "good life," but confused as to how to find it. Conflict between images in the mass media and what the local minister is preaching. Enter the therapist . . . who may or may not help. . . . What next?	• If live together, relationship is sexually and emotionally nonexclusive. • Creative singlehood, or if marriage, some similar kind of open-ended arrangement such as the alternatives described in this book. • A *decision* to be open or closed in various areas of marriage, with the ongoing process of renegotiation of the marital contract. Marriage as a process rather than a static set of promises. • Various open marriages with comarital or satellite relationships viewed as supportive of the pair bond rather than as a threat to it. • Swinging — from recreation to utopian. • Group marriage. • Communal living with or without sexual sharing. • Compartmentalized marriage — with "night off" from marriage. • If divorce, joy rather than sadness (creative divorce). • Synergy: 1 + 1 = more than 2. (See O'Neill & O'Neill, 1972.)

It is not uncommon for those socialized in the traditional script to later decide to take on different roles and to adopt some of the emerging alternatives to the monogamous image of the cheating reality . . . so some switching back and forth between scripts prior to and after marriage(s) is common. The above scripts are two *ideal types* on a continuum rather than dichotomies. However, many people still fit the traditional extreme of the "primrose path."

divorce. Since divorce is more prevalent among the remarried (Nye and Berardo, 1973, p. 529), it would appear that people will be spending more of their adult lives in some single status.

Furthermore, we cannot assume that those who do not divorce are happily married. The marriage and family literature (including longitudinal studies) reveals that only about 10 to 20 percent of marriages are self-reported as happy throughout most of the marriage, and wives report less satisfaction than husbands. Also, more men than women remarry; five-sixths of divorced men and three-fourths of women aged thirty-five to forty-four remarry (Glick, 1975). Apparently the double standard of aging, whereby women tend to be considered less attractive sooner than men (Susan Sontag, 1972), and the larger proportion of women to men with increasing age account for such a sex differential in remarriage rates. Since women tend to be less satisfied with marriage, it may also be that they are less anxious to remarry. The relaxation in divorce laws (although many so-called "no-fault" laws are not as the label implies, Weitzman, 1974) and the decreasing social stigma of divorce make singlehood a more viable alternative for both sexes. In spite of the increased economic independence of women through increased employment, women still appear to have more liabilities such as children and fewer assets to bargain for remarriage. Finally, it appears that the period between divorce and remarriage is increasing for young people of both sexes.[3] Even though most divorced people still remarry, an increase in the time interval after divorce, which has been about three years, may indicate a trend toward post-marital singlehood without remarriage for a growing population.

EMPIRICAL STUDIES

In addition to demographic statistics, studies of attitudes about marriage contribute to predictions about future life style choices. Although the social psychology literature indicates that attitudes alone are not very accurate predictors of behavior, when considered with behavioral intention and selected situational, reference group, and social support variables, attitudes do contribute to the prediction of behavior (Fishbein and Ajzen, 1975; Acock and DeFleur, 1972). Peter Stein (1973) collected data on a population of college students (N of nearly 500, with a response rate of 75 percent of the college's class of 1973). He found that 3 percent of freshman women did not expect to marry as compared to 8

---

3. This is not yet a demonstrated fact (Paul Glick, discussion with author, 1976), but I believe this trend will be documented in the near future.

percent of senior women. Most impressive was his finding that 40 percent of senior college women did not know whether or not they should marry, and 39 percent of seniors felt that traditional marriage is becoming obsolete (Stein, 1973). Yankelovitch (1972) has noted a similar increase in disillusionment with marriage among college student samples over the years.

Whitehurst (1977) and White and Wells (1973) have also studied university students' attitudes toward various life styles. These investigators concluded that some changes were in the making but that dramatic, widespread changes in life style choices should not be expected. Twelve percent of Whitehurst's nonrandomly selected students felt that monogamy is dying; of these 88 percent were single. Whitehurst found that 58 percent agreed it is possible to love (including sexually) more than one person at a time, but more marrieds than singles felt this way.[4] The implications of such beliefs for extramarital and comarital sex, as well as for eventual divorce and choice of singlehood or remarriage, are obvious. Furthermore, less than half intended to have conventional marriages like those of their parents, and nearly a fifth would be willing to try group living arrangements. Generally, then, Whitehurst's student subjects perceived some need for change in conventional monogamous marriage.

In the past few years, some research directly concerned with singlehood and sexuality has been undertaken. Stein (1975) conducted in-depth interviews with ten women and ten men (median ages of thirty-five and twenty-nine, respectively). All but two subjects had been married or involved in some type of exclusive sexual relationship prior to choosing a nonexclusive single life. Stein purposefully limited his sample to those who were nonexclusive, who did not plan to marry in the near future, and who did not hope to live with one person in an exclusive relationship in the near future. Thus, singles in this sample were defined as those who were sexually available to multiple partners after having experienced exclusivity. This is an obvious bias; one would expect such a sample strongly to endorse singleness, due in part to their previous unhappiness in exclusive relationships. Not surprisingly, Stein's sample felt that exclusive and/or marital relationships restricted human growth. One wonders what would be reported by other types of singles including those who had never experienced an exclusive relationship, or those who had been involved in an open marriage, com-

---

4. Jessie Bernard's discussion of younger couples stressing exclusivity and older couples opting for permanence without exclusivity is relevant here. See Bernard (1977).

munal living, group marriage, or some other alternative to traditional monogamous marriage or exclusive cohabitation.

Stein identifies some of the pushes and pulls toward and away from singlehood and monogamous marriage. Stein rightly points up the need for an ideology to make singlehood more viable as an option to marriage, and he identifies the lack of control which single people have over their existence (due to economic exploitation by such businesses as singles' bars, for instance). Stein's list of pulls toward singlehood (which might more precisely be called rewards from an exchange theory view) includes career opportunity, variety of experiences, self-sufficiency, sexual availability, exciting life style, freedom to change and experiment, mobility, sustaining friendships, and supportive relationships such as men's and women's groups, group living, and specialized groups. Pushes toward singlehood (or costs associated with other life styles) include suffocating one-to-one relationships, obstacles to self-development, boredom, unhappiness and anger, role playing, and conforming to expectations of others. Some other pushes toward singlehood could be poor communication with a mate, sexual frustration, lack of friends, isolation and loneliness, limitations on mobility and possible experiences, and influence of or participation in the women's movement (Stein, 1975, pp. 493-4). Stein also lists pulls and pushes toward marriage, most of which involve economic, emotional, and sexual security, and the influence of parents.

While Stein's study does offer some insights into one segment of the singles population, it also has several limitations. First, Stein did not present his findings in the context of any well-developed theoretical framework. In addition, he refers to singlehood as an emerging social movement (a response to sources of discontent, a set to goals, and a program to implement the goals, as defined by Killian, 1973). This claim is not justified; it would be more accurate to conceive of singlehood as one of several intimate life styles receiving increased social and legal support from the human potential, women's liberation, and population control social movements. A more comprehensive treatment of Stein's study is available in his book, *Single In America* (1976). Stein's ideas for future research, presented in his article and book, are likely to spur more systematic and theoretically based empirical investigations into singlehood.

Fishel and Allon (1973) carried out an extensive ethnographic study of singles' bars. They utilized participant observation and open-ended interviews with 100 people in eight singles' bars in New York City. Their conceptualization of single people was consistent with those of Stein and of such singles' publications as *Single Magazine*. Being single meant not being married or living together and not being engaged, pinned, or going steady. Taking the self-definitions of the participants in the bars, a "constant, steady relationship" implied attachment and not single-hood. There were some who were married or suspected of being married who frequented the singles' bars. For these people, the researchers concluded that singlehood was situational — that one could appear single and behave according to that social image. Actual interaction patterns were stressed and a situational definition of singlehood used. However, coupling was found to be a primary goal of participants in the singles' bars — success was often measured by achieving coupling and leaving singlehood behind. In this sense, singlehood as choice or stage is a critical research question.

Fishel and Allon's research is based in social theory, largely drawing on Georg Simmel's sociability theory of interaction patterns and Irving Goffman's analysis of interaction. The researchers concluded that sin-gles' bars were full of those seeking companionship as an answer to their self-estrangement and isolation from others. The picture was one of disillusionment with self and others, dissatisfaction with the pre-scribed role playing in the singles' bar, and a sense of boredom which the participants hoped to replace with excitement, ego support for being attractive, and some semblance of intimacy with others.

Fishel and Allon's findings are consistent with another study of singles in Chicago by Starr and Carns (1973). A nonrandom availability sample of seventy single people was interviewed in 1970 and 1971; all in the sample were college graduates in their early to mid-twenties who had done graduate work and then moved to the big city to work. Nine had been married and most had no previous conception of the singles scene. The relative ease in meeting people during college had not been experienced in the urban single life.

The frequency with which the subjects went to singles' bars dropped off the longer they lived in the social context of urban singlehood; this was particularly true of women. Single men were often in search of instant sex, and many had sex with women of lower social status. Men were more sexually oriented, while women tended to be interested in friendship and permanent relationships. Starr and Carns found that singles' bars, neighborhood apartment living complexes, and parties did not offer much in the way of companionship or satisfactory ways to meet people. The majority of cross-sex friendships resulted from having been introduced to someone when at work (usually to someone who did not work in the same office). The researchers viewed the work world as the most significant context in which singles could develop a strong sense of self. The carefree swinging singles image was not supported. The contrast between the relatively happy singles in Stein's select sample in New York City and those in the samples collected by Starr and Carns and by Allon and Fishel is suggestive of the broad range of life styles and degrees of singlehood.

The process of adjusting to a new single life includes relating to old and new friends and meeting companions for intimacy and sex. Yet the traditional sociological research on friendship patterns fails to include sexual expression as a dimension of some friendships. For example, Booth and Hess (1974) failed to deal directly with the issue of sex in friendship in their data collection on eight hundred middle-aged and elderly urban residents. Booth and Hess apparently assumed that friendship by definition excludes sex. Ramey and other investigators have shown this to be false. Friendship studies should consider the full range of friendship types rather than narrowing their observations to conform with their narrow world views (Implications for the sociology of knowledge are rampant).

Research on personality characteristics and adjustment to marital or nonmarital life gives some clues to the viability of singlehood for women as compared to men. Spreitzer and Riley (1974) carried out a secondary analysis of a sample to 2454 applicants for social security benefits. The median age of the sample was fifty-five, and less than 3 percent were under thirty-five (1974, p. 534). They found that higher intelligence, education, and occupation were associated with singlehood for females, while single males tended to have poor interpersonal relations with parents and siblings (1974, p. 541).

Several other studies compare singlehood and marriage in terms of relative adjustment and happiness for men and women. Genevieve Knupfer, Walter Clark, and Robin Room (1966) found that single men were more antisocial and maladjusted than married men. They also concluded that single women aged thirty and over were less depressed, neurotic, passive, and maladjusted than their married counterparts. In agreement with the conclusions of Knupfer et al., Jessie Bernard (1972) summarized four studies and concluded that single men were less happy than married men. Luther Baker's (1968) results similarly supported those of Knupfer et al. He found that never married women without children had above average personal and social adjustment based on the national norms established for the California Test of Personality. Finally, Lenore Radloff's (1974) study of depression indicated that single women were less depressed than divorced or separated women, but that single men were more depressed than divorced or separated men.

In contrast to the above, Norval Glenn (1975) found that married persons of both sexes reported greater global happiness than any category of unmarried persons, and that the difference in happiness between marrieds and unmarrieds was greater for females than for males. The Glenn study utilized self-report data from 1972, 1973, and 1974 social surveys of the U.S. conducted by the National Opinion Research Center. Glenn's study suggests that the data from the above researchers should be cautiously interpreted; however, as Bernard (1975) has noted, the self-reported global happiness of the married women in Glenn's study may be suspect, partly due to the social desirability of reporting greater happiness than is actually felt. Bernard concludes that such data tend to obscure "the dismal picture of the mental health of married women so convincingly documented in the research literature" (1975, p. 600).

The conclusion to be drawn from most available data is that marriage is probably better for men than it is for women. Existing studies of the relative adjustment and happiness of single women and men do not warrant sweeping conclusions about the dire state of single men as argued by journalists such as George Gilder, but it does seem that single women are happier than single men.[5] Perhaps this pattern will change as more men become independent and liberated; male dependency on mother and then on wife as pseudo-mother may account for the greater unhappiness of single men.

JOURNALISTIC REPORTS

Journalists, on the other hand, have carried out some more thorough (though not methodologically precise) investigations of singlehood than have social scientists. One journalistic investigation of singlehood is the now classic study of the world of the formerly married by Morton

---

5. Commenting on this article, Gilbert Nass offered a contrasting point of view. He stated: "Single life may not be better for single women than single men. In fact, given society's bias in favor of men, the male bachelor has much more going for him. However, in a world in which the advantages lie with married men, the man who is single is more likely to be among the population who can't take advantage of this good deal because of personal handicaps (there are exceptions of course). Thus, it is probably the better selection of single women over single men that causes them to function better despite an environment geared toward men. As Knupfer, et al. (1966) point out, a well adjusted woman may be unmarried because no one asks her — the same cannot be said for single men."

Hunt (1966). In that study Hunt identified a broad range of life style for formerly married people — from the "abstainers" to the "addicts." It is significant that Hunt's book is still in print ten years later, and that he has been asked to carry out a new study to update his earlier book. For the updated study, Morton and Bernice Hunt collected questionnaire data on a nonrandom, availability, mail-in sample of separated and divorced people in order to compare parents with nonparents. They looked at the process of adjusting to a new single life, including relation to old and new friends, meeting companions for intimacy and sex, and planning to remain single or to remarry.

Studies on increased premarital and extramarital sex, though only indirectly relevant to singlehood, indicate support for Sprey's (1969) argument that there is an increasing autonomy of sex from marriage, the family, and parenthood. Daniel Perlman's (1974) study, for example, documents the rise in sexual activity among unmarried college students. He found that his liberal sample reported both high self-esteem and more coital partners when compared with subjects of earlier studies by Stratton and Spitzer (1967) and by Reiss (1966). It remains for future research to identify how much of what is commonly called premarital or extramarital sex is really nonmarital and thus part of the single life.

Between the extreme images of the swinging and always elated single and the desperately lonely, suicidal single lies a continuum of single people with joys and sorrows similar to those of people electing other life styles. Since Martin Panzer's article, "No World for a Single," appeared in Coronet Magazine (April 1955), singlehood as a choice rather than a residual category of undersirables has become a reality for some. As the article suggests, it may be that most single people are not happy; this is the view of George Levinger who notes that more do not opt for singlehood because they "need deep attachments that go beyond the 'modular man' [or woman] syndrome implied as normative by Toffler" (letter to author, November 1975). Levinger noted that his research with University of Massachusetts students "indicates that almost none would look forward to a future in which he or she remains permanently single." Of course, the attitudes expressed by a sample of college sophomores may not be adequate predictors of the later behavior of this same group.

Similarly, Jeanette Ames McIntosh and Gilbert D. Mass (1975) studied 109 females at Wheelock College, and it was found that 5 percent were willing or very willing to remain unmarried throughout their lives. As Wheelock has a fairly conservative student body, it might be hypothesized that more liberal samples would yield larger minorities who desire lifelong singlehood. Furthermore, it is possible that the proportion of women selecting singlehood along with careers will increase over time.

We are left, then, with the impression that singlehood (like marriage) is not a lifelong commitment for most people. Choices are usually replaced by new choices. After all, singlehood could not be a binding choice, for to whom would one be bound by such a choice? To oneself? Perhaps theoretical choices vary more than real options, but we will not really know the range of either choices or options without more comprehensive, theoretically grounded research. In the meantime, social scientists leave speculation and descriptive studies to journalists, for the most part, just as they previously left the study of sex to Kinsey, a zoologist. One wonders how long social scientists will wait to study the realities of the twentieth century.

One journalist (Phyllis Raphael, 1975) has argued that twentieth century woman's dilemma is whether to marry or not, but that she need not worry about sex since it is available to the single person who wants it. Raphael feels that most people want to be married and that they attempt to act on that want. Furthermore, she argues that people are what they *do* rather than what they *say* they do. As simple as this may seem, it indicates the importance of comparing attitudes, behavioral intentions, and reported behavior with actual interactive behavior. Such comparison is essential if we are to determine how satisfied people really are with various life styles.

A Theoretical Approach to Singlehood

It will be helpful to consider singlehood within a theoretical framework. Four figures have been developed as aids in presenting theoretical models of different aspects of singlehood. The first figure presents various dimensions of singlehood and a continuum of degrees of singlehood. The second figure depicts the transitions in relationships over time. The third and fourth figures describe the process of evaluation and reevaluation of life style decisions. The theoretical approach taken here integrates elements from symbolic interaction, role, and exchange theories.

The degrees and dimensions of singlehood presented in Figure 1 are some of the many considerations that enter into decisions made about sexual life styles and role transitions. They help define the relative rewards and costs associated with decisions. However, Figure 1 is limited in that it does not identify the process of role and exchange transactions over a sexual career. (These factors are dealt with in the remaining figures.) Before explaining Figure 1, the relevance of exchange theory will be discussed.

As Libby and Carlson (1976) indicate, the relative costs and rewards of any relationship or decision in a relationship include not only observable rewards and punishments, but inner feelings, motives, and other less tangible but extremely important emotional and cognitive states. For example, one factor which contributes to a person's perception of fairness in relationships is the relative degree of interdependence (with reciprocity) or dependency. Usually dependency entails an unbalanced interaction with one person both incurring greater costs than the other person and being less satisfied with the relationship. As will be explained, such a lack of reciprocity usually results in a reevaluation of the relationship (see Figure 3), although some people remain in relationships with little apparent profit.

There are several ways to conceptualize a sequence of interactions and decision making in terms of exchange theory. Thibaut and Kelley (1959) used reward-cost matrices to depict the possible outcomes of social interaction. Outcomes are evaluated through comparison levels (CL) which are "the lowest level of outcomes a member will accept in the light of available alternative opportunities" (such as other more attractive people to relate to), and by comparison level for alternatives (CL alt.), which is "the standard the member uses in deciding whether to remain in or leave the relationship" (or, when comparing other relationships or potentials for relationships with current relationships) (Thibaut and Kelley, 1959, p. 21). Decisions are based on the assumption that people enter and remain in relationships (or life styles) only as long as the relationships and life styles are evaluated by the interactants to be profitable (profit in exchange terms is rewards minus costs).

Secord and Backman (1974) have pointed out that changes occur in the perception of rewards and costs for any given relationship:

> Rewards and costs may change as a function of (1) past exchanges which shift reward-cost values of current behaviors, (2) changes in the characteristics of the dyad members occurring through training, education, or other experiences, (3) changes in external circumstances that introduce new rewards and costs or modify the values of old ones, (4) sequential factors in the relation itself, such as the augmentation of satisfaction in current relations as a result of previously rewarding experiences in the dyad, and (5) associations with other behaviors having different reward-cost values (Secord and Blackman, 1974, p. 234).

Reward-cost benefits in one's relationships are illustrated by the categorization of sexual life styles in Figure 1. Reading down from

FIGURE 1. Degrees and dimensions of sexual life styles

Decentralized commitment and interdependency

Degrees: **Creative Singlehood**	Dimensions:
→Singlehood as choice with multiple relationships which are temporary and secondary →Singlehood as choice with multiple relationships which are both primary and secondary, but not temporary	Living alone or with roommates Financial independence Sexual independence Emotional independence Self as determinant of budgeting of time
Cohabitation	
→Open primary relationship with mutual intentions to enter open cohabitation or open marriage →Open cohabitation or open marriage	Open cohabitation (with or without legal marriage) Financial interdependence Sexual interdependence Emotional interdependence Primary but not exclusive relationship(s) to budget time
Exclusive Monogamous Model	
→Closed cohabitation →Premarital courtship (exclusive) →Serial monogamy →Permanent monogamy	Exclusive cohabitation (with or without legal marriage) Financial dependence Sexual dependence Emotional dependence Primary and exclusive relationship to budget time together (constant togetherness or couple front)

Centralized commitment and dependency

The dotted lines with arrows indicate feedback loops to other life styles if one chooses to or is forced to leave a particular life style. The continuum from creative singlehood to the exclusive monogamous model does *not* assume a regular progression. People do not necessarily go from top to bottom of the figure, one may stop at any point, or skip life styles (they may begin with traditional premarital courtship and end with serial monogamy or permanent monogamy, skipping cohabitation). The arrows indicate the entry points into the various life styles.

"singlehood" to "permanent monogamy" one can see the lessening degrees of autonomy from others. Choosing singlehood may include multiple relationships of a transitory nature, or more intense and enduring bonds (such as primary relationships). The "Dimensions" section of Figure 3 identifies some of the costs and rewards associated with various sexual life styles. The range of life styles is collapsed into three major prototypes: creative singlehood, cohabitation, and monogamy. These three prototypes are useful in comparing the partitioning of one's time, money, emotions, and sexual expression in various life styles. Many people, of course, are in gray areas outside these prototypes involving some different combination of the dimensions.

Figure 2 was created to illustrate the sequential effects of rewards and costs in relationships over time. The reevaluation of the relative costs and rewards of relationships over time is central to the exchange theory conceptualization used as a basis for explaining and predicting transitions in relationships. Thibaut and Kelley (1959) and others have published various interpretations of exchange theory (sometimes called interpersonal attraction or equity theory) which have recognized the importance of the sequential effect of past decisions on present and future decisions about relationships. Without considering sequential effects from past exchanges in a matrix of relationships, one cannot identify satiation of a given stimulus situation (for example, when one is bored with the same person doing the same things). A researcher must be aware of present and past exchanges as well as the matrix of likely outcomes for a particular exchange. In the sexual realm this means one must be aware of past and present exchanges with sexual, emotional, and ego values. To do this we need a biographical and current analysis of the relative costs and rewards associated with the myriad of relationships in each person's life. Such data could be collected over time, or from retrospective accounts (Libby and Carlson, 1976). It is imperative to carry out a sequential analysis in order to explain — let alone predict — the nature of decisions leading to role transitions.

The implications for exchange outcomes for competing sexual choices appear in Figure 2, where a sample overview of the development and demise of a person's relationships over time is provided. The costs and rewards associated with each relationship as the individual's personal and social situations, expectations, needs, and desires change; this affects whether the person maintains or abandons various relationships. Some patterning of role expectations and behaviors can usually be identified through such a natural history analysis of one's relationships over time, and projecting into the future may be possible.

Figure 3 illustrates the reevaluation of current relationships. A person in the reevaluation stage of potential "unbonding" must consider the rewards and costs of the various life style options. When and if a person selects singlehood, there are both pulls and pushes which affect the new single identity. The process of coupling, dissolution of coupling (or unbonding), and identification of "crucial events" and "turning points" (Turner, 1970, pp. 12–13) resulting in role transitions and transformations in choices of life styles appears in Figure 3. As can be seen in the figure, ongoing decisions about roles, needs, and self-identities involve a series of role bargains where discrepancies between actors' sexual and emotional expectations and behavior contribute to perceived costs and rewards for various role behaviors.

When there are discrepancies and crucial events concerning identities, needs, or role definitions in a relationship, the actors typically consider hypothetical alternative relationships or life styles. Hypothetical comparisons may be complemented by actual comparative experiences with others serving as role models to consider alternative roles and ways of interacting and making commitments. After reentering the interactional space of the troubled relationship, the actors (Persons A and B) must decide whether to leave the relationship, change it, or continue living with unfulfilled needs. The hypothetical process of role-need-identity-taking with peers and significant others as models or mirrors of the self aids in weighing the costs and rewards of putting energy into the troubled relationship. For example, Figure 3 would allow us to hypothesize that Person A and Person B have a primary relationship (it might be two cohabiting people, two single people, or a married couple). Due to various crucial events, one or both people may be unhappy enough to reevaluate the worth or the nature of the relationship. The evaluation line indicates that Person A is exposed to others who can serve as role models. These role models (possibly close friends or even movie stars) provide a basis to compare the costs and rewards being experienced in the relationship with Person B, with the costs, rewards, and role expectations connected with the roles of the models.[6] The reevaluation line leading back to the primary relationship

---

6. Elizabeth Havelock and Bob Whitehurst have suggested (letter, January 1976) that married people view single people as role models, too. Their observation is that marrieds both vicariously identify with the "swinging singles" image, and at the same time pity singles for their isolation and assumed loneliness. The married may find the freedom of the single person appealing, but at the same time the single person may view the married person as happy because of the companionship of the marital partner. These contrasting images of the costs and rewards associated with both singlehood and marriage perpetuate the existence of both as choices.

FIGURE 2.   Transitions in relationships over time

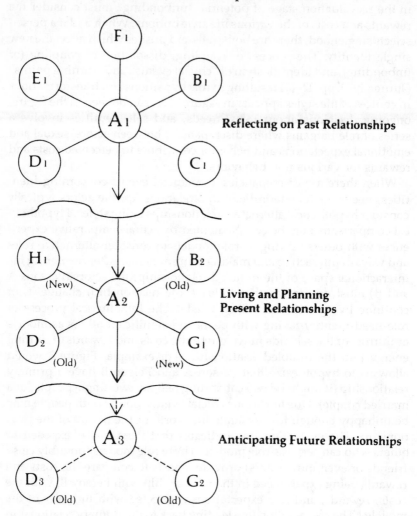

Reflecting on Past Relationships

Living and Planning
Present Relationships

Anticipating Future Relationships

Person A_1 (past) is traced to the present (A_2) and the future (A_3). Person A forms
relationships with Persons B–G at one stage or another. The biography of relationships
can be used to reflect on one's past, to analyze the present configuration of old and new
relationships, and to hypothesize about future relationships. Some relationships might
be primary, coprimary, secondary, transitory, or simply acquaintanceships. According
to exchange theory, reflecting on past relationships, living with present relationships,
and anticipating future relationships all influence the perception of relative costs and
rewards of relationships.

FIGURE 3.   Reevaluation of role expectations for a relationship

Key
C. E. = Crucial Event
A = One Person
B = Another Person

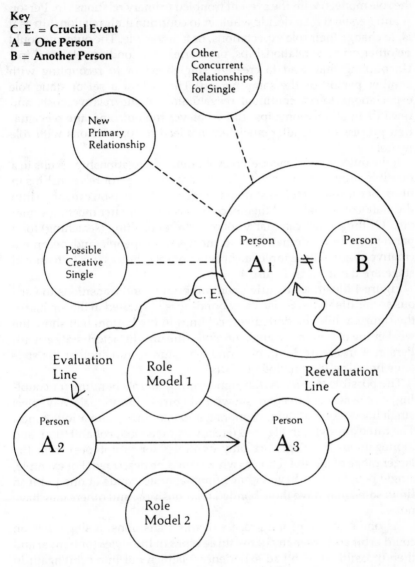

Here we can see Person A's evaluation of needs and possible roles and future identities prompted by difficulty in the relationship with Person B. Among the options are to stay in the present relationship or to become creatively single. Person B may go through an evaluation process similar to that illustrated for Person A.

symbolizes the comparison of alternative relationships (as shown by the role models) with the present troubled primary relationship. Person A and Person B then decide whether to continue their relationship as it is, to change their role expectations, or to uncouple. The outcome could be other primary relationships, or a series of secondary relationships. Uncoupling may lead to creative singlehood or to recoupling with another person or the same person. The lack of a set of static role expectations forces continual reevaluation of the relative costs and rewards in all relationships. But whatever the outcome, the reevaluation process occurs after crucial events lead to comparisons with role models.

If the outcome of someone's reevaluation of a relationship results in a possible single, that person has further role choices for relationships in his or her sexual career, as shown in Figure 4. The person can move into the status of a single and then become a cohabitor after meeting someone. Or the person can marry someone after orbiting (searching) for a partner. A third alternative is to meet several people and become a creative single. These three major types of role choices in a transitional stage are depicted in Figure 4.

Figure 4 illustrates bonding and unbonding and transitions to various sexual life styles. Satisfactory bonding is illustrated in the top half of the figure, while the dotted vertical lines to the bottom half show the weakening of bonds in a given life style (the unsatisfactory state as with Person A in Figure 3 and how one may launch into another life style after breaking the previous bond(s).

The possible *transitions* (through orbiting) in role bonding (or coupling) over a sexual career are shown in Figure 4. Individuals may select singlehood, cohabitation, or monogamous marriage at various times. The three life styles in Figure 4 (creative singlehood, cohabitation, and monogamous marriage) are only examples (or prototypes) from the larger range of life style choices which could be described. For example, single people don't have to have four separate bonds at one point in time; some may have three bonded relationships, and others may have none.

As one example of the process of role transitions, a single person could orbit and enter any of the three types of life styles (or bonds) and then (possibly due to bad experiences) launch out into orbit again in search of another relationship or another life style. Any entry into a given choice may in turn by followed by another launching into the orbit of life styles and reentry into another life style with greater prom-

FIGURE 4:   Transitions in role bonding

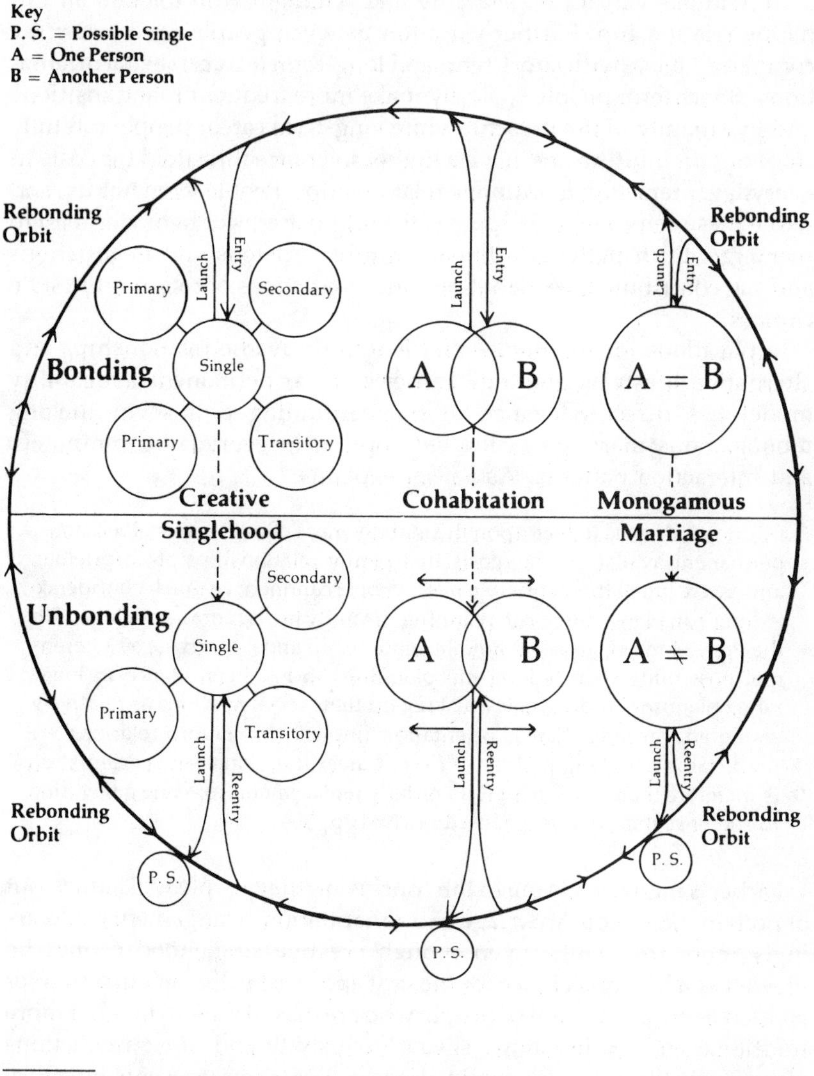

Key
P. S. = Possible Single
A = One Person
B = Another Person

In the lower half of the circle, the single person may launch into orbit seeking a new bond after losing a primary relationship; the cohabitors may launch into orbit because they have grown apart; and the married couple may seek new bonds due to dissatisfaction with their relationship.

ise of rewards. The nature of the entry and launching process depends in part on one's comparison level for alternatives.

Individuals vary in their ability and willingness to tolerate an unhappy relationship. Further variation between people can be seen by comparing those with short-term and long-term (career) sexual orientations. Short-term people typically make more frequent role transitions and live mainly in the present, while long-term career people carefully chart out their future and have a higher tolerance threshold for costs in everyday interaction in intimate relationships. People learn habits, and while these can change, it appears that old patterns of behavior tend to reemerge. Such patterns influence future decisions and negotiations and can contribute to explanations and predictions of role and life style choices.

Implications for the nature and length of dyadic relationships and alternative lifestyles abound. Farber's (1964) permanent availability model has direct relevance to the continuing demise of lifelong monogamous marriage as the *only* option in everyday commitment and interaction patterns. As Farber explains:

> . . . depending as it does upon the tentativeness of interpersonal relations, permanent availability suggests that family relationships are capricious and as a result of this capriciousness, people cannot have much confidence in long-run plans. Short-run planning in family life is more consistent with the view of marriage as a voidable relationship and remarriage as a perennial possibility than is long-run planning. To have confidence in long-range planning, individuals must regard their social relations as relatively stable and orderly. Career orientation implies that family relations are predictable over long periods of time. Career [i.e., long-term] orientation is therefore more consistent with orderly replacement from one generation to the next than is role orientation (1964, p. 306).

Farber's model leads me to the conclusion that people will launch out of both monogamous marriage and cohabitation arrangements increasingly more frequently. Even though creative singlehood cannot be viewed as a life-long choice for most, it appears to offer an attraction for an increasing proportion of people who are dissatisfied with other more tradtional choices involving sexual exclusivity and other restrictions often in conflict with the need to be free. Figure 4 represents the entry and launching process; it may be that more people will be in orbit (far out?) as they make short-term commitments in a life style and then seek happiness through quick role transitions to other choices. Toffler (1970) predicted that we would move toward a series of transitory and casual sexual relationships or encounters; these could be illustrated in Figure 4, as could the option to remain in a given life style such as cohabitation or monogamy for longer periods of time. Future research may reveal that the pleasure of new sexual and emotional experiences, along with the comfort and affection of long-term love relationships which are minus the hassles of cohabitation, will be a strong "pull" toward creative singlehood in the future.

Some Research Questions

Currently there are many more questions than answers about singlehood as a sexual life style. Some examples of research questions include:

1. How do the happiness, adjustment, and interaction-commitment patterns of singles vary by size of city; by ratio of women to men; by marital status, such as never married, separated, or divorced; by parenthood or nonparenthood; by education, occupation, and income; and by migration patterns?

2. How do those who select singlehood make such a choice? Who are their role models? How do variant time periods affect modeling effects and role transitions? How do specific reference groups, attitudes, situations, significant others, and various mass media affect the choice and relative viability of singlehood? What are the key social supports and negative sanctions for singlehood?

3. What is the interrelationship between the various dimensions of singlehood (financial, sexual, emotional, time budgeting, career orientation, etc.)?

4. What are the proportions of people who either select or "fall into" the various lifestyles in Figure 1? What is their relative happiness, controlling for sex and age?

5. To what extent do various samples of people from all marital categories view creative singlehood as moral, appropriate, or as a threat to marriage? How do social labels mesh with self-definitions of singles?

6. What are the crucial events and turning points which lead to role transitions and changing commitments as one moves in and out of various social situations, occupations, cities, new social contacts, etc.? How does the single experience vary by sex, age, biographical history, and current social situation? How does the opportunity

structure vary in terms of meeting and maintaining relationships? Who is best and worst suited to creative singlehood and why?

7. What are the correlates leading to high self-acceptance as opposed to high self-esteem? Do singles commonly distinguish between these two self-concepts? Why are some single by choice and others by default? How do these two groups differ?

8. What interpersonal experiences (such as encounter groups) are helpful in maintaining emotional stability and personal happiness and combating anomie?

9. When one chooses singlehood, is the choice binding to anyone? To the self? What is the nature of personal commitments to singlehood? Is singlehood viewed as a temporary state or as a commitment for an extended period of time? What differences are there between those who see singlehood as a temporary state and those who have no intention of changing their life style?

10. To what extent is singlehood a state of mind? Do married and cohabiting people consider themselves to be at least part-time single? On what basis? How do their claims relate to their actual interactive behavior?

11. When comparing what singles say they feel and do with what they really do, are they honest with others and with themselves about their happiness?

12. What are the differential experiences of those who have primary, coprimary, secondary, and transitory sexual relationships as singles? How are short-term and long-term commitments defined in various kinds of friendships and other sexual and nonsexual relationships? If distinctions are made between commitments to sexual and nonsexual friends or acquaintances, on what basis are such distinctions made, and what are the implications for intensity and permanence of these relationships?

The questions could go on, but the challenge before social scientists is to pose more theoretically grounded questions, to develop theoretically based hypotheses, and to carry out studies that will indicate how theories should be modified in light of data. Retrospective life histories (as recommended by Stein, 1975), combined with longitudinal and cross-sectional studies should yield valuable data on what it means to be single in urban and suburban America. In-depth interview studies of single people with a broad range of personal, family, and social backgrounds, and engaged in a variety of personal and professional pursuits should provide a basis for comparisons, explanations, and ultimately for some predictions about the future of creative singlehood. Interview studies will have to be complemented by participant observation studies carried out in the single's work world, restaurants, bars, hotels, and clubs, as well as in other social settings which cater to a mixture of single and married people. Analyses of attitudes, feelings, and behaviors in such a range of public settings with the use of multiple research methods such as interviews and participant observation should yield results which have some theoretical value. Large attitude and opinion surveys (such as that by *Psychology Today* on happiness, October 1975) could also contribute to knowledge, if not theory, about the costs and rewards associated with the single life as compared with marriage.

Perhaps in the end we will find that single people are not as different in their goals as many would contend. It may be that most people, regardless of life style or marital status, really just want to be happy and seek pleasure. Creative singles may be saying that they don't need marriage or cohabitation to find sexual and emotional happiness. For those who choose creative singlehood, marriage is not a necessary rite of passage for legitimizing one's sexual identity.

REFERENCES

Acock, A., and DeFleur, M. "A Configurational Approach to Contingent Consistency in the Attitude-Behavior Relationship." *American Sociological Review*, 37 (1972): 714–26.

Adams, M. "The Single Woman in Today's Society: A Reappraisal."·*The American Journal of Orthopsychiatry* 41 (1971): 776–86.

Baker, L. "The Personal and Social Adjustment of the Never-Married Woman." *Journal of Marriage and the Family* 30 (1968): 473–79.

Bernard, J. *The Future of Marriage*. New York: World Publishing Company, 1972.

Bernard, J. "Infidelity: Some Moral and Social Issues." In *Marriage and Alternatives: Exploring Intimate Relationships*, edited by R. W. Libby and R. N. Whitehurst. Glenview, Ill.: Scott, Foresman, 1977.

Bernard, J. "Note on Changing Life Styles, 1970–1974." *Journal of Marriage and the Family* 37 (1975): 582–94.

Booth, S., and Hess, E. "Cross-Sex Friendship." *Journal of Marriage and the Family* 36 (1974): 38–47.

Clanton, G. Letter to Roger W. Libby. January, 1976.

Dullea, G. " 'Marriage Tax': It Has Couples in a Rage (and Even Divorcing)." *The New York Times*, March 27, 1975, 26.

Farber, B. *Family: Organization and Interaction*. San Francisco: Chandler Publishing Company, 1964.

"First Singles' Church." *Newsweek*, June 12, 1972.

Fishbein, M., and Ajzen, I. *Belief, Attitude, Intention and Behavior*. Reading, Mass.: Addison-Wesley, 1975.

Fishel, D., and Allon, N. "Urban Courting Patterns: Singles' Bars." Paper presented at the American Sociological Association Annual Meeting, Summer 1973.

Gilder, G. *Naked Nomads*. New York: Quadrangle, 1974.

Gilder, G. *Sexual Suicide*. New York: Bantam Books, 1973.

Glick, P. Personal discussion with Roger Libby. March, 1976.

Glick, P. "Some Recent Changes in American Families." *Current Population Reports*, Bureau of the Census, Special Studies, Series P-23, no. 52, U.S. Government Printing Office, 1975.

Havelock, E., and Whitehurst, R. N. Letter to Roger W. Libby. January, 1976.

Hunt, M. *The World of the Formerly Married*. New York: McGraw-Hill, 1966.

Killian, L. "Social Movements." *Society Today*, 2d ed. Del Mar, Cal.: CRM Books, 1973.

Knupfer, G., Clark, W., and Room, R. "The Mental Health of the Unmarried." *American Journal of Psychiatry* 122 (1966): 841–51.

Levinger, G. Letter to Roger W. Libby, November 1975.

Libby, R. W. "Changing Sexual Mores." In *International Text in Sexualtiy*, edited by J. Money and H. Muspah, Amsterdam, Holland: Excerpta Medica Press, 1976.

Libby, W., and Carlson, J. "Sexual Behavior as Symbolic Exchange: An Integration of Theory." Unpublished manuscript, 1976.

McIntosh, G., Ames, J. and Noss, D. "Career Orientation and Heterosexual Autonomy Attitudes of Wheelock Students." Paper presented at Wheelock College Colloquium, May 1975.

Mazur, R. Unpublished notes to Roger W. Libby. October 1975.

Nass, G. Letter to Roger W. Libby. October 1975.

Nye, I. Personal discussion with Roger W. Libby. February 1976.

Nye, I., and Berardo, F. *The Family: Its Structure and Interaction*. New York: Macmillan, 1973.

Panzer, M. "No World for a Single." *Coronet Magazine* 37 (April, 1955).

Perlman, D. "Self-Esteem and Sexual Permissiveness." *Journal of Marriage and the Family* 36 (1974): 470–73.

Radloff, L. "Sex Differences in Mental Health: The Effects of Marital and Occupational Status." Paper presented before the American Public Health Association, October 1974.

Raphael, P. "Twentieth-Century Women's Dilemma." *Female Forum* (*Penthouse* Special Edition), 1975.

Reiss, I. *Heterosexual Relationships Inside and Outside of Marriage*. Morristown, N.J.: General Learning Press, 1973.

Reiss, I. "The Sexual Renaissance in America." *Journal of Social Issues* 22 (1966): 123–37.

Roy, R. and Roy, D. "Is Monogamy Oudated?" In *Marriage and Alternatives: Exploring Intimate Relationships*, edited by R. W. Libby and R. N. Whitehurst. Glenview, Ill.: Scott, Foresman, 1977.

Secord, P. F., and Backman, C. W. *Social Psychology*, 2d ed. New York: McGraw-Hill, 1974.

Sontag, S. "The Double Standard of Aging." *Saturday Review* (September 23, 1972): 29–38.

Spreitzer, E., and Riley, L. "Factors Associated with Singlehood." *Journal of Marriage and the Family* 36 (1974): 533–42.

Sprey, J. "On the Institutionalization of Sexuality." *Journal of Marriage and the Family* 31 (1969): 432–41.

Starr, J., and Carns, D. "Singles in the City." In *Marriages and Families* edited by H. Lopata. New York: D. Van Nostrand, 1973.

Stein, P. "Changing Attitudes of College Woman." Unpublished study, Rutgers University, 1973.

Stein, P. "Singlehood: An Alternative to Marriage." *Family Coordinator* 24 (1975): 489–505.

Stein, P. *Single in America*. Englewood Cliffs, N.J.: Prentice-Hall, 1976.

Stratton, R., and Spitzer, S. "Sexual Permissiveness and Self-Evaluation: A Question of Method." *Journal of Marriage and the Family* 29 (1967): 434–42.

Straus, M. Letter to Roger W. Libby. November 1975.

Thibaut, J., and Kelley, H. *The Social Psychology of Groups*. New York: John Wiley, 1959.

Toffler, A. *Future Shock*. New York: Bantam Books, 1970.

Turner, R. *Family Interaction*. New York: John Wiley, 1970.

U.S. Bureau of the Census, Marital Status and Living Arrangements: March, 1974. *Current Population Reports*, Series P-20, no. 271, U.S. Government Printing Office, 1974.

"What Makes You Happy: A *PT* Questionnaire." *Psychology Today* (October 1975).

Weitzman, L. J. "Legal Regulation of Marriage: Tradition and Change." *California Law Review* 62 (1974): 1169–1288.

Whitehurst, R. N. "Youth Views Marriage: Awareness of Present and Future Potentials in Relationships." In *Marriage and Alternatives: Exploring Intimate Relationships*, edited by R. W. Libby and R. N. Whithurst. Glenview, Ill.: Scott, Foresman, 1977.

White, M. and Wells, C. "Student Attitudes toward Alternate Marriage Forms." In *Renovating Marriage*, 1st ed., edited by R. W. Libby and R. N. Whitehurst. Danville, Cal.: Consensus Publishers, 1973.

Yankelovich, D. *The Changing Values on Campus*. New York: Washington Square Press, 1972.

COHABITATION

[9]

I REMEMBER one day circa 1950 when my friends and I were looking at the photo of a Chicago policeman circa 1925 dragging off an agitated female bather into the "paddy wagon." Her crime? Indecent exposure! The bottom of her bathing suit revealed several inches of thigh though it terminated well below the crotch. We laughed when we saw the picture because we found the poor woman indecently *conservative* in her bathing suit. We felt so liberated and sophisticated compared to 1925. Still, it didn't strike us as ludicrous at the University of Miami that women had to be in their dormitories by 11:00 P.M. and, after a warning whistle (or was it a warning blinking of the lights?), the key was turned in the lock and maidens who had the misfortune to be still outside the door were locked out for the night to face reprobation (expulsion?) on the morrow.

It was no joke to the Barnard coed who in 1962 was expelled from school because she cohabited with a graduate student in an apartment off campus. The comprehensive review by Macklin that follows will make even the comparatively recent experience of the Barnard coed seem as if it happened in an earlier century.

Now that cohabitation is an established part of courtship, it all seems so logical: extended education for both sexes; biological and ideological readiness for sex by the time students enter college, if not before; improved contraception available right on campus; and the abandonment by the colleges of the chaperone system and *in loco parentis* functions. All that is lacking now is for the first college to start building dorms expressly geared for cohabitation. And yet, amazingly, the

196

majority of parents do not know what is going on and would strongly disapprove if they did.

In this rich article, Macklin tackles all the tough questions including, Is cohabitation a substitute for marriage? A trial marriage? How do cohabitors differ from noncohabitors? Is cohabitation perceived as a good experience in retrospect? I will not spoil the article by giving you her answers. I will just leave you with the question I wondered about after reading the chapter. If the behavior patterns of the young can turn around so completely in *ten years*, what will be the next big event in interpersonal relationships?

Review of Research on Nonmarital Cohabitation in the United States

ELEANOR D. MACKLIN

The Social Setting

D URING THE past decade, observers of the social scene and researchers in the area of marriage and courtship have become increasingly aware of a growing increase of unmarried heterosexual persons living together. Although the phenomenon of men and women living together without "benefit of marriage" is not new, either in this country or in other cultures (Berger, 1971; Rodman, 1961, 1966), it has certainly not been common to Western middle-class society. In fact, nonmarital cohabitation is still held to be a crime, complete with fine and jail sentence, in many states in this country (see Massey and Warner, 1974; Weitzman, 1974; King, 1975; Hirsch, 1976; Lavori, 1976 for a review of the legal situation).

Despite the fact that cohabitation has not been a common practice until recently, trial marriage as a concept has been a topic of public debate for some time. In the mid-twenties, Judge Ben B. Lindsey (1926,1927) promoted the idea of "companionate marriage," a legalized relationship involving no children, with the option of divorce by mutual consent. Bertrand Russell (1929), then in this country, carried the proposal one step further, arguing that a legal structure for such a relationship was unnecessary: if a man and woman chose to live together without children, it should be no one's business but their own. He recommended a relationship for university students very similar to cohabitation on the university campus today, believing that one should not marry without first having some sexual experience, and that work and sex were better combined "in a quasi-permanent relationship than in the scramble and excitement of parties and drunken orgies" that he saw as prevalent at the time. The time was not ripe, however, for such a change. The public was strongly opposed to both ideas, and in fact, Judge Lindsey lost his judicial bench.

It took another forty years for society to evolve to the point where it was ready to think seriously about nonmarital cohabitation as a possibly appropriate arrangement. Margaret Mead, in a series of *Redbook* articles in the mid-sixties, heralded this next stage. Noting that it was no longer fair or feasible to expect physically mature young persons to postpone sex until their middle twenties, that individuals could be expected to grow and change during their early twenties and so should not be locked into a first relationship, and that children need to be assured of a lifetime relationship with both parents, she proposed a "two-stage marriage." Couples would first enter an "individual marriage . . . a licensed union in which two individuals would be committed to each other as individuals for as long as they wished to remain together," but without children. This first stage could be easily entered into, would involve no economic obligation if the marriage broke up, would allow the couple the kind of intimacy necessary to grow together, and could be terminated without the burden of guilt and failure associated with divorce. Stage two, "parental marriage," would be explicitly directed to forming a family. It could not be entered into without a prior satisfactory individual marriage, and divorce would be more difficult (Mead, 1966). Her ideas were echoed by other writers of the period (Caldwallader, 1966; Satir, 1967; Packard, 1968).

Again, the idea of cohabitation was condemned as impractical, unconstitutional, immoral, and unnecessary. Mead's article elicited such questions and comments as: How will you prevent the couple from having children until the parental marriage stage? Who will judge when a couple is ready for the second stage? No marriage will work unless the couple is committed to making it work. More effort should be placed on preparing persons for the ideal marriage rather than on legalizing an immature relationship. Sex is not a shoe to be tried on and, if it doesn't fit, try another. And from the young: Why get married? Why can't we simply live together until we are ready to get married? (Mead, 1968).

As the adult world argued pro and con, there was increasing evidence that young persons (and some not-so-young persons) were not sitting patiently waiting for the verdict. Quietly, and on their own, they were beginning to experiment with new ways of living together and relating to one another. The public media were the first to report ("Unstructured Relationships," 1966; Grant, 1968; "Linda, the Light Housekeeper," 1968; McWhirter, 1968; Schrag, 1968; Bloch, 1969; Karlen, 1969; Sheehy, 1969). And slowly, on many different campuses around the country, researchers also began to note the changing mores, and, simultaneously and independently, to gather data that suggested that a new dimension was being added to the traditional courtship pattern. In 1968, the first graduate thesis on cohabitation was completed (Johnson, 1968), and in 1972, the first published research appeared (Lyness *et al.*, 1972; Macklin, 1972).

Why now and not in 1927? One can only hypothesize the myriad possible factors which together created an atmosphere conducive to change. The women's movement, gathering fresh steam after lying dormant for many decades, renewed its challenge of the double standard and its demand that women be granted the same rights and privileges as men. An important by-product was the increasing equalization of parietals and housing regulations for male and female students, making it possible for large numbers of college women to live off-campus or to reside in dormitories without curfew. The phenomenon of extended adolescence (with individuals experiencing puberty earlier while being required to complete many years of education before becoming eligible for the adult labor market), the radical tenor of the late 1960s, which encouraged college students to question their continued treatment as children and to demand that they be granted the same privileges as their age-mates who were not in college, all led to a slow erosion of *in loco parentis* and a gradual acceptance of a policy of twenty-four-hour visitation within the dormitories.

While these factors made it physically feasible for large numbers of young persons to cohabit, concurrent social changes made it likely that many would take advantage of this opportunity. The increase in divorce, and the changing conception of the function of marriage, caused many young single people and divorcees to move more cautiously into that state. The increased acceptance of sexuality outside marriage and improved contraception made it easier for nonmarried persons to engage openly and comfortably in a sexual relationship. And the increased emphasis on relationships and personal growth called into question the superficiality of the traditional dating game, and led to a search for styles of relating that allowed for change, growth, and a high degree of total intimacy.

The First Ten Years of Research (1968–1977)

Research on cohabitation has become increasingly popular. Over twenty-five graduate theses on topics related to cohabitation were completed during the years 1968-1977, most of them in the latter portion of this period, and numerous others are currently in progress. The first issue of the *Cohabitation Research Newsletter* (designed to facilitate communication among researchers in the field) was published in October, 1972, and the first workshop on cohabitation research was held at the Groves Conference on Marriage and the Family in May, 1973.

Types of Studies

Research to date has fallen, in general, into three major categories:

1. *Interviews or questionnaires given to nonrandom samples of individuals who had cohabited*. The goal was to gain basic information about the nature of the cohabitation relationship and about the characteristics of persons who cohabit. Samples were usually obtained through a snowball or reputational technique, or through advertisements in classes or campus newspapers, and respondents were usually members of the college community.

2. *Surveys on college or university campuses*. These used either random or convenience samples in order to investigate attitudes toward cohabitation, to estimate prevalence rates, to compare demographic characteristics of cohabitors and noncohabitors (e.g., gender, academic major, religious background, quality of parental marriage, sexual values and political attitudes, sexual and drug experience, attitudes toward marriage, perceived peer support), and to gain information about the nature of the cohabitation relationship (e.g., how it was initiated, degree of commitment and exclusivity, length of relationship, type of living and financial arrangements, household responsibilities, birth control usage, parental knowledge, problems and benefits experienced, and future plans).

3. *Studies that compared cohabitation and noncohabiting couples.* In general these have compared married couples and couples who were living together unmarried, but there have also been comparisons of going-together, engaged, and cohabiting couples, and one study (Stevens, 1975) compared heterosexual and homosexual cohabiting couples. Increasingly, studies have compared married persons who have and have not cohabited prior to marriage, in an effort to determine whether premarital cohabitation is related to differences in the quality of the later marriage.

Couples have been compared on such variables as degree of commitment, extent to which the couple espouses and practices equalitarian spousal roles, degree of satisfaction with the relationship, evidence of sexual nonexclusivity, amount of self-disclosure, and nature and extent of problems experienced. Much of the couple research has involved small sample sizes (with twenty to thirty couples in each status category), and too often there has been no evident effort to ensure that the comparison groups were initially similar on such important variables as age, length of time together, and social class. Thus it is often difficult to be sure that any reported differences between the couples are in fact due to one set having lived together unmarried while the other has not.

LIMITATIONS OF RESEARCH TO DATE

Research to date has been hampered by numerous problems. The most obvious has been the lack of any standard operational definition of cohabitation.* Early researchers did not even use the same term to refer to the new phenomenon. Among the terms tried were "consensual union," "trial marriage," "unmarried liaison" (or "unmalias"), "quasi-marriage," and "nonmarital living arrangement," although most researchers now use "nonmarital cohabitation" or the less formal

---

*Legally, cohabitation refers to "two persons of opposite sexes living together as husband and wife without benefit of marriage" (Massey and Warner, 1974, p. 18), and one who lives in such a relationship is a *meretricious spouse*. "The usual elements of such a relationship are: (a) two members of the opposite sex, (b) living under the same roof, (c) in a conjugal or sexual relationship, (d) for any length of time, (e) without benefit of marriage" (King, 1975, p. 10). In those states where common-law marriage is legal, the essential distinction between cohabitation and common-law marriage appears to be whether the man and woman represent themselves to the world as married. Cohabitors may live together in the same way as a husband and wife but must always advertise themselves as being single if they wish to remain legally single in these states (King, 1975, pp. 122-23).

"living together/unmarried." Society also struggled for some time to find an appropriate term, and journalists tried such phrases as "unwed couples," "young-unmarrieds," "premarital-marriage," "unmarried-marrieds," "living together without benefit of marriage" (or "without benefit of clergy"), "the arrangement," "living in sin," and "shacking up." There was even uncertainty about how to refer to the individual with whom one was having such an arrangement, although most now simply say, "the person with whom I am living." (The *New Emily Post's Etiquette*, acknowledging the reality of nonmarried cohabitation, spends some time discussing the social dilemma caused by lack of an appropriate term. Post suggests the term "covivant" as the most appropriate way to refer to one's roommate of the opposite sex, although one suspects this would sound a bit too formal for most.)

But although the terminology is becoming more standardized, what is actually meant by these terms still remains ambiguous and varies from user to user. To review a few of the operational definitions used in research to date (see Cole, 1977, for a more complete listing):

1. A heterosexual couple consistently sharing a living facility without legal contract (Macklin, 1973; Clatworthy, 1975).

2. Two unrelated persons of the opposite sex living together without being legally married (Henze and Hudson, 1974).

3. Two persons of the opposite sex living together in a relatively permanent manner similar in many respects to marriage but without legal or religious sanctions (Lautenschlager, 1972).

4. A heterosexual couple living together seven days a week, for at least four months, in the same dwelling, not legally or religiously married, and having sexual relations (Berger, 1974).

5. Sharing a bedroom and/or bed with someone of opposite sex to whom not married, for four or more nights a week for three or more months (Macklin, 1972, 1974b, 1976b).

6. A heterosexual couple who are not married to each other, spending four or more nights a week in the same room for at least one month (Lyness, 1974; Budd, 1976).

7. Spend five nights a week with someone of the opposite sex to whom one is not married, individuals keep their clothes at a common residence (Guittar and Lewis, 1974).

There are those researchers who feel that self-definition is an adequate criterion for determining whether one is cohabiting. They would argue that, irrespective of how much time is spent together, if an individual feels he or she is living with someone else, he or she should be classified as a cohabitant. There are others who urge greater specificity, believing that there should be a minimum amount of time spent together in order to qualify, but there is disagreement as to what this minimum should be. Some reserve the term for those couples who share a common residence (with common lease and address) and who keep their personal possessions at that residence. Others will extend the term to individuals who may maintain separate residences but spend the majority of their nights together. It is clear that as one seeks to interpret and compare research findings, it is important to know to which group one is referring and which operational definition has been used.

Another major problem has been the difficulty of obtaining adequate samples. All of the surveys to date have been done on college and university campuses (or with the parents of students on such campuses). The expense involved in surveying a probability sample of the general population, and in adapting the U.S. Census to provide adequate information on the incidence of cohabitation, has so far been prohibitive. And the negative attitude toward cohabitation of some of the general public has tended to make researchers hesitate before venturing out of the college community with their questionnaires.

The initial college surveys used convenience samples (large undergraduate classes to which the researchers had ready access, or questionnaires distributed to as many individual students as could be persuaded to participate). Increasingly, however, surveys have involved more adequate random or systematic samples of the student body and, hence, provide more generalizable data. Studies that compared cohabiting and noncohabiting couples have usually been limited to volunteer samples with an average age of less than twenty-five years, have often not involved carefully matched comparison groups, and have usually not extended beyond the college community.

Almost without exception, all published research to date has been cross-sectional, and results have been limited to information about the present or the remembered past. Except for the 23 dating and 15 living-together couples whom Lyness recontacted eight months after they filled out an initial questionnaire (Lyness, 1976a), there are as yet no available data on couples or individuals over time. Two on-going longitudinal projects should eventually yield some helpful information: Rubin's (1975) sample of 231 college-age dating couples includes some individuals who had cohabited at some point in their relationship; Cole and Bower (1974) have collected interview and survey data from over 100 cohabiting couples whom they are in the process of reinterviewing at one-year intervals.

- Most of the initial studies on cohabitation were of an exploratory, descriptive nature, as might be expected when research is just beginning in an area (exceptions were Johnson, 1968, 1973; Storm, 1973). It is only recently that research on cohabitation has been designed to test explicit hypotheses, or the researchers have sought to relate their research to theory. Similarly, there was little initial attempt to develop objective measures of the effects of cohabitation or to obtain behavorial indices of the variables studied, leaving researchers dependent upon the accuracy of the self-reports of respondents. Now, however, there is an increasing sensitivity to these problems and an increasing effort to use operational definitions of cohabitation, noncollege samples, carefully matched control groups, hypothesis-testing designs based on theoretical conceptualization, validated instruments, and behavioral assessment over time.

PREVALENCE RATES

Estimates of prevalence are only available for college students, and these estimates vary to some extent as a function of the definition of cohabitation used, when the data were collected (year and time of year), method of sample selection, and whether prevalence is taken to mean the percent in the particular population who at any given time have *ever* cohabited or the percent who at that point in time are *currently* cohabiting. But the most important determining factors are the nature of the institution itself and the population from which it draws. Rates of "ever having cohabited" vary from near 0 percent at those institutions that are single-sex or have rigid parietals and requirements that all students live on campus, to about one-third in some larger state universities where housing restrictions are more liberal (see Table 1).* The one study (Bower and Christopherson, 1977) that sought to compare prevalence by region found no significant differences, but the samples were small and

---

*It is indicative that the four institutions having the lowest cohabitation rates for women in Table 1 are those institutions with limited visitation hours. It may also be significant that these tend to be institutions located in the midwest and north central areas of the country.

primarily consisted of students in family relations courses at large state universities.

Because of the tremendous variation from campus to campus, one is hesitant to give an overall estimate or prevalence. However, if one averages the rates for "ever having cohabited" given in Table 1, one gets 24 percent, which is very close to the 25 percent rate reported by Bower and Christopherson (1977) in their survey of convenience samples in 16 state universities in eight regions of the U.S. Therefore, for now, it would probably be safe to conclude that about one-quarter of all undergraduate students across the country have already had a cohabitation experience at some point in their life. At most institutions, men have higher rates than women (perhaps one-fifth of the women and one-third of the men nationally), although this difference may disappear if one considers only individuals who have lived together for three or more months (males tending to have a higher percentage of the short-term overnight relationships). The rate would undoubtedly be much higher by the time these students graduate (or marry), since percentages tend to increase with class standing.

Statistics from non-college populations are much harder to come by and must be estimated from census data. Paul Glick, senior demographer with the U.S. Bureau of the Census, reported, "A spectacular eight-fold increase occurred during the 1960s in the number of household heads who were reported as living apart from relatives while sharing their living quarters with an unrelated adult 'partner' (roommate or friend) of the opposite sex" (Glick, 1975, p. 24). Table 2 indicates for 1960 and 1970 the number of household heads who shared their living quarters with an unrelated partner of the opposite sex (no relatives present), showing an increase from 17,000 in 1960 to 143,000 in 1970. Of these 143,000, almost 30,000 were under 25 years of age, 45,000 were 25 – 44 years old, 42,000 were 45 – 64, and 26,000 were 65 and older, indicating that large numbers of persons at all stages of the life cycle are sharing their living quarters with an unrelated heterosexual partner. To what extent these increases are due to more accurate reporting as opposed to a real change in living patterns is not clear.

Comparable figures for the years since 1970 are not yet available, but the data we do have suggest that the numbers of unmarried persons living together is still rising sharply. In 1960, there were 242,000 two-person households consisting of an unmarried adult sharing his or her living quarters with an unrelated adult of the opposite sex; In 1970, there were 327,000, and in 1976, 660,000. One must remember, however, that

TABLE 1. Summary of cohabitation surveys on college campuses

Author	Region	Size of School	Male/Female Ratio	Housing Policy	Time of Study	Type of Sample
1. Arafat & Yorburg (73)	urban northeast	13,000 UG (18,000 UG/G)	42% female 58% male	commuter	1971	convenience
2. Bower & Christopherson (77)	national	16 state universities in 8 regions of the U.S.	n/a	n/a	Spring, 1975	convenience (classes in marriage & family)
3. Cole (personal communication)	midwest	2,000 UG	49% female 51% male	all but 10% on-campus; 24-hour visitation	Spring, 1973	probability (UG student body)
4. Cole (personal communication)	midwest	1,700 UG	47% female 53% male	on-campus; noncoed dorms; no 24-hour visitation (except 1 senior dorm)	Winter, 1974	probability (UG student body)
5. Henze & Hudson (74)	southwest	30,000 UG/G	43% female 57% male	majority off-campus; 12 noon to closing visitation	1971–72	structured interviews with random sample (UG & G student body)
6. Huang (74)	midwest	17,000 UG/G	60% female 40% male	majority on-campus; visiting hours vary with dorm	1972	sociology classes and residence halls
7. Kalmbach (73)	midwest	14,270 UG	7,335 females 6,935 males	majority off-campus; some coed dorms; 24-hour visitation	Fall, 1973	stratified random (soph/senior)
8. Lautenschlager (72)	west	24,000 UG/G	46% female 54% male	majority off-campus; coed dorms on-campus	Winter, 1972	11 classes in marriage & family
9. Macklin (74b; 76b)	northeast	11,500 UG 16,000 UG/G	35% female 65% male	off-campus option, 24-hour visitation	Spring, 1972	stratified systematic (soph/senior, males & females)
10. Macklin (74a)	northeast	11,500 UG 16,000 UG/G	35% female 65% male	off-campus option, 24-hour visitation	Spring, 1974	systematic sample of Human Ecology juniors
11. Marzoni & Deaux (75)	midwest	26,000 UG/G	35% female 65% male	off-campus option; some semicoed dorms; limited visiting hours	Spring, 1975	stratified systematic (soph/senior)
12. McCauley (personal communication)	northeast	15,000 UG/G	51% female 49% male	off-campus option; some coed dorms; 24-hour visitation	Spring, 1975	(a) random (UG student body) (b) classes in sexuality & family
13. Peterman, Ridley, & Anderson (74)	northeast	22,000 UG (29,000 UG/G)	34% female 66% male	off-campus option, 24-hour visitation	Winter, 1972	stratified random (male/female UG)
14. Shuttlesworth & Thornman (73)	southwest	28,000 UG/G	40% female 60% male	off-campus option, 24-hour visitation		8 UG courses
15. Steiner (75)	north central	6,800 UG/G	40% female 60% male	off-campus option after freshman year; visiting hours limited to 1 pm–1 am	1974	random sample of women in dorms

Original Sample Size	Rate Return	Definition Used	Rate of Living Together	
			Current	Ever
1. 900 UG	85%, (762)	living together relationship with a member of the opposite sex	20% (17% female 23% male)	n/a
2. unknown	1216 (948 females, 268 males)	lived with someone in a cohabitation relationship	n/a	25% (22% females 34% males) Range: females = 15%-27% males = 0%-44%
3. 200 UG	95%	same as survey no. 9	n/a	17% (15% females 18% males)
4. 175 UG	97%	same as survey no. 9	n/a	9%
5. 350 UG/G	80% (117 females, 174 males)	two unrelated persons of the opposite sex living together without being legally married	n/a	18% females 29% males
6. unknown (everyone present when survey distributed)	100% (429 females, 214 males)	have cohabited	n/a	7% females 23% males
7. 40	100% (20 females, 20 males)	same as survey no. 9	n/a	28%
8. unknown	519 UG/G	two persons of the opposite sex living together in a relatively permanent manner similar in many respects to marriage but without legal or religious sanctions	9% females 10% males	25% (21% females 30% males)
9. 400 UG	75% (161 females, 138 males)	share bedroom and/or bed with someone of opposite sex to whom not married, for 4 or more nights a week for 3 or more months	n/a	31% (40% females 20% males)
10. 75	70% (47 females, 5 males)	Same as survey no. 9	n/a	45%
11. 400	38% (79 females, 73 males)	Same as survey no. 9	n/a	11%
12. (a) 473	(a) 397 (84%) (213 females, 179 males)	(a) hetrosexual couple consistently sharing a living facility without legal contract	n/a	(a) 23% (19% females 26% males)
(b) 177	(b) 173 (98%) (116 females, 56 males)	(b) a heterosexual couple consistently sharing a living facility without legal contract	n/a	(b) 25% (22% females 32% males)
13. 2,500 UG	44% (626 females, 473 males)	are now or have ever lived with someone of the opposite sex	n/a	33% (32% females 33% males)
14. unknown	431 UG/G	am or have been living with a person of the opposite sex to whom not married	n/a	36%
15. 150	87% (130 females; 75% of them were fresh & soph)	Same as survey no. 9	n/a	5%

in addition to partners (as outlined in Table 2), these figures include lodgers and live-in employees. (U.S. Bureau of the Census, p.5)

Further clues as to the prevalence of cohabitation among nonstudent populations come from a recently reported study by Clayton and Voss (1977). During the period 1974–1975, interviews were held with a nationwide random sample of 2,510 men, between the ages of twenty and thirty, who had registered with the Selective Service in 1962 through 1972. Of these men, 18 percent reported having lived nonmaritally with a woman for a period of six months or more. Two-thirds of them had had only one such relationship and only 5 percent were currently cohabiting, suggesting that most such relationships terminate or end in marriage. Cohabitants were more likely to be men who were not attending college or had less than a high school education, indicating again that cohabitation is not only a college campus phenomenon.

TABLE 2.   Household heads, with no relatives present, sharing their living quarters with an unrelated partner of opposite sex: United States, 1970 and 1960.

| Sex and age of head of household | Sharing quarters with unrelated partner of opposite sex | | |
	1970	1960	1970 / 1960
Total	142,848	17,320	8.2
Male head	104,516	9,359	11.1
Under 25 years	22,183	444	50.0
25-44 years	36,661	3,252	11.3
45-64 years	28,773	3,320	8.7
65 and over	16,899	2,379	7.1
Female head	38,332	7,925	4.8
Under 25 years	7,733	469	16.5
25-44 years	8,792	1,316	6.7
45-64 years	12,795	3,828	3.3
65 and over	9,012	2,312	3.9

Source: U.S. Bureau of the Census, *1970 Census of Population*, Vol II-4B, *Persons by Family Characteristics*, Table II; and *1960 Census of Population*, Vol. II-48, *Persons by Family Characteristics*, Table 15.

ATTITUDES TOWARD COHABITATION

There have been a number of studies designed primarily to measure attitudes of college students to the new life styles and to determine factors associated with these attitudes, and many of the more general surveys have included questions regarding attitudes. All available evidence suggests that, in general, students tend to approve of cohabitation outside marriage.

At City College in New York in the early 1970s, almost 80 percent of a large convenience sample said they would live with someone of the opposite sex if given an opportunity to do so (Arafat and Yorburg, 1973). At Arizona State University at about the same time, almost 60 percent of the men who had not cohabited and 35 percent of such women answered "yes" when asked if they would want to (Henze and Hudson, 1974). Bower and Christopherson (1977), in their national survey of convenience samples in sixteen state universities, found that more than 50 percent of those who had not cohabited indicated they would consider doing so. At the University of Delaware, only 28 percent of the undergraduate random sample said they would probably or definitely not cohabit (McCauley, 1977). At Illinois State University in 1972, only 23 percent of the females and 8 percent of the males in a large convenience sample said they would definitely not cohabit, even if in love (Huang, 1974). At Cornell University in 1972, only 7 percent of those who had not cohabited said it was because of moral reasons. The most common reasons indicated for not having cohabited were: "Have not yet found a partner with whom I would like to stay for four or more nights a week," and "Am geographically separated from partner" (Macklin, 1976b).

Drawing upon these varied data, one is tempted to project that, across the country as a whole, probably about 25 percent of the undergraduate population has cohabited; 50 percent would if they were to find themselves in an appropriate relationship and in a situation where they could; and 25 percent feel they probably would not do so even if it were possible (more of these being females and underclassmen).

Not only does a majority of the student population apparently approve of cohabitation outside marriage and would cohabit given an opportunity and the right circumstances, but most feel no long-term commitment to the person is necessary before doing so (see Table 3). The most commonly held attitude appears to be that cohabitation is acceptable as long as there is a strong, affectionate, preferably monogamous relationship between the two persons involved. There is

TABLE 3.   Relationship that should exist before a person cohabits with someone of the opposite sex.*

	Macklin (1976b) N: 299	Cole ** N: 190	Kalmbach (1973) N: 40	McCauley (1977) N: 397
Married	5%	2%	5%	14%
Officially engaged	1	10	19	3
Tentatively engaged	6	16	0	14
Strong affectionate, monogamous relationship	45	42	38	34
Strong affectionate relationship, but may be dating others	13	13	18	10
Good friends	10	7	17	8
No relationship need exist	19	10	3	17

* Data are from surveys of random or systematic samples of various undergraduate populations, using the same questionnaire item.
** Personal communication.

some suggestion, again depending upon the institution, that males as a group may be somewhat more accepting of cohabitation than females and may not feel the need for as strong an emotional involvement before cohabiting.

How do those who approve of cohabitation differ from those who do not? Religion and personality factors have been the two differentiating variables most frequently discussed in reports to date. As well as being one of the best predictors of who will cohabit, religion (in particular, present religious preference and strength of that preference) has been found to be one of the most powerful predictors of attitude (Arafat and Yorburg, 1973; Huang, 1974; Strong and Nass, 1975). Those who receive high religiosity scores are less likely to approve of cohabitation, while those who indicate they have no current religious affiliation are more likely to approve.

Personality and, in particular, self concept may also be important variables. For instance, Strong and Nass (1975) found that females who viewed their mothers as being more rejecting and less satisfied in the marital relationship, and who held less traditional sex-role orientations, tended to be more accepting of cohabitation. This would appear to fit well with the Arafat and Yorburg (1973) finding that those women who approved of cohabitation were more likely to characterize themselves as independent, outgoing, and aggressive. It is also consistent with the finding by Guittar and Lewis (1974) that cohabiting females tend to see themselves as more managerial, competitive, and aggressive than do engaged, noncohabiting women, and are more likely to report less closeness to the same-sex parent. It has frequently been hypothesized that women who are more independent, have more need to achieve, and are less accepting of traditional feminity tend to see their mothers as colder and less supportive (Bardwick, 1971). It would make sense that these less traditional women would more easily accept nontraditional courtship patterns. Mosher's finding (1975) that disbelief in romantic love and value placed on self-actualization were major personality variables related to endorsement of trial and contract marriage would seem consistent with these general conclusions.

While students have been found to have generally positive attitudes toward cohabitation, parents do not. Three studies are known to have compared the attitudes of parents and students (Macklin, 1974a; Smith and Kimmel, 1970; Steiner, 1975) and, in all three cases, the gap between the generations has been dramatic. When the attitudes of 70 students (mostly female) at a northeastern university were compared with those of their parents, 6 percent of the students and 63 percent of the parents indicated that persons should marry before living together (Macklin, 1974a). When a more conservatiave group of women was surveyed at a north central university, the difference was equally significant, with 41 percent of the daughters and 88 percent of the mothers indicating that cohabitation without marriage was morally unacceptable under any circumstances (Steiner, 1975). In neither study did a single parent indicate they would approve of their daughter's cohabitation (although some would accept it). Interestingly enough, when students were asked to predict their parents' attitudes, they were able to do so with considerable accuracy (for example, in the Steiner research, 80 percent of the daughters correctly predicted their mothers' response regarding cohabitation).

NATURE OF THE RELATIONSHIP

It has become clear that there is no single entity known as "the cohabitation relationship." The concept as now used covers a wide variety of relationships, differing not only in amount of time spent together and nature of the living arrangement, but also in the partners' degree of commitment.

Several attempts have been made to develop a useful typology of cohabitation relationships. The cohabitation research group that met at the Groves Conference on Marriage and the Family in 1974 sought to classify cohabitation relationships along a continuum of dyadic commitment, and identified the following six points: (1) temporary convenience or mutual benefit; (2) affectionate relationship but open to other simultaneous relationships; (3) affectionate, monogamous relationship (i.e., "going steady"); (4) trial marriage or the conscious testing of a relationship; (5) temporary alternative to marriage (e.g., while awaiting divorce settlement or graduation); and (6) permanent alternative to marriage (*Cohabitation Research Newsletter*, No. 4, June 1974, p. 2).* Others, for ease of analysis, have reduced the types to three: casual or temporary involvement, preparation or testing for marriage, and substitute for or alternative to marriage (Lewis *et al.*, 1975; Petty, 1975). It is now generally accepted by most researchers that it is unrealistic to treat all unmarried cohabitants as one homogeneous group, but there is still a strong tendency to do so.

The percentage of cohabitants who fall within each of the above categories is not clear. When *college* cohabitants have been asked in surveys to identify the nature of their relationship at the time they *began* living together, a small number described themselves as simply friends or persons living together purely for convenience (probably under 10 percent). A somewhat larger group (somewhere between 10 and 20 percent generally) indicated that they were seriously contemplating marriage or living together until it was convenient to marry. The great majority fell in between these two extremes, describing themselves as involved in a strong, affectionate, but as yet uncommitted relationship (with between 50 and 60 percent indicating that they were monogamous or "going steady"). Rarely did undergraduate cohabitors see themselves as involved in a permanent alternative to marriage. Consistent with this perception was the fact that most college cohabiting couples maintained two separate residences, at least during the first year of their relationship, and did not spend every night together.

It is the above that has led researcher after researcher to declare that

---

* This typology, which uses exclusivity as one clue to increasing commitment, may require some rethinking as society becomes more accepting of nonmonogamous marital relationships. Monogamy may no longer be an adequate indicator of degree of commitment to a relationship.

cohabitation on the college campus is merely an added step in the courtship process — a kind of "living-out of going steady" (e.g., Henze and Hudson, 1974; Johnson, 1968; Macklin, 1972, 1974b, 1976b; Bower and Christopherson, 1977). The partners generally share a deep emotional relationship with each other but have not yet reached a point of long-term commitment. Most have not even considered marriage as a viable alternative to their present relationship, not because they disapprove of marriage (study after study has confirmed that the great majority of cohabiting students see themselves as being married at some point in their life), but because they do not feel personally ready for marriage or are not ready to commit themselves to that particular person. As Bower and Christopherson indicate when reporting their national survey: "Cohabitation, as it seems to be practiced today by middle-class college students, is defined as a replacement for marriage by only a small minority of its participants . . . . Cohabitants seem not to be rejecting marriage itself, but merely adding to some of the processes by which the marriage bond is formed" (1977, pp. 450-51).

DEMOGRAPHIC DIFFERENCES BETWEEN COHABITANTS AND NONCOHABITANTS

Much of the research effort to date has been directed toward answering the questions: Who cohabits? And are there identifiable predictors of who will and who will not cohabit? The most common method has been to give a questionnaire to a sample of students and to compare the answers of those who have cohabited with those who have not. The two groups have been found to differ significantly on:

1. Religious preference and religiosity — a higher percentage of cohabitants indicate no religious preference or low church attendance (Arafat and Yorburg, 1973; Henze and Hudson, 1974; Huang, 1974; Macklin, 1976b; Peterman, Ridley, and Anderson, 1974).

2. Attitudes — cohabitants tend to hold more liberal attitudes toward sexuality, politics, and drugs (Henze and Hudson, 1974; Macklin, 1976b).

3. Reference groups — cohabitants are more likely than noncohabitants to report having friends who have had intercourse or who have cohabited (Macklin, 1976b; Marzoni and Deaux, 1975).

4. Perceived campus norms — cohabitants are likely to predict a

higher incidence of nonvirginity and cohabitation on campus than do noncohabitants (Macklin, 1976b).

5. Sexual experience — cohabitants are more likely to be nonvirgins, to have had intercourse in the past month, and to have had more sexual partners over time (Macklin, 1976b).

6. Field of study — cohabitants are more likely to be in the arts and social sciences, and less likely to be in engineering and the physical sciences (Macklin, 1976b; Peterman, Ridley, and Anderson, 1974).

7. Personality variables — consistent with the above discussion regarding personality as predictive of attitude toward cohabitation, research has found personality, as measured by self-report, to be related to whether or not one has cohabited. Arafat and Yorburg (1973) found that cohabiting *females* were less likely than noncohabitants to describe themselves as shy, introspective, isolated, and dependent. Similarly, Guittar and Lewis (1974) found that cohabiting females, when compared with engaged noncohabiting females, perceived themselves as more managerial-autocratic and more competitive-exploitative. On the other hand, cohabiting *males* perceived themselves as less managerial-autocratic and less competitive-exploitative than did engaged noncohabiting males, and as warmer and more supportive. Peterman, Ridley and Anderson (1974) found that, on the basis of self-report, cohabitants evidenced better personal adjustment and higher quality heterosexual relations when measured by such variables as openness of communication and need-satisfaction.

It is important to mention that, because of the cross-sectional design of studies to date, it is impossible to tell from the present research to what extent the above differences are a function of the cohabitation experience and to what extent they preceded it.

Significant differences between cohabitants and noncohabitants have generally *not* been found for: perceived success of parents' marriage, parental educational or income level, academic performance, or attitude toward marriage (while cohabitants are more likely to indicate a willingness to engage in nontraditional postcollege living arrangements, they still tend to give marriage as their first choice (Peterman, Ridley, and Anderson, 1974).

Most researchers have been more impressed by the similarities between cohabitants and noncohabitants than by the differences. Although the research to date is far from definitive, it appears from available information that, on a campus where the incidence of cohabitation is high and a large percentage of persons engage in the experience at some point in their undergraduate life, persons who cohabit are not dramatically different from those who do not. In many ways, these students seem characteristic of the general undergraduate population, with their cohabitation more a function of the opportunity for such a relationship than a function of any demographic charactertistics, although there is a tendency for them to be persons whose sexual and religious values allow them to be open to this life style, and whose personal skills allow them to take advantage of it.

As cohabitation becomes a more common phenomenon in our culture, it seems likely that the majority of those who experience a love relationship will at some point in their lives experience a cohabitation relationship. The more crucial question may, therefore, become: What are the differences between persons who are able to initiate and sustain a love relationship and those who cannot? Although noncohabitants are likely to give lack of opportunity as their primary reason for noncohabitation, it is not clear to what extent lack of opportunity reflects real external barriers and to what extent it is an indication of personal inadequacies and lack of interpersonal skill. It may well be that "capacity for intimacy," or "heterosexual competence" (Ridley and Peterman, 1975), or "degree of interpersonal anxiety" (Gilmartin, personal communication) may become more relevant differentiating variables than many of those researched to date.

COMPARISON OF COHABITING AND NONCOHABITING COUPLES

In addition to efforts to tease out those factors that differentiate *persons* who cohabit from those who do not, research has been directed toward exploring differences between *couples* who cohabit and those who do not. The major variables explored have been: commitment, androgyny, sexual exclusivity, and degree of experienced satisfaction. It is important to remember that the samples in the couple research to date have consisted almost entirely of volunteers. It is not clear to what extent one is justified in generalizing the results to the broader population of cohabiting and noncohabiting couples in our society.

COMMITMENT. Commitment as a variable has probably been discussed more fully and repeatedly in the cohabitation literature than any other variable. Much of the interest would appear to stem from an assumption that a degree of commitment is necessary for success in an interpersonal relationship and the popular concern that cohabitation involves insufficient commitment. Indicative of interest in the topic is the fact that the first cohabitation thesis (Johnson, 1968, 1973) compared the degree of commitment in cohabiting and married relationships. Johnson's theoretical analysis of the commitment variable, and his attempt to operationalize it, has influenced much of the research since. He combined two meanings of commitment: *personal commitment* ("the extent to which an actor is dedicated to the completion of a line of action") and *behavior commitment* ("those consequences of the initial pursuit of a line of action which constrain the actor to continue that line of action"). Behavior commitment is further subdivided into *social commitment* (one's awareness of the normative expectations which have developed as a result of his behavior, his relationship with those who hold these expectations, and the perceived legitimacy of the expectations) and *cost commitment* (the costs to the actor should he discontinue his line of action).

All research to date has demonstrated that married couples evidence more commitment to their relationship than do nonmarried cohabiting couples, even when the two groups are matched for length of time together (Johnson, 1973; Lewis et al., 1975; Budd, 1976). Married couples feel more strongly about continuing the relationship with their partner, name more persons who know about the relationship and who would disapprove of its termination, and have made more major joint purchases than have unmarried cohabitants. However, when asked to indicate the extent of change that they anticipate they would have to make in present plans and living conditions were the relationship to end, and the degree to which they would be unhappy about this, there was no significant difference between the groups (Johnson, 1973; Budd, 1976). It is suggested that living together, married or unmarried, has a significant influence on one's daily living patterns, and hence, a separation will inevitably involve important changes even if the couple is not married and has tried to avoid large monetary investments in the relationship. Separating if married is difficult, but one should not assume that separating after cohabiting will be easy.

Married couples who had and had not lived together before marriage showed minimal differences with regard to degree of commitment to their relationship. It was only on measures of social commitment (extent to which opinions of others and societal standards would influence one to continue the relationship) that differences appeared. Cohabiting couples and marrieds who had cohabited were less likely to see others' opinions as influencing the continuation of their relationships than were marrieds who had merely dated. It may be that those who engage in a deviant life style place less value on the opinions of society to begin with, and that this attitude carries over into marriage (Budd, 1976).

As might be expected, degree of commitment varies with the type of cohabitation relationship. Personal commitment is higher for those cohabiting couples who see themselves in an "alternative to marriage" relationship than for those who see themselves in a trial marriage, and higher for those in a trial marriage than for those who are in a temporary involvement (Lewis *et al.*, 1975). When cohabitants were compared to a matched group of engaged couples who had not cohabited, there were no significant differences in degree of determination to continue the relationship, although the engaged persons were more committed to becoming married to their partner (Lewis *et al.*, 1975). A provocative finding from this research was that the predictors of level of pair-commitment differed for cohabiting, engaged, and married couples. Whereas the best predictors for degree of commitment for engaged couples were such quantitative variables as length of acquaintance and amount of mother's education, the predictors for commitment in cohabiting couples were more qualitative in nature (e.g., degree of perceived happiness and amount of dyadic consensus). Interestingly enough, these two combined variables — couple happiness and length of time together — were the best predictors of pair-commitment for married respondents (Lewis *et al.*, 1975).

One of the frequently voiced popular concerns is that cohabitation leads to exploitation of the female partner by the male, who is seen as less emotionally involved and less personally committed. Research to date has tended to document these predicted differences in commitment. Lyness *et al.* (1972), in a study of eighteen living-together couples, noted that the males showed less commitment to marriage than did the females. Johnson (1973) found that cohabiting females were more likely than cohabiting males to indicate that they "very strongly" wanted to stay with their partner at least five years. Similarly, Budd reports that, whereas cohabiting males rank themselves as significantly less committed to continuing the relationship than married males, cohabiting females do not significantly differ from married females. She concludes, "This may be an indication of more investment on the part of cohabiting females than males" (Budd, 1976, p. 114). However, studies have not always found this gender difference (e.g., Lewis *et al.*, 1975; Kieffer, 1972), leaving the question of relative commitment of males and females an open one.

ANDROGYNY. Because cohabitation has been seen by many as an innovative life style, and because at least originally those who cohabited tended to be more liberal in their general attitudes and life styles, it has been hypothesized that cohabitation relationships would be more androgynous in nature, possibly leading to more androgynous marriages. The available evidence does not suggest this to be the case. Study after study has found that cohabiting couples tend to mirror the society around them and to engage in the same sex roles that are characteristic of other couples, although there is a tendency for both cohabiting and noncohabiting persons to be somewhat more androgynous today than previously.

In a survey of a random sample of college students, Makepeace (1975) compared cohabiting and married students and found that cohabiting students were no more equalitarian in the performance of household activities than married students, but that cohabiting students and married students without children were more equalitarian than those married students with children. Whether more traditional college couples tended to have children, or whether children created a situation that encouraged sex role differentiation, is not clear.

Stevens (1975), in her study of heterosexual and gay cohabiting couples, found that "decision-making as well as role-division in the household is trending toward equalitarianism for all categories, although married couples and to a lesser degree heterosexual cohabitants are more traditional in their role than are gay couples."

Segrest (1975), in her study of household-managerial and decision-making role expectations of 30 married and 22 cohabiting couples, found that both married and cohabiting subjects were more equalitarian than traditional. Where there were differences between the groups, married subjects (both student and nonstudent) were more equalitarian than the cohabiting subjects, and married males more so than cohabiting males.

Bower (1975), in his study of 126 cohabiting individuals, asked them to rate whose responsibility it was to perform fourteen jobs around the house. He concluded, "The division of labor along traditional lines of gender is apparent here, just as it was in previous studies of cohabitation sex roles . . . . In the general area of labor division, cohabitation looks much like marriage" (p. 73). Cole and Bower (1974c) report similar findings from a study of thirty cohabiting couples done in the early 1970s. An interesting aside is the observation that there was considerable difference of opinion within couples as to whose responsibility it was to do different tasks, with males tending to claim that they had equal or more responsibility for most jobs, and females believing it was they who did most of the work. Some objective assessment will be required to know what really happens on a day-to-day basis.

Using data from a questionnaire administered to a random sample of 1,100 *married* students at a western university. Olday (*Cohabitation Research Newsletter*, No. 5, p. 38) compared the degree of reported equalitarianism within the households of 184 individuals who had cohabited before marriage and 524 who had not. He reports, "Cohabitation was unrelated to all indicators of equalitarianism (i.e., which spouse actually took primary responsibility for housekeeping activities, organization of family recreation, and initiation of sexual activity, as well as opinions with regard to who should do these activities)."

Stafford *et al.* (1977) administered a questionnaire regarding sex roles and division of labor to a stratified sample of upperclass courses at a western university. A range of household tasks was enumerated and the respondent was asked to indicate his responsibility for and actual performance of each task. Among the respondents were 54 cohabiting and 57 married men and women. In summarizing the implications of the data, the authors state:

> Cohabitation apparently is not the cure all for traditional sex role inequality. . . . Although ultimate responsibility for many tasks is shared, generally wives and female partners do the women's work and husbands and male partners do men's work. This division leaves the women most of the household duties whether or not they are also employed in the labor force. . . . the more research that is done, the more the cohabitants seem like ordinary students and their relationship, at least in its household division of labor, seems like an ordinary marriage. (1977, pp. 54–55)

Because mother's labor force participation and father's time spent on household tasks were found to be related to the sex role ideology of the respondents, they conclude that "it is the non-conscious ideology developed from parental modeling that preserves traditional sex roles."

McCauley (1975), in a survey of student attitudes, found that there were "no significant differences in attitudes toward egalitarian sex roles between cohabitants and non-cohabitants of the same sex. However, there was a significant difference in egalitarian atitudes *between males and females* who are or have been involved in a living-together relationship" (p.4), suggesting that this may become an area of potential disagreement and discontent within these relationships. He concludes, "As cohabitation becomes more normatively accepted, it may also become institutionalized as another double-standard relationship" (p.6).

In a recent paper on sex-roles in cohabitation, Whitehurst makes the observation that "one cannot make the assumption that because people violate conventional norms and engage in cohabitation, they are therefore 'liberated' and striving for sex role equality. [In the near future] sex role equality as a goal in either marriage or cohabitation is unlikely to occur for any large number of people" (1974, pp. 2-3). Available evidence would certainly support his view.

SEXUAL EXCLUSIVITY.   Again, on the assumption that persons who cohabit are more liberal and innovative than others, it has been hypothesized that cohabitants would be less monogamous in their relationships than other persons their age. Huang (1974), in interviews with 70 cohabiting couples, found that although most couples maintained a monogamous relationship, 16 of the couples engaged in open nonmonogamy. She states that these couples tended to believe that a destructive force in many relationships is the jealousy and possessiveness that keeps partners from communicating with others socially and sexually.

> They assume that even if they get married some day, they will not follow the traditional exclusive monogamous rule which, they claim, is the basic difficulty in the high rate of broken marriages. . . . These couples wish to deromanticize heterosexual relationships, and to season them with honesty and realism instead of fantasy and hyprocrisy . . . . They are, in general, open, communicative, adaptable to new situations and unafraid of their own feelings and emotions and respectful of those in others. Non-exclusive sexual cohabitation among unmarried couples may be considered a period of novel and flexible experimentation toward more daring varieties of heterosexual relationships. They may be a pace-setter for a smoother transition into such patterns as mate-swapping, group marriage, or extra-marital sex contracts. (pp. 20-22)

Bower found, in his study of 126 cohabiting individuals, that "31 percent of the females and 39 percent of the males had dated outside the relationship, and 19 percent of the females and 31 percent of the males had had sex with one or more persons other than their cohabitor since the cohabitation began" (1975, p. 76). He does not indicate whether this behavior was known and condoned by the partner.

In a study of 31 cohabiting couples, Montgomery (1974) found that the degree of importance attached by the couple to sexual exclusivity was related to the degree of importance attached to personal freedom within the relationship. A minority felt that continuation of the relationship was dependent upon sexual exclusivity. Another small group emphasized the personal growth and emotional well-being of the individuals involved and, hence, felt they should be able to handle any extra-cohabitant sexual activity that the partner felt necessary for his or her happiness. The majority felt that sexual freedom should ideally be available, but at the same time, each person voluntarily restricted his own sexual activity as evidence of his commitment to the relationship. Only five of his 62 current cohabitors (8 percent) indicated that they had been involved in extra-cohabitant sexual activity.

Clatworthy and Scheid (1977), in a study of married couples who had and had not cohabited before marriage, found that the same percentage of each group (about 25 percent) had had outside sexual partners during the marriage, and concluded that the more liberal sexual behaviors of the premarital cohabitants did not carry over into their marriage, at least not during the early years.

SATISFACTION. At least four studies have compared degree of satisfaction reported by cohabiting and noncohabiting couples. C.M. Cole (1975) investigated the overall satisfaction or happiness expressed by a matched sample of 20 married and 20 cohabiting couples. Satisfaction was measured by (a) a set of inventories relating to couple satisfaction (e.g., general types of problems experienced, shared activities, time spent together, sexual behavior); (b) a seven-day checklist of "pleasing" and "displeasing" behaviors engaged in by both partners; and (c) a videotape of a problem-solving task involving typical conflict situations. The findings revealed no major differences between married and living-together couples in terms of satisfaction or happiness. Cole concluded, "The only difference was that living-together couples perceived, on the average, fewer barriers to terminating their relationship. Apparently it is not so much the legal nature of the relationship that encourages or discourages satisfaction. Instead, it is more likely a factor of how the partners behave toward each other and define their roles that is predictive of happiness within an individual relationship" — a conclusion that is echoed by much of the other research in the area.

Polansky *et al.* (1975) interviewed a sample of 25 cohabiting couples and 26 married couples on three factors associated with degree of mutual satisfaction experienced by partners (amount of affective support provided, degree of mutual knowledge, and degree of overall satisfaction) and found no significant differences between the groups on any of the three. Similarly, Stevens (1975), in her study of gay male and female cohabitants, heterosexual cohabitants, and married couples, reported that all four types were equally satisfied with their relationships. Cole and Bower (1974*b*), in a comparison of 25 cohabiting and 25 married nonstudent couples (matched for length of time together and age), found little difference with regard to level of sexual satisfaction or desire for change in sexual activity.

Olday (*Cohabitation Research Newsletter* No. 5, p. 38) compared 184 married students who had cohabited prior to marriage and 524 married students who had not and found that cohabitation before marriage was virtually unrelated either to degree of expressed marital satisfaction or degree of marital conflict. Two measures of satisfaction were used: "What is the likelihood that you would ever leave your spouse?" and "Please describe how you feel about your marriage" on a scale from 1 to 7, with 1 meaning emotionally close and 7 emotionally distant. Several indicators of marital conflict were employed: spending money, family recreation, sexual activity, and housekeeping chores.

When Budd (1976) compared 54 cohabiting couples, 48 married couples who had cohabited before marriage, and 49 who had not on the degree to which they had experienced each of 28 different problem areas within their relationship, she found minimal differences among them. Only two problem areas showed significant differences among groups: (a) cohabitors were more likely than marrieds to indicate having been upset by "feelings of overinvolvement in the relationship" and by lack of privacy (due perhaps to the fact that cohabiting couples are more likely than marrieds to share their residence with other persons); and (b) cohabitors and marrieds who had not cohabited were more likely than married who had cohabited to report having been upset by feelings that their partner did not love them as much as they once did. Budd hypothesizes that perhaps unmarried couples and couples who dated before marriage have more romantic expectations of their relationships than do cohabitants who end up marrying. The author suggests that the similarity among the three groups with regard to extent of problems experienced may well be due to the fact that the problems investigated (such as lack of opportunity to be with others) are intrinsic to heterosexual relationships no matter what the nature of the living situation.

In summary, as when we compared the characteristics of individuals who had and had not cohabited, one is primarily impressed by all the many ways in which cohabiting and noncohabiting couples appear to be alike. The findings cited above would suggest that, when one controls for age and length of time together, cohabiting and noncohabiting couples are more similar to one another than they are different. Or, what may be even more accurate, the differences within each group are greater than the differences between them. Again, one is moved to suggest that cohabitation per se is not the central determining or differentiating variable.

FORMATION OF THE COHABITATION DYAD

Living together, at least on the college campus, is seldom the result of a considered decision, at least not initially. Most relationships involve a gradual (and sometimes not so gradual) drifting into sleeping together more and more frequently. Only 25 percent in one study (Macklin, 1974*b*) indicated that they had discussed whether to live together before starting to do so. If and when a decision with conscious deliberation is made, it is usually precipitated by some external force (e.g., need to make plans for the summer or next fall, graduation, unexpected pregnancy, or a necessary housing or room change). Until that time, there is only a mutual, often unspoken, recognition of the desire to be together — a natural progression of the relationship.

Some attention has been given to identifying those factors that influence, encourage, or facilitate this drift into living together. At the first meeting of the cohabitation research group (at Groves Conference in 1973), it was suggested that the variables most predictive of cohabitation were: low perception of social disapproval, low internalized guilt regarding premarital sexuality and living together, and high availability of opportunity (*Cohabitation Research Newsletter*, No. 3, October, 1973). Working from this idea, Clatworthy (1975) suggested that if one were to place amount of guilt and perceived degree of social disapproval on separate scales from one to ten points each, and if an individual received a total of more then ten points from the two scales together, he or she would find living together to be more anguish than benefit. This is an interesting idea that awaits testing.

Meeting again in 1974, the research group further delineated those factors that might be predictive of drift. The following were among those hypothesized (see *Cohabitation Research Newsletter*, no. 4, June, 1974, pp. 2-3):

1. Factors which affect the degree to which an individual *experiences or perceives the opportunity to cohabit*:

   a. Environmental opportunity (e.g., availability of potential partners; geographic distance from partner; permissive housing regulations).

   b. Socio-cultural norms within immediate environment (e.g., peer norms, salience of peer norms, perception of reference group support, awareness of others cohabiting).

   c. Isolation from conventional social control agents (e.g., geographic distance from parents; predictability of parental visits). Importance will be conditional upon degree of financial and emotional independence of these agents.

   d. Interpersonal attractiveness (e.g., interpersonal competence, physical attractiveness).

2. Factors which affect the likelihood that an individual *will avail him/herself of the opportunity to cohabit*:

   a. Religiosity (degree to which one identifies with religious groups or beliefs which are consistent with cohabitation).

   b. Personality variables (e.g., degree of need for autonomy, capacity for intimacy, disbelief in romantic love, acceptance of non-traditional sex roles, value placed on self-actualization, aggressiveness, comfort with ambiguity and change) will vary somewhat with gender.

   c. Degree of previous sexual or dating experience.

   d. Degree of affection for partner and perceived happiness when with individual.

The above are, in general, factors that research to date has found tend to differentiate between cohabitants and noncohabitants, or that have been reported by individuals as reasons for or for not cohabiting. No attempt has yet been made to weigh the variables or to develop some path analysis indicating which variables may be more basic and determinant than others.*

---

*Ward, in a paper called *Cohabitation and Drift*, elaborated on this theory of drift into cohabitation, and hypothesized a slightly different relationship among the variables. He suggested that attitudes toward cohabitation, perception of opportunity to cohabit, and degree of affection for partner would determine one's likelihood of cohabiting (Ward, 1975).

Montgomery (1973) has also given some thought to the path by which relationships move from their typically casual beginnings to deeper and more permanent involvements. He argues that cohabitation requires more commitment ("internally generated cohesion") than does marriage in order to continue, for there are fewer external unifiers and numerous external forces that work against the relationship. And since commitment is only evident through some behavorial manifestation, there must be behavioral manifestations of gradually increasing commitments if the cohabitation relationship is to grow and survive. Each step toward increased commitment requires that the individual experience some evidence that his increased commitment is going to be worth it to him. Evidence of the other's deepening commitment provides that reassurance. Montgomery suggests the following hierarchy of "commitment evidence":

1. Sharing fun and pleasant social activity.
2. Limiting of social activity to the one other person.
3. Establishment of joint residence.
4. Sharing of activities necessary for the continuation of the relationship (e.g., the sharing of household tasks).
5. Sharing expenses.
6. Working out personal problems in ways that strengthen the relationship.
7. The making of marriage plans.
8. Marriage.
9. Having children.

DISSOLUTION OF THE COHABITATION DYAD

Ganson (1975) surveyed a sample of 30 male and 41 female students who had experienced the termination of a cohabitation relationship, in an effort to identify the causes of termination, and the differences between males and females in their reasons for breaking up. Respondents were given a list of 43 possible reasons for the termination of a living-together relationship and were asked to indicate the extent to which they felt each factor had contributed to their own break up. Factors related to infringement on freedom and personal incompatibility were most often seen as the cause of dissolution, with women more likely than men to feel that the factor had played a role. The following items were those on which men and women differed significantly in their responses:

	Percent indicating reason for terminating	
	% males	% females
Infringement on personal freedom		
I felt trapped	32	63
There were times I couldn't be me	32	58
My partner wanted me to be different	36	48
I felt I was losing my identity	32	48
My partner dominated me	24	43
Personal characteristics of partner		
We just grew apart/our personalities were no longer compatible	39	73
I got bored with my partner	13	45
Our sexual needs weren't compatible	16	33
Inability to cope with situation		
Parents dead set against relationship	7	19
My values opposed to cohabitation	0	10
Living situation		
Didn't have privacy I needed	32	45
Insufficient income	13	35
Commitment discrepancy		
I was too dependent on partner	19	41

Why females were consistently more likely than males to feel that a factor had contributed to dissolution is not clear. Ganson hypothesized that women are more emotionally involved in relationships than men, and hence more sensitive to problems. Noting that many of the reasons given by women for breakup revolve around infringement on personal freedom, she hypothesizes that women have traditionally given up more autonomy than men when they move into a relationship, and that women are increasingly unwilling to do so. If indeed their relationships were as traditional as has been suggested earlier in this chapter, and women are indeed more interested in androgynous relationships than men (as suggested by McCauley, 1975), then perhaps these women did feel unduly trapped and inhibited, and were in fact more in need of freedom from the relationship than their male partners.

One is reminded of the findings reported by Zick Rubin (1975), who followed a sample of 231 college-age couples for two years. Like Ganson, he also noted that when the relationships dissolved, the women tended to cite more problems in the relationship than did the men (74 percent of the women and 61 percent of the men cited "my need for independence" as a contributing factor). Like Ganson, Rubin hypothesized that women may be more sensitive to the quality of their interpersonal relationships, but he suggested a somewhat different reason. Rubin argued that because a woman's future status in our society is so dependent upon the kind of husband she marries, she must evaluate her courtship relationship more frequently and more carefully than a man. Rather than finding women to be more emotionally involved than men, his data suggest that men fall in love more quickly and suffer more emotional pain at dissolution than do women. Although his research dealt only peripherally with cohabitation, he did report that those of his couples who lived together were no more or less likely to stay together than couples who had not lived together—suggesting once again that the mere fact of cohabitation may be somewhat irrelevant.

In a paper based on interviews with six cohabiting couples, Hennon (1975a) theorized about the role that conflict-management plays in the development and maintenance of cohabitation relationships. Building on concepts developed originally by Jetse Sprey, Hennon argued that any pair-bond relationship, including the cohabitation relationship, must be seen as "a system in conflict." How conflict is dealt with will vary with the degree of mutual desire to maintain the relationship and with the extent to which there are shared procedural rules for negotiating the conflict. This will, in turn, determine whether conflict leads to dissolution or to enhanced intimacy and pair-bond strength.

Hennon raised the following important, but as yet unanswered, questions: Are cohabiting couples, because they cannot take the relationship for granted and must "work" in order to maintain it, more likely than married couples to be aware of areas of disagreement and their techniques for dealing with these? Or do they tend to be in a romantic stage and, hence, less able to face their conflicts realistically? Or, because they are less secure in their relationship (with less perceived mutuality of commitment, and less conviction that the partner will cooperate to negotiate the conflict in a way that will preserve the relationship), will they be more hesitant to disclose and confront areas of conflict? These are interesting research questions, deserving attention, but one could predict that the answer will vary with the particular skills and personality attributes of the individual couple and that it will be difficult to generalize about cohabiting couples as a group.

How many cohabitation relationships break up and how many continue on as permanent relationships is not yet known, and the answer awaits more longitudinal research. One study of college cohabitation (Macklin, 1976b) reported that at time of data collection, 5 percent of the relationships had resulted in marriage, 25 percent were at the point of tentative or formal engagement, 50 percent were still ongoing but not as yet committed, and 20 percent had dissolved.

EFFECTS OF COHABITATION

ON THE INDIVIDUALS INVOLVED. Most of the research to date on effect of cohabitation on the individuals involved has been a matter of self-report, with the cohabitants indicating either by questionnaire or interview what they considered to be the pros and cons of the cohabitation experience. By and large, cohabitants have given overwhelmingly positive ratings to their experience. In one study (Macklin, 1976b), when college cohabitants were asked to indicate the degree to which their cohabitation was successful, pleasurable, and maturing, 78 percent indicated that it was successful or very successful (10 percent unsuccessful); 93 percent rated it pleasurable or very pleasurable (1 percent unpleasurable); and 91 percent rated it as maturing or very maturing (no one rated it as "not at all maturing"). When asked to rate the effect of the experience on a number of specific growth areas (e.g., self-confidence, emotional maturity, ability to understand and relate to others, and insight into the opposite sex), 80 percent or more indicated that the experience had had a positive effect in each area. Over three-quarters indicated that they would never marry without living with the person first and no one said that they would never again cohabit outside of marriage.

These findings are corroborated by other research. When Bower (1975) asked a similar question of his 126 cohabitants, 66 percent said that they would never marry without cohabiting first, and 68 percent said they would cohabit again with the same person. Shuttlesworth and Thorman (1973) report that 64 percent of their sample of college cohabitors rated the relationship as "very happy," 30 percent as "pretty happy," and only 6 percent as "not very happy." Eighty percent checked that "the experience gave me a deeper understanding of myself" and "fostered my own emotional growth." Eighty-three percent indicated that they held no regrets about having cohabited; only three percent regretted having done so. Fifty-six percent "indicated that they would not consider marriage without having first lived with the prospective marriage partner."

Peterman, Ridley, and Anderson (1974) conclude their report on college cohabitation by saying, "There are no immediately obvious negative effects of cohabitation, at least in terms of self-described personal adjustment or functioning as a student. If anything, cohabitation is associated with more positive self-attitudes and heterosexual relating." Lautenschlager (1972) concludes, on the basis of her survey of college students, that although "there are risks involved to the individual as there are in any human relationship . . . consensual union for the young college student appears to have definite functional value" (e.g., providing emotional support, financial practicality, sexual fulfillment, opportunity for personal growth, and the chance to assess compatibility).

In reviewing all available data, one is repeatedly impressed by the very strong positive attitudes toward cohabitation that are held by those who have experienced it. The main message that one consistently gets from cohabitants is the many ways in which the experience served to foster their own personal growth and maturity. Yet to date, no one has attempted to develop or apply over time any objective measures to test to what extent cohabitation does in fact lead to enhanced personal growth.

Ridley and Peterman (1975) have hypothesized that cohabitation is most likely to be a growth-producing experience and to lead to improved heterosexual competence when the following conditions are present: (a) the individuals do not have strong needs for emotional security, which might serve to prevent them from openly acknowledging and dealing with any disagreements for fear of endangering the relationship; (b) the couple enters the relationship with increased self-understanding as a goal; (c) one has a basis of prior heterosexual experience on which to build; and (d) one does not isolate oneself from a broader network of friends. They suggest that should a termination result, it will be less traumatic if (a) the individual has already affirmed his/her social desirability and developed good interpersonal skills in earlier relationships; (b) the step into cohabitation was a natural developmental extension from earlier relationships; and (c) the individuals maintain a "cushion" of friends to fall back upon. All of these are hypotheses that deserve to be tested.

ON MARRIAGE.   The critical issue for many laymen has been: What effect does cohabitation have on later marriage? Does it, by serving as a screening device and laboratory for personal growth, enhance the chances of later marital success? Or does it instead encourage persons to place a priority of self-fulfillment and personal happiness and, hence, make them less likely to make the sacrifices necessary for a successful relationship? To answer this question will require agreed-upon criteria of marital success (longevity and lack of evident conflict are not necessarily adequate criteria) and longitudinal research on carefully matched samples of unmarried cohabiting and noncohabiting couples. At present, we must rely instead on comparisons of currently married couples who had and had not cohabited before marriage. Four such studies come to mind.

Lyness (1976b) compared 11 married couples who had cohabited before marriage with 13 married couples who had not on sixteen variables representing concepts from "open marriage" and found few differences between the groups. Olday (Cohabitation Research Newsletter, No. 5, p. 38) surveyed 184 married students who had cohabited before marriage and 524 who had not, controlling for such variables as income, length of marriage, and relationship to parents, and also found practically no significant difference between the groups. Specifically, cohabitation before marriage did not seem to be related to degree of emotional closeness, satisfaction, conflict, or equalitarianism in marriage. The only significant difference was age at marriage, with the premarital cohabitants marrying about a year later than the others.

Budd (1976) studied 151 volunteer couples (54 cohabiting couples, 48 marrieds who had cohabited, and 49 marrieds who had not). Like Olday, when she compared those marrieds who had cohabited with those who had not on problems experienced, amount of self-disclosure, and degree of commitment, she found few significant differences. Marrieds who had cohabited did indicate less social commitment to the relationship (i.e., opinions of others would have less influence on making them stay together); males showed less concern about their partners not loving them as much as they used to; females indicated more concern about feeling trapped; and males indicated their partners had more often seen them use "poor communication" methods (e.g., walking out or refusing to talk). But caution is urged in interpreting these results, for they were not strong differences and could well be due more to personality factors than to the experience of having cohabited.

Clatworthy and Scheid (1977), while noting many similarities between couples who had and had not lived together before marriage, also found important differences: Those who had cohabited premaritally were less likely to acquiesce in disagreements; disagreed more often on such things as finances, household duties, and recreation; were less dependent on their spouses; considered their marriage a less intrinsic part of their lives; had broken up more often; and a higher percentage had sought marriage counseling. Again, it seems likely that these differences might well have existed even if the couples had not cohabited and are more likely due to preexisting personal predispositions than to the experience of cohabitation per se. In fact, the very factors that led them to be attracted to cohabitation in the first place (more liberal attitudes and greater tendency toward independence and assertiveness on the part of the females) might lead them to reveal less acquiescence in marriage and to see marriage as less essential to their well-being.

Clatworthy and Scheid go on to report that, while all the married couples studied who had cohabited before marriage considered the experience to have been beneficial, there was no evidence that their marriages were any better or any less conventional than the marriages of those who had merely dated. They conclude that, while there is no evidence that cohabitation causes any problems in later marriage, it certainly should not be seen as a cure-all for the problems facing marriage in today's society.

There has as yet been no research that will let us say with any certainty what effect the movement from cohabitation to marriage has on a relationship. Berger (1974) concludes, on the basis of retrospective data gained from interviews with 21 middle-aged couples who had cohabited premaritally, that marriage leads to no dramatic change in the relationship. The quality of the relationship after marriage duplicates to a large extent the apparent quality of the relationship before marriage. One finds no real consensus on this point, however, (see, for example, Keaough, 1975). Some observe that marriage made things better by removing social and parental pressure; others complain that they found themselves falling into traditional roles and expectations with a resulting loss of identity. On the basis of what evidence we do have, it seems likely that in many cases, movement into marriage brings escalation of commitment and increased ease with relatives and other members of the larger community. However, because of our socialization, marriage also brings an increased tendency toward role-playing and possessiveness, and reduction in personal identity and autonomy unless the couple makes a strong effort to counteract this tendency. How the couple defines the relationship for themselves may well be more important than the legal label attached to it.

ON SOCIETY. Many have feared that cohabitation will lead to erosion of the family, reduction in marriage rates, and an increase in children born without the security of committed parents. However, these fears have not been validated. Although there has been a decrease in percent of women currently married over the past fifteen years (62.1 in 1960; 58.4 in 1970; 57.5 in 1974), and an accompanying increase in single and divorced women (28.6 percent of women aged 20–24 were single in 1960, while 39.6 percent were single in 1974), there is no reason to think that large numbers are permanently substituting nonmarital relationships (Bernard, 1975).

When students are asked about their attitude toward marriage, the vast majority continue to indicate that they hope some day to marry. In Bower and Christopherson's national survey (1977), only 4 percent of the cohabitants and 1 percent of the noncohabitants indicated they wished never to marry. This is consistent with findings of surveys at two large eastern universities (Macklin, 1976b; McCauley, 1977) where only about 1 percent indicated no desire ever to marry. Although about 25 percent said they might marry someday but did not feel marriage was necessary for their happiness, the great majority plan to marry at some point in their life.

Many have pointed to Sweden and used that country's social history as cause for alarm, noting the decided decrease in marriage rates (the number of marriages decreased from 61,000 in 1966 to 38,251 in 1973—a decrease of 37 percent in seven years) and the accompanying increase in cohabitation rates (12 percent of all "syndyasmos"* in Sweden were unmarried in 1974 as opposed to 6.5 percent in 1970). Trost suggests that Denmark and the United States probably also have a fairly high rate, and that the same tendency is occurring in many parts of the world. He argues that these three countries may simply have gone through the change earlier and, because Sweden is such a small country with good

---

*Trost reports that Scandinavian researchers reserve the term "unmarried cohabitation" to refer to "two adult persons of different sex living together under marriage-like conditions in the same household without having officially confirmed their relation through marriage" (unlike this country where the term often refers to more transient relationships). "Syndyasmos" is a term coined by P. Locsei (Syndyasmos in Contemporary Budapest, Budapest, 1970, mimeographed) and used by Trost to refer to all long-term marriage-like living arrangements, whether or not the couple is legally married (Trost, 1975).

official statistics, the change has been easier to document there. He concludes that:

> rather than replicating marriage, unmarried cohabitation will eventually become a social institution with its most important function being that of a test or trial-marriage. If this assumption is correct—that unmarried cohabitation will become a trial-marriage institution—the marriage rate will increase again and eventually reach a level slightly lower than the level in the middle sixties. If this is the case, many marriages between two partners who do not fit well together will never be formed, those marriages which are formed will be "happier" and the divorce rate will be lower. (Trost, 1975, p. 682)

We cannot yet say whether cohabitation before marriage will eventually reduce the divorce rate in this country. It is true that it may provide for more effective screening and lead to persons marrying at a more mature age. But the mere fact that a couple has had an opportunity to test their initial compatibility through living together, even if they make maximum use of that opportunity, may have little effect on whether that couple manages to spend a life time together. There are so many factors that affect the course of relationships in our society that cohabitation before marriage would logically play a very minor role when compared with the multitude of other influences.

As yet, there are no data to tell us what effect growing up with cohabiting parents will have on children. Bernice Eiduson and her associates are currently involved in a longitudinal comparison of 200 children reared in cohabiting, communal, single-parent, and two-parent nuclear families. Evidence to date suggests that the needs of the infant are such strong determiners of how children are reared during the first year of life, that caretaking practices in nontraditional and traditional families do not differ significantly during this period. At the end of one year, the development of the total sample generally fell within the normal range, with life style not a differentiating factor (Eiduson, personal communication, 1977). It will be interesting to see the extent to which life style appears to affect the later development of these children.

What Can We Conclude?

1. Cohabitation as a stage in the courtship process is fast becoming a part of the dominant culture—at least among college-educated

persons—and may be a natural, to-be-expected outcome when two persons care about one another and enjoy being together. It seems likely that, in time to come, the majority of persons in this country will experience nonmarital cohabitation at some point in the life cycle.

2. We have as yet little information about the extent to which cohabitation will become an alternative to marriage, but the prediction is that it will be chosen as a permanent life style by a very small proportion of the total population. The social, economic, and legal supports for marriage in this country continue to be very strong.

   On the other hand, it seems plausible to predict that society's movement toward increased premarital cohabitation will be accompanied by a gradual increase in permissiveness and experimentation within the marriage relationship itself. For instance, as there is more acceptance of sexuality before marriage, there may be more acceptance of nonmarital sexuality after marriage. But this must remain pure speculation at the moment, and the cause and effect relations are not clear.

3. Persons who experience premarital cohabitation have personality and demographic profiles very much like those who do not; opportunity (and the social factors that influence opportunity) probably plays a greater role in determining who cohabits than any personality or demographic variables, although predisposing attitudes and a minimum of interpersonal skills may be requisite. We can as yet say very little about persons who live in a relatively permanent alternative to marriage.

4. When matched for length of time together and for position on the courtship continuum, cohabitation relationships look very much like noncohabitation relationships, and the interactions that occur within them seem in many ways to be fairly traditional. In fact, one is more impressed by the degree to which they mirror noncohabitation relationships than by their difference from these relationships.

5. While persons who have cohabited tend to report the experience as having been maturing and growth-producing, there is no information at present that it is more growth-producing than any of the more traditional courtship patterns. While it can afford the couple an opportunity to practice important relationship skills, there is nothing about cohabitation per se that necessarily ensures that this will happen. And if cohabitation is to serve as an impor-

tant screening device in the courtship process, it is essential that external social forces not press the couple into a premature decision to marry, and that continuation of the relationship not be seen as the major criterion of its success or value.

6. Society needs to move ahead to catch up with the reality of cohabitation. Studies show that large numbers of college couples hestitate to tell their parents of their cohabitation and, hence, cannot benefit from the give and take, and the emotional support, that might come if it were more acceptable to the older generation. College dormitories are not built to facilitate the development of healthy intimate heterosexual relationships and the capacity to handle such relationships, nor does the college community provide the educational or counseling support systems that might help college cohabitors gain maximum growth from their experiments in interpersonal relations.

7. Research must move ahead in new directions. Much of the proposed graduate research continues to repeat the same questions and to use research designs similar to the studies that have already been done. The real need for longitudinal research—and for objective, behavioral measures — on non-college and older populations is not yet being met.

8. We should perhaps stop using cohabitation as a central variable in our future research. Although there are important questions that still deserve to be answered more definitively (such as the long-range social and personal effects of living with someone while unmarried and the kinds of attitudes toward relationships that this life style may promote), it seems likely that cohabitation per se will not prove to be the crucial determining factor. The quality of the interaction, the socioemotional characteristics of the individuals involved, and the extent to which a conscious effort is made to assess and grow through the relationship, seem much more important than the mere fact of whether one has lived with someone to whom one is not married.

It seems indicative that many of the original cohabitation researchers are now focusing their attention on what I have come to call "capacity for intimacy," or what Ridley and Peterman call "heterosexual competence," and are searching for ways to conceptualize and operationalize these variables adequately, and for methods to facilitate their development. The ability to initiate and sustain meaningful and mutually satisfying relationships seem central if one is to find happiness in any intimate relationship—traditional or innovative—and it is these inner qualities and skills rather than the outward form on which we must now focus. To know simply that a couple is cohabiting tells us very little about that couple—either about the individuals involved or the relationship itself.

REFERENCES

Ald, R. *Sex Off Campus*. New York: Grosset and Dunlap, 1969.

Arafat, I. and Yorburg, B. "On Living Together Without Marriage." *Journal of Sex Research* 9 (1973): 97–106.

Bardwick, J. *The Psychology of Women: A Study of Bio-Cultural Conflict*. New York: Harper and Row, 1971.

Berger, M. E. "Trial Marriage: Harnessing the Trend Constructively." *The Family Coordinator* 20(1971):38–43.

Berger, M. E. *Trial Marriage Follow-Up Study*. Unpublished manuscript, 1974.

Bernard, J. "Note on Changing Life Styles, 1970–1974." *Journal of Marriage and the Family* 37(1975):582–93.

Bloch, D. "Unwed Couples: Do They Live Happily Ever After?" *Redbook* (April, 1969): 90, 140–44.

Bower, D. W. *The Determinants of Dyadic Commitment Among Cohabiting Couples: A Pilot Study*. Unpublished manuscript. Denison University, 1974.

Bower, D. W. *A Description and Analysis of a Cohabiting Sample in America*. Unpublished master's thesis University of Arizona, 1975.

Bower, D. W. and Christopherson, V. A. "University Student Cohabitation: A Regional Comparison of Selected Attitudes and Behavior." *Journal of Marriage and the Family* 39 (1977):447–53.

Brown, G., Cottle, B., Donooy, F., Daiboch, C., and Murphy, M. *Heterosexual Cohabitation Among Unmarried College Students at San Diego State University*. Unpublished master's thesis. San Diego State University, 1975.

Budd, L. S. *Problems, Disclosure, and Commitment of Cohabiting and Married Couples*. Unpublished doctoral dissertation. University of Minnesota, 1976.

Cadwallader, M. "Marriage as a Wretched Institution." *Atlantic Monthly* (November, 1966):62–66.

Clatworthy, N.M. "Couples in Quasi-Marriage." In *Old Family/New Family: Interpersonal Relationships*, edited by N. Glazer-Malbin. Princeton: Van Nostrand, 1975.

Clatworthy, N. M. and Scheid, L. *A Comparison of Married Couples: Premarital Cohabitants with Non-Premarital Cohabitants*. Unpublished manuscript. Ohio State University, 1977.

Clayton, R. R. and Voss, H. L. "Shacking Up: Cohabitation in the 1970s." *Journal of Marriage and the Family* 39(1977):273–83.

Coffin, P. "Young Unmarrieds: Theresa Pommett and Charles Walsh, College Grads Living Together." *Look* (January 26, 1971):634.

Cole, C. L. *Dyadic Commitment and the Cohabitation Bond: A Progress Report.* Unpublished manuscript. Denison University, 1973.(a)

Cole, C. L. *Living Together and the Implications of Heterosexual Socialization.* Unpublished manuscript Denison University, 1973.(b)

Cole, C. L. *Non-Marital Cohabitation Research: Strategies and Prospects.* Unpublished manuscript. Denison University, 1973.(c)

Cole, C. L. *Training Human Service Personnel for Work with Cohabiting Couples.* Unpublished manuscript. Denison University, 1975.

Cole, C. L. *Living Together as an Alternative Life Style.* Unpublished manuscript. Iowa State University, 1976.

Cole, C. L. "Cohabitation in Social Context." In *Marriage and Alternatives: Exploring Intimate Relationships,* edited by R. W. Libby and R. N. Whitehurst. Glenview, Ill.: Scott, Foresman and Co., 1977.

Cole, C. L. and Bower, D. W. *Cohabitation as Life Style and Its Implications for Marriage and Family Counseling.* Unpublished manuscript. Denison University, 1974.(a)

Cole, C. L. and Bower, D. W. *Cohabitation Pair Bond: Intimacy Requirements and Love Life Development Differences.* Unpublished manuscript. Denison University, 1974.(b)

Cole, C. L. and Bower D. W. *Role Disparity in the Cohabitation Pair Bond.* Unpublished manuscript. Denison University, 1974.(c)

Cole, C. M. *A Behavioral Analysis of Married and Living Together Couples.* Unpublished manuscript. University of Texas Medical Branch at Galveston, 1975.

Collins, B. *Complementary, Symmetrical and Rhythmic Relationship Patterns Among Married and Cohabiting Heterosexual Couples.* Unpublished doctoral dissertation. United States International University, 1977.

Croake, J. W., Keller, J. F., and Catlin, N. *Unmarrieds Living Together: It's Not All Gravy.* Dubuque, Iowa: Kendall/Hunt Publishing Co., 1974.

Danziger, C. *Unmarried Heterosexual Cohabitation.* Unpublished doctoral dissertation. Rutgers University, 1976.

Danziger, C. and Greenwald, M. *Alternatives: A Look at Unmarried Couples and Communes.* New York: Institute of Life Insurance, 1973.

Davids, L. "North American Marriage: 1990." *The Futurist* 5(1971):190–94.

DeLaet, D. *Cohabitation: A Study of a Few Aspects of the Living Together Unmarried of a Heterosexual Couple.* Unpublished master's thesis. University of Gent, 1975.

DeLora, J. R. and DeLora, J. S. *Social Structure and Satisfaction of Heterosexual Cohabiting Dyads.* Unpublished manuscript. San Diego State University, 1975.

Drabkin, R. "Living Together and the Law." *Marriage and Divorce* (August, 1974):18–20.

Edwards, M. P. *College Students' Perceptions of Experimental Life Styles*. Unpublished master's thesis. Oklahoma State University, 1972.

Eiduson, B. T. "Looking at Children in Emergent Family Styles." *Children Today* 3(1974):2–6.

English, D. A. *Alternate Role Relationships: A Study of Attitudes and Behavior Relating to Family Life Styles*. Unpublished master's thesis. Baylor University, 1975.

Ganson, H. C. *Cohabitation: The Antecedents of Dissolution of Formerly Cohabiting Individuals*. Unpublished master's thesis. Ohio State University, 1975.

Garza, J. *Living Together and the Double Funnel Theory of Courtship*. Unpublished manuscript. Georgia State University, 1974.

Gavin, M. C. *The Living-Together Phenomenon*. Unpublished master's thesis. Washington State University, 1973.

Glick, P. C. "A Demographer Looks at American Families." *Journal of Marriage and the Family* 37(1975):15–26.

Grant, A. "No Rings Attached: A Look at Premarital Marriage on Campus." *Mademoiselle* (April, 1968): 208.

Gross, G. *Cohabitation and Marriage: A Study of Relationships*. Unpublished master's thesis. San Francisco State University, 1976.

Guittar, E. C. *Family Background and Personality Factors of Unmarried, Living-Together, and Engaged Couples*. Unpublished master's thesis. University of Georgia, 1974.

Guittar, E. C. and Lewis, R. A. *Self Concepts Among Some Unmarried Cohabitants*. Unpublished manuscript. Pennsylvania State University, 1974.

Hennon, C. B. *Open-Systems Theory and the Analysis of Non-Marital Cohabitation*. Unpublished manuscript. West Virginia University, 1974.

Hennon, C. B. *Conflict Management Within Pairing Relationships: The Case of Non-Marital Cohabitation*. Unpublished manuscript. University of Utah, 1975.(a)

Hennon, C. B. *Self-Conception of Cohabitors*. Unpublished manuscript. West Virginia University, 1975.(b)

Henze, L. F. and Hudson, J. W. "Personal and Family Characteristics of Non-Cohabiting and Cohabiting College Students." *Journal of Marriage and the Family* 36(1974):722–26.

Hirsch, B. *Living Together: A Guide to the Law for Unmarried Couples*. Boston: Houghton Mifflin, 1976.

Hobart, C. W. *Trial Marriage Among Students: A Study of Attitudes and Experience*. Unpublished manuscript. University of Alberta, n.d.

Huang, L. J. *Religious Background of College Students and Attitudes Toward Living Together Before Marriage*. Unpublished manuscript. Illinois State University, 1972.

Huang, L. J. *Some Patterns of Non-Exclusive Sexual Relationships Among Unmarried Cohabiting Couples*. Unpublished manuscript. Illinois State University, 1973.

Huang, L. J. *Research with Unmarried Cohabiting Couples: Including Non-Exclusive Sexual Relations.* Unpublished manuscript. Illinois State University, 1974.

Hudson, J. W. and Henze, L. F. "A Note on Cohabitation." *The Family Coordinator,* 22(1973):495.

Johnson, M. P. *Courtship and Commitment: A Study of Cohabitation on a University Campus.* Unpublished master's thesis. University of Iowa, 1968.

Johnson, M. P. "Commitment: A Conceptual Structure and Empirical Application." *Sociological Quarterly* 14(1973):395–406.

Kalmbach, C. *Replication Study of Heterosexual Cohabitation Among Unmarried College Students: Cornell University vs. Central Michigan University.* Unpublished manuscript. Central Michigan University, 1973.

Karlen, A. "The Unmarried Marrieds on Campus." *New York Times Magazine* (January 26, 1969):31.

Keaough, D. "Without Knotting the Tie." *The Arizona Republic* (July 27, 1975): 8–15.

Kieffer, C. M. *Consensual Cohabitation: A Descriptive Study of the Relationships and Sociocultural Characteristics of Eighty Couples in Settings of Two Florida Universities.* Unpublished master's thesis. Florida State University, 1972.

King, M. D. *Cohabitation Handbook: Living Together and the Law.* Berkeley, California: Ten Speed Press, 1975.

Kopecky, G. "Unmarried, But Living Together." *Ladies Home Journal* (July, 1972):66–71, 138.

Lautenschlager, S. Y. *A Descriptive Study of Consensual Union Among College Students.* Unpublished master's thesis. California State University at Northridge, 1972.

Lavori, N. *Living Together, Married or Single: Your Legal Rights.* New York: Harper and Row, 1976.

LeHecka, C. F. *Premarital Dyadic Formation in West Germany and the United States: A Cross-National Comparison.* Unpublished master's thesis. University of Georgia, 1974.

LeShan, E. L. *Mates and Roommates: New Styles in Young Marriages.* Public Affairs Pamphlets, No. 468, 1971.

Lewis, R. A., Soanier, G. B., Storm, V. L., and LeHecka, C. F. *Commitment in Married and Unmarried Cohabitation.* Unpublished manuscript. Pennsylvania State University, 1975.

Liddick, B. "Practicing Marriage Without a License." In *Marriage Means Encounter,* edited by G. Roleder. Dubuque, Iowa: William C. Brown, 1973.

"Linda, the Light Housekeeper." *Time* (April 26, 1968):51.

Lindsey, B. B. "The Companionate Marriage." *Redbook* (October, 1926; March, 1927). (a)

Lindsey, B. B. *The Companionate Marriage.* Garden City, New York: Garden City Publishers, 1927.(b)

Lobsenz, N.N. "Marriage vs. Living Together." *Modern Bride* (April/May, 1973):124.

Lobsenz, N. N. "Living Together: A New-Fangled Tango or an Old-Fashioned Waltz?" *Redbook* (June, 1974): 86–87, 184–186.

Lyness, J. F. *Aspects of Long-Term Effects of Non-Married Cohabitation.* Unpublished manuscript. Purdue University at Fort Wayne, 1974.

Lyness, J. F. *Happily Ever After: A Follow-up of Living Together Couples.* Unpublished manuscript. Pennsylvania State University, 1976.(a)

Lyness, J. F. *Open Marriage Among Former Cohabitants: "We Have Met the Enemy: Is It Us"?* Unpublished manuscript. Pennsylvania State University, 1976. (b)

Lyness, J. F., Lipetz, M. E., and Davis, K. E. "Living Together: An Alternative to Marriage." *Journal of Marriage and the Family* 34 (1972): 305-11

Macklin, E. D., ed. *Cohabitation Research Newsletter,* Issue No. 1, October, 1972; Issue No. 2, April, 1973; Issue No. 3, October, 1973; Issue No. 4, June, 1974; Issue No. 5, April, 1976.

Macklin, E. D. Heterosexual Cohabitation Among Unmarried College Students. *The Family Coordinator* 21(1972):463–72.

Macklin, E.D. *Report of Grove Conference Cohabitation Research Workshop.* Myrtle Beach, South Carolina, 1973.

Macklin, E. D. *Comparison of Parent and Student Attitudes Toward Non-Marital Cohabitation.* Unpublished manuscript Cornell University, 1974.(a)

Macklin, E. D. "Students Who Live Together: Trial Marriage or Going Very Steady?" *Psychology Today* (November, 1974):53–59.(b)

Macklin, E. D. "Campus Cohabitation: Toward a Rational Response to a Reality." *Journal of the National Association of Student Personnel Administrators* (Spring, 1976):21–37.(a)

Macklin, E. D. "Unmarried Heterosexual Cohabitation on the University Campus." In *The Social Psychology of Sex,* edited by J. P. Wiseman. New York: Harper and Row, 1976.(b)

Makepeace, J. M. *The Birth Control Revolution: Consequences for College Student Life Styles.* Unpublished doctoral dissertation. Washington State University, 1975.

Marciano, T. D. *Qualitative Studies on Women with Advanced Degrees: Older Women and Their Younger Lovers, and Post-Marital Living Patterns Among Women with Advanced Degrees.* Unpublished manuscript. Fairleigh Dickinson University at Teaneck, 1975.

Marzoni, M. R. and Deaux, K. *Cohabiting Students in Perspective and Comparison with Married Couples on Territoriality, Privacy, and Division of Labor.* Unpublished manuscript. Purdue University, 1975.

Massey, C. and Warner, R. *Sex, Living Together and the Law: A Legal Guide for Unmarried Couples (and Groups).* Berkeley, California: Nolo Press, 1974.

Maxa, R. "Living Together: The Aftermath." *The Washington Post (Potomac)* (April 14, 1974): 14–15, 33–34.

McCauley, B. *Sex Roles in Alternative Life Styles: Egalitarian Attitudes in the Cohabiting Relationship.* Unpublished manuscript. University of Delaware, 1975.

McCauley, B. *Self-Esteem in the Cohabiting Relationship.* Unpublished master's thesis University of Delaware, 1977.

McWhirter, W. A. "The Arrangement at College." *Life* (May 31, 1968):56.

Mead, M. "Marriage in Two Steps." *Redbook* (July, 1966):48–49, 84–86.

Mead, M. "A Continuing Dialogue on Marriage: Why Just Living Together Won't Work" *Redbook* (April, 1968): 44–52, 119.

Michael, J. J. *Petal and Me: A Survival Manual for Unmarried Live-Togethers.* Lisle, Illinois: Turtle Creek Publishing Co., 1972.

Montgomery J. P. *Towards an Understanding of Cohabitation.* Unpublished doctoral dissertation. University of Massachusetts, 1972.

Montgomery, J. P. *Commitment and Cohabitation Cohesion.* Unpublished manuscript. University of Edmonton, 1973.

Morrison, J. L. and Anderson, S. M. "College Student Cohabitation." *College Student Journal* 7(1973):14-19.

Mosher, J. B. *Deviance, Growth Motivation and Attraction to Marital Alternatives.* Unpublished doctoral dissertation. University of Connecticut, 1975.

Packard, V. *The Sexual Wilderness.* New York: McKay, 1968.

Peterman, D. J., Ridley, C. A., and Anderson, S. M. "A Comparison of Cohabiting and Non-Cohabiting College Students." *Journal of Marriage and the Family* 36(1974):344-354.

Petty, J. A. *An Investigation of Factors Which Differentiate Between Types of Cohabitation.* Unpublished master's thesis. Indiana University, 1975.

Polansky, L. *A Comparison of Marriage and Cohabitation on Three Interpersonal Variables.* Unpublished master's thesis. Ball State University, 1974.

Polansky, L., Johnson, W., McDonald, G., and Martin, J. K. *A Comparison of Marriage and Heterosexual Cohabitation with Respect to the Variables of Interpersonal Knowledge, Affective Support and Satisfaction.* Unpublished manuscript. Ball State University, 1975.

Reuben, D. "Alternatives to Marriage." *McCall's* (February, 1972):38.

Ridley, C. A. and Peterman, D. J. *Beyond Cohabitation: A Case for Heterosexual Competence.* Unpublished manuscript. Pennsylvania State University, 1975.

Rodman, H. Marital Relationships in a Trinidad Village. *Marriage and Family Living.* 23(1961):166-70.

Rodman, H. "Illegitimacy in the Carribbean Social Structure: A Reconsideration." *American Sociological Review.* 31(1966):673-83.

Rosenblatt, P. C. and Budd, L. G. "Territoriality and Privacy in Married and Unmarried Cohabiting Couples." *Journal of Social Psychology* 97(1975): 67-76.

Rubin, Z. *Dating Project Research Report* (Vol. 2, No. 1). Cambridge, Massachusetts: Harvard University, 1975.

Russell, B. *Marriage and Morals*. New York: Liveright, 1929.

Satir, V. *Marriage as a Statutory Five-Year Renewable Contract*. Unpublished manuscript. 1967.

Schrag, P. "Posse at Generation Gap: Implications of the Linda LeClair Affair." *Saturday Review*. (May 18, 1968):81.

Segrest, M. A. *Comparison of the Role Expectations of Married and Cohabiting Students*. Unpublished master's thesis. University of Kentucky, 1975.

Sheehy, G. "Living Together: The Stories of Four Young Couples Who Risk the Strains of Non-Marriage and Why." *Glamour*. (February 1, 1969):136-137, 198-202.

Shuttlesworth, G. and Thorman, G. *Living Together Unmarried Relationships*. Unpublished manuscript. University of Texas at Austin, 1973.

Silverman, I. *Unmarried Students Who Lived Together: A Comparison of Two Campuses*. Unpublished manuscript. University of South Florida, 1974.

Smith, J. "The Arrangement: As Acceptable as Going Steady." *Wisconsin State Journal* (April 27, 1969):1.

Smith, P. B. and Kimmel, K. "Student-Parent Reactions to Off-Campus Cohabitation." *Journal of College Student Personnel* 11(1970):188-93.

Snodgrass, J. *Without Benefit of Clergy: An Exploration of Non-Institutionalized Marital Roles*. Unpublished master's thesis. University of Illinois at Chicago Circle, 1975.

Stafford, R., Bachman, E., and diBona, P. "The Division of Labor Among Cohabitating and Married Couples." *Journal of Marriage and the Family* 39(1977):43-57.

Steiner, D. *Non-Marital Cohabitation and Marriage: Questionnaire Responses of College Women and Their Mothers*. Unpublished master's thesis. North Dakota State University, 1975.

Stevens, D. J. H. *Cohabitation Without Marriage*. Unpublished doctoral dissertation. University of Texas at Austin, 1975.

Storm, V. *Contemporary Cohabitation and the Dating-Marital Continuum*. Unpublished master's thesis. University of Georgia, 1973.

Strong, L. and Nass, G. *Correlates of Willingness Among College Students to Participate in Prolonged Cohabitation*. Unpublished manuscript. University of Connecticut, 1975.

Thorman, G. "Cohabitation: A Report on the Married-Unmarried Life Style." *The Futurist* 7(1973):250-54.(a)

Thorman, G. *Cohabitation: A Report on Thirty Living-Together Couples at a Texas University*. Unpublished manuscript. University of Texas at Austin, 1973.(b)

Trost, J. *Various Forms of Cohabitation and Their Relation to Physical and Social Criteria of Adaptation*. Unpublished manuscript. Uppsala University, 1972.

Trost, J. "Married and Unmarried Cohabitation: The Case of Sweden with Some Comparisons." *Journal of Marriage and the Family* 37(1975):677-82.(a)

Trost, J. *Married and Unmarried Cohabiting Couples in Sweden–Attitudes on Their Degree of Integration.* Unpublished manuscript. Uppsala University, 1975.(b)

Trost, J. *A Renewed Social Institution: Cohabitation Without Marriage.* Unpublished manuscript. Uppsala University, 1976.(a)

Trost, J. *Attitudes to and Occurrence of Cohabitation Without Marriage.* Unpublished manuscript. Uppsala University, 1976.(b)

"Unstructured Relationships: Students Living Together." *Newsweek* (July 4, 1966):78.

U.S. Bureau of the Census, "Marital Status and Living Arrangements: March 1976," *Current Population Reports*, Series P-20, No. 306. Washington, D.C.: U.S. Government Printing Office, 1977.

Van Deusen, E. L. *Contract Cohabitation: An Alternative to Marriage.* New York: Grove Press, 1974.

Ward T. J. *Cohabitation and Drift: A Conceptual Model.* Unpublished manuscript. Baker University, 1975.

Weitzman, L. J. "Legal Regulation of Marriage: Tradition and Change: A Proposal for Individual Contracts and Contracts in Lieu of Marriage." *California Law Review.* 62(1974):1169-1288.

Wells, T. and Christie, L.D. "Living Together: An Alternative to Marriage." *The Futurist.* 4(1970):50-51.

Whitehurst, R. N. *The Double Standard and Male Dominance in Non-Marital Living Arrangements: A Preliminary Statement.* Unpublished manuscript. University of Windsor, 1969.(a)

Whitehurst, R. N. *The Unmalias on Campus.* Unpublished manuscript. University of Windsor, 1969.(b)

Whitehurst, R. N. *Living Together Unmarried: Some Trends and Speculations.* Unpublished manuscript. University of Windsor, 1973.

Whitehurst, R. N. *Sex Role Equality and Changing Meanings in Cohabitation.* Unpublished manuscript. University of Windsor, 1974.

HOMOSEXUALITY

[10]

WE LAUGH today at the erroneous thinking of the past. Did people really believe that wearing garlic around the neck would ward off colds? That a woman menstruating during planting season might ruin the crops? Nowhere has misinformation or prejudice existed more strongly than in the area of sex. Even in the nineteenth century the most learned physicians and sex experts were misleading their readers as to when a woman's period of fertility occurred, and were stating forthrightly that sexual desire in women led to sterility (Murstein, 1974).

By the twentieth century, homosexuality could no longer be viewed as evidence of the invasion of the body by Satan. Like witchcraft and insanity, homosexuality was turned over to the physicians, who declared that homosexuals were not evil, only sick. Our two papers on homosexuality illustrate that the medical model must be replaced by the more neutral label of "different," and "different" only in the statistical sense, without any necessary implications for adjustment.

Much of the reason for such homosexual maladjustment as it exists may be attributed to societal pressure and prejudice. Indeed, as Bullough's Salt Lake City sample indicates, where it was easy to hide the fact that one was a lesbian, the women were quite as conventional as their neighbors and remained undetected throughout their lives.

Nevertheless, the pressures and prejudices of society against "deviancy" can lead to maladjustment so that the perception of the homosexual as "sick" can become a self-fulfilling prophecy. Michael Burk has ingeniously borrowed from Kübler-Ross's stages of coming to terms with dying to demonstrate from the experiential point of view

244

how the courageous homosexual allows his false personna to die in allowing life to his true "self."

It may well be that our treatment of the homosexual has ramifications for our progress as a civilization. When we can accept our own sexuality we shall no longer have need to project our own fears and weaknesses on to those who are different from the norm.

REFERENCE

Murstein, B. I. *Love, Sex, and Marriage through the Ages*. New York: Springer Publishing Company, 1974.

Variant Life Styles: Homosexuality

VERN L. BULLOUGH

MANY INDIVIDUALS, when they first hear of the existence of variant intimate life styles, assume that the phenomenon is a new one. One of the tasks of an historian is to indicate that only rarely is this the case. Communes, for example, have been around for thousands of years, and the most durable survival of them in the Western world is the monastic unit. Obviously the modern monastery is radically different from the Twin Oaks Commune, but then it is also different from some of the fifth-century monasteries that included both sexes in the same unit and emphasized the need for love among its members. American history has witnessed several communal movements, both asexual ones such as the Shakers and sexually promiscuous ones such as the Oneida Community. Many societies have had far more open marriages than ours, at least as far as sex is concerned, and group marriages appeared in structured forms among the Mormons of the nineteenth century and in less structured forms in the relationship of the so-called prostitutes in naval ports (where a good wife had a sailor on every ship) and in the far western frontier communities. The term "so-called prostitute" is used because this is what society tended to class such women, although they did not regard themselves as prostitutes, nor did the men regard their multiple wives in this way. Cohabitation in American society has a long history as evidenced by the development of common-law marriage precedents to recognize unions not marked by a marriage license or clerical blessing.

When this is said, what is new today is the social class of those involved in the new variant life styles, at least those openly involved, and general acceptance by part of the middle-class establishment of such life styles. Even those intimate life styles previously most severely punished by societies are beginning to surface, although they still have a long way to go to achieve widespread public acceptance. This is particularly true of homosexuality which, of the variant life styles discussed here, has a history of being the most condemned. Even today, according to a survey of 3018 Americans, some 70.2 percent felt sexual acts between two persons of the same sex was wrong even though the two loved each other. Only 11.4 percent of the sample were willing to indicate that such activities were not wrong at all (Levitt and Klassen, 1974). Still public attitudes toward homosexuality are changing, and the best evidence for this is change in laws making sexual behavior between consenting adults in private, including homosexuality, a matter of individual choice, not legal limitations.

If attitudes toward homosexuality can change, and homosexuality has been the most feared of the intimate life styles, then it should seem obvious that greater public tolerance will be extended to many forms of previously stigmatized sexual behavior. In fact so all-punishing has society been in the past of homosexual activity that only rarely did it exist as an exclusive form of sex relationships. Rather, what we have is the existence of bisexuality, and though many in the past might well have had a person of the same sex as the desired love object, he or she usually also mated with an individual of the opposite sex if only in order to have children. This is somewhat different from those who call themselves bisexual today who, of their own choice might have sex both with persons of the same sex and the opposite sex. Usually, however, after a period of experimentation, most settle down to being either homosexual or heterosexual.

Before I can argue that basic attitudes are changing, it is essential to show the sources of these attitudes in the Western world, again my historical training showing. In general, in Western culture non-procreative sex has been regarded as signifying either a sin or an illness, with the homosexual being particularly sinful or sickly. The origin of the concept of the sinful nature of such conduct lies deep in the Jewish tradition, but this was reinforced in the Christian period by Greek concepts. In the Jewish scriptures the story of Sodom (*Genesis* 9:22-24) and Onan (*Genesis* 38:8-10) provided the foundation, even though Biblical scholars have argued that the equation of the story of Sodom with homosexuality was a postexilic interpretation (Bailey, 1955). Christianity accepted such concepts, amalgamating them with Greek dualistic beliefs which emphasized that the pleasures of the mind or the soul were to be preferred to those of the body. Inevitably sex as the most bodily of pleasures, and the one least susceptible to control by the mind, was frowned upon (Bullough, 1976).

Institutionalizing such beliefs in Christian theology was St. Augustine (Augustine, 1948, 1955), who argued that celibacy was the best way for men and women to live, but for those who could not live in celibacy, married sex was allowable providing the intent of the partners was to engage in procreation. Again, procreation was the essential factor and, based upon this supposition, St. Augustine established a sort of list of forbidden sexual activities, although some were not as bad as others. Least sinful of the alternatives was fornication outside the bounds of matrimony providing it did not intentionally exclude procreation. This was followed by adultery, then incest, and finally all those sex activities against nature. This last was a catch-all category including avoidance of procreation through use of contraceptives or by *coitus interruptus* or similar activities, the use of a member not designated for such a purpose (i.e., the anus or the mouth), sex between members of the same sex, between humans and animals, and solitary sex, that is masturbation (Gratian, 1879–1881, St. Thomas Aquinas, 1947). These concepts were deeply inculcated in the Western psyche through the penitential literature and through the law codes, both ecclesiastical and secular (McNeill and Gamer, 1938; Bullough, 1976).

Though there were some variatons over the next 1400 years (by the Protestants on celibacy, for example), the attitudes expressed by the religious model of sexuality dominated Western thought until supplemented by the medical model of sexuality. Unfortunately the medical model took over intact most of the concepts associated with sex as a sin and relabeled these same concepts as an illness. Based on the observable fact that sex in the male results in an emission and a feeling of lassitude, the medical model came to accept as proven the belief that sex was debilitating. To engage in it with any great frequency or with too much zest would ultimately result in the wasting away of health, ultimately leading to disease if not death. The medical model had the advantage over the previous religious model of encouraging research, and in some cases it implied that a cure for a disease was possible. In this last, however, it merely shifted to physical remedies what the priest and minister had attempted to do with spiritual ones. It was this medical model of sexuality that many people of my generation were taught, and which concentrated on the horrors of masturbation as well as upon the dangers of touching, feeling, or more intimate forms of contact with members of the opposite sex or same sex, although it should be added that much of the scientific basis for the medical model of sex had been undermined by 1920 (Bullough, 1974, 1975).

Western law accepted the sin model of sexuality so that those who departed from societal norms could come into conflict with the law and be punished or incarcerated either in prison or in mental hospitals. There were, of course, challenges, and in Roman law countries (i.e., continental Europe) the laws dealing with sex were largely liberalized as part of the changes wrought by the French Revolution in the revision popularly known as the Napoleonic Code. In England, however, the laws tended to become more stringent, and in the last part of the nineteenth century England and English common-law countries (including the U. S.), based in part on medical discoveries, moved to make solicitation, prostitution, intercourse in the "wrong" position, use of contraceptives, and even masturbation against the law (Gigeroff, 1968; Stephen, 1878).

The organized movement to repeal some of the harsher sex laws, particularly those dealing with homosexuality, had its origin in Germany where the Prussian code was much less lenient in dealing with sex activities than some of the other German states more deeply influenced by the Napoleonic liberalizing revisions. Magnus Hirschfeld is perhaps the best known of the individuals involved in changing the laws, but he was not alone, and the reformers gathered signatures and support from all walks of German life (Jahrbuch). The campaign to modify sexually repressive laws in the English-speaking countries was slower to appear and slower to gain momentum. In spite of some early sporadic efforts, the effective campaign for legal reform might be said to date from the Wolfenden report in 1957 in England (Wolfenden, 1957) which essentially argued for decriminalizing of sexual activities that did not do involuntary harm to others. In this country, with the post World

War II efforts of the American Friends Service Committee, the American Law Institute, and the American Civil Liberties Union (Bullough, 1976), demands for change are just beginning to result in legal modifications.

Why the change in attitudes? Several reasons should be noted. Moreover, though homosexuality is still less socially acceptable than many other forms of intimate sex behavior, attitudes toward homosexuality are closely related to attitudes toward other forms of sexuality. Thus one of the major factors in changing attitudes toward nonprocreative sex has been the dissemination of information about contraception. This chapter is not the place to give a history of the contraceptive movement, but one of the effects of the widespread public acceptance of contraception is the recognition of sex for pleasure, particularly for women. When the inevitable consequence of premarital or extramarital sex is not necessarily pregnancy, then some of the restrictions that society has put upon women, as well as the sexual restrictions that women put upon themselves, are no longer necessary. Thus the mere fact that sex pleasure is recognized as a female right forces changes in attitudes toward sex in general.

Another factor involved in lessening some of the inhibitions about sexuality has been the control of venereal disease. Undoubtedly one of the factors that caused the nineteenth century to be so anxious about sex was their realization of the dangers of syphilis, particularly since the third stage of syphilis was only understood at that time. It was fear of venereal disease which also gave momentum to the move to abolish prostitution in this country, and which gave emotional support to the repressive sex laws. It was fear of the disease that also gave rise to efforts to find cures, and the twentieth century has seen a series of preventive measures from the use of silver nitrate to prevent blindness in infants born of gonorrheal mothers, to Paul Ehrlich's salvarsan and neosalvarsan, to the dissemination of prophylactic kits, and finally to the discovery of more effective treatments with the advent of sulfonamides and penicillin. While venereal disease exists, it is no longer the inhibiting factor in sexual relationships it once was.

Traditionally, also, most of Western culture has been based upon rather strict sex roles. Men were active in the world at large, women were confined to the home, and within these large categories there were even further limitations. Undoubtedly many of the people forced into a particular role model were either unhappy or unable to meet all the expectations required, particularly since such role models were culturally and socially defined and enforced rather than personally chosen (Money and Ehrhardt, 1972; Bullough, 1973). Though we have become very conscious of the limitations of role models through the agitation associated with women's liberation, the effect has been not only to make role modification possible for women but for men as well. In the process of redefining roles, alternative life styles have become much more possible, both in the world at large and in more intimate ways.

One of the alternative intimate life styles is homosexuality, although it usually is not regarded as such (Sussman, 1975). I choose the descriptive term of homosexuality rather than bisexuality because I think the homosexual intimate life style implies a greater deviation from the norms of the past than does an occasional homosexual experience for a generally heterosexual person. Moreover, since homosexuality has clearly been a stigmatized behavior, it has usually involved a subculture which encouraged identification as homosexual rather than bisexual, although in the past many people adopted a bisexual identity because they felt this was the only way they could survive. In short, homosexuality went underground. Today, as some of the restrictions are removed, homosexuality is becoming more obvious, although the process, as Michael Burk indicates, is still not easy. Homosexuality then is not a new life style, but one that suffers somewhat less from society than it once did. Although we have no way of knowing whether homosexuality is increasing or decreasing, it is becoming more open and people who might once have taken tremendous personal effort to disguise their life style are now willing to be more open about their sexual identity.

Signs of this changing attitude are evident through the organization of such groups as the gay academics, gay librarians, gay militants, gay students, gay artists, and ultimately, of course, the gay churches. These movements, I think, are a step toward ultimate integration, since the assertion of one's difference and the acceptance of this difference, no matter how difficult this might be personally, is a necessary prerequisite to joining society on one's own terms. Obviously there has long been a gay underground culture centered in the bars and the baths for males, although the female culture has been much less noticeable. My research (Bullough, 1976) indicates the existence of such bars in America at least as early as the post-Civil War period, and in England they date back at least to the eighteenth century. At the same time the vast number of homosexually inclined individuals have led fairly constructive lives, as several recent studies have indicated. The pioneering study in this respect for the United States was by Evelyn Hooker, who, in a small selected sample of gays, found that they were generally well adjusted to the norms of society (Hooker, 1957). A wider sample of lesbian women by Heald and Finley (1975) agreed with these findings.

I hold, however, that this is not a recent phenomenon, but a traditional one. Homosexuality was never, in my mind, a conscious rebellion against society's emphasis on procreation as Herbert Marcuse has argued (Marcuse, 1955). Rather, homosexuals, from my studies, have generally been law-abiding, conforming citizens, sometimes overconforming, who were conscious of their differences in sex preference, but in other ways accepted societal norms. I recognize, of course, that there were always exceptions to this generalization, but if one accepts the hypothesis, then it implies there have been large numbers of people who were homoerotically inclined who have passed unnoticed through the pages of history. The only alternative hypothesis I think would be to argue that conditions in today's society create more homosexuals than ever existed before. This second hypothesis seems less likely than the first for several reasons: the sex ratios of today are more equal than ever before, due in part to greater attention to female infants and a fall in maternal mortality; this means there are more opportunities to find a partner of the opposite sex than ever before instead of trying to be celibate or having to resort to prostitutes. I also am not conscious of any radical change in society that would cause a greater increase in homosexuality. I do believe, however, that whenever pressure to conform in certain directions is relaxed, people who might have felt a need to make an effort to conform openly will no longer do so, and will become more obvious in the formerly disapproved conduct. The greater tolerance shown an alternative life style might lead to greater experimentation by adolescents with same-sex relations, but ultimately I think such experiments will prove a passing phase for most individuals who, after a period of bisexuality, will settle into the traditional heterosexual life pattern, or a new variant of the heterosexual life pattern. In fact, the challenging of the rigid stereotyped sex roles will make it somewhat easier for many to adjust to a heterosexual relationship, since it becomes more of a sexual relationship and less of a sex role one.

The real reason I doubt that conditions of today create more homosexuals than ever before is that I have very strong suspicions that significant groups of homosexuals existed before. This becomes a debatable point because scientific investigations of the topic have only taken place in the last hundred years and most of these investigations until the last few decades were by physicians. The result was an emphasis on the pathological nature of homosexuality and a misunderstanding of its extent. There were some potentially larger samples in the longitudinal studies projected by Magnus Hirschfeld, but most of this information was never released and was unfortunately destroyed. All we have are individuals reported on by Magnus Hirschfeld, as well as a similar collection of cases by Havelock Ellis, neither of whom accepted a pathological explanation of homosexuality. Most of the studies we have also concentrated on the male homosexual, leaving some authorities to imply that female homosexuality was almost nonexistent. I think this last statement is inaccurate, and I have some evidence to document my challenge and to emphasize the widespread existence of unreported homosexual communities.

Recently my wife and I were given an unpublished study of female homosexuals undertaken in the 1920s and 1930s. The sample of twenty-five was about the same size as Hooker's study of male homosexuals, but antedates it by approximately thirty years. Interestingly, the sample comes from Salt Lake City rather than a major metropolitan center. While we have written up and reported on this study elsewhere (Bullough and Bullough, in press), some information is worth repeating here. Essentially, the sample was compiled by a lesbian who wanted to demonstrate the basic normality of her condition. There are some interesting insights into the lesbian psyche. For example, the group she studied did not welcome the 1928 publication of Radclyffe Hall's *The Well of Loneliness*, now usually regarded as a significant fictional breakthrough in the portrayal of lesbian relationships. Instead they felt that the publicity given the novel caused people to be more observant of women living together, and to classify every woman who wore a suit (with a skirt) and was seen more than once in the company of another woman as a lesbian. They much preferred their life of outward respectability where their sexual preference was never suspected by the public at large, an essential perquisite for them since they held responsible jobs and positions in the community. Six of the twenty-five women in the group indicated they had realized they were homosexual at a very early age and had made no attempt to orient themselves toward men as love objects. The rest of the group had struggled against accepting a homosexual identity until much later in life. Six had actually married in an effort to prove they were not lesbians, and three remained married at the time they were interviewed although they now accepted their lesbian identities. Four others had become engaged but had never formally been married, while four others had experimented with heterosexual intercourse before accepting their homosexuality. Two others had been seduced as girls in rather traumatic experiences, and one of these seductions had resulted in a pregnancy. Except for the three married women (whom the other members of the group regarded as opportunists) all of the respondents felt they would never try marriage in the future, if only because it would be unfair to the man. To our knowledge, none of them ever did marry.

In examining the lives of these twenty-five women, it becomes evident that they were for the most part highly respectable women, accepted by the community at large as spinsters or old maids. Though the majority lived with a partner in a fairly stable relationship, this might or might not have been typical of other lesbians, and might have reflected the Salt Lake City environment rather than something else. The median age of the sample interviewed sometime in the late 1920s and early 1930s was twenty-nine. Politically and socially the group was conservative and their sexual outlook, with the exception of their lesbianism, was generally repressive. Masturbation, for example, was condemned, and one of the physical education teachers in the sample felt it her duty to prevent any of her students from engaging in this kind of "perversion." We know that other lesbian groups existed in the city at this time, but how this group differed from the others is not entirely clear.

Since many of the lesbians in this group had at least been born into the Mormon Church, although not all of these were still active Mormons, we have some indication of their discretion. The Mormon Church excommunicates homosexuals in a psychologically traumatic and degrading process, but none of these women ever came into conflict with the Church. Instead the lesbian women complained that the Mormon Church was continually trying to get them to be more active, regarding them as "strayed" Mormons suitable for intensive missionary efforts. In short, in a rather sexually repressive atmosphere, lesbians lived openly without much interference and with hardly anyone aware of their sexual preference. What was true of the Salt Lake City lesbian community, I think, must have been true of other groups across the country, although the male homosexual might have had more difficulty in concealing his sexual preference. This is because women in a sense had an easier time in engaging in homosexual liaisons than men. The laws toward women were not only more permissive, but society accepted as natural the fact that two women would live together and regarded it as preferable that they do so rather than live alone. The male-oriented world accepted as fact that women would be unable to do much sexually without a man. Indicative of these attitudes is the fact that, although two women who allegedly engaged in lesbian activities in Plymouth colony in 1649 were charged with lewd conduct and one of them was found guilty (Shurtleff, 1855–61), this seems to have been the only successful prosecution in American history of lesbian activities (Kinsey, *et al.*, 1953).

The same lack of prosecutorial zeal can be noted in England where, as in America, female homosexuals had a different standing in the law. In 1855, for example, when the Criminal Law Amendment Act was passed to provide for more effective prosecution of prostitution and homosexuality, lesbianism was excluded. The major attempt to rectify this exclusion was made in 1921, but the action was defeated in the House of Lords. Some of the arguments in that august chamber served as another illustration of both the male's misunderstanding of the female and his bemused tolerance of the female's "inadequacies." The rejection of any action against women was moved by the Earl of Malmesbury, who argued that women were "entirely different" from men.

> Women are by nature more gregarious. For instance, if twenty women were going to live in a house with twenty bedrooms, I do not believe that all the twenty bedrooms would be occupied, either for reasons of fear and nervousness, and the desire for mutual protection. On the other hand, I know that when men take shooting boxes the first inquiry is that each will have a room to himself.

The Director of Public Prosecutions who had initiated proceedings against Oscar Wilde admitted that, while there might be some lesbian women, they composed an extremely small minority. "For parliament to expose this minority," he added, "would result in the whole world knowing there was such an offence, to bring it to the notice of women who had never heard of it, never thought of it, never dreamed of it." The Lord Chancellor, Lord Birkenhead, summed up the prevailing view of female innocence. He held that outside sophisticated circles in the most metropolitan of cities there was not more than one woman out of a thousand who had ever

> heard a whisper of these practices. Amongst all these, in the homes of this country, where, in all innocence, and very often as a necessary consequence of the shortage of small houses, they have to have the same bedroom, and even sleep together in the same beds, the taint of this noxious and horrible suspicion is to be imparted, and to be imparted by the Legislature itself, without one scintilla of evidence there is any widespread practice of this kind of vice (Hansard, 1921; Hyde, 1970).

Even men more skeptical of female virtue saw little to bother about in lesbian practices. The anonymous author of *My Secret Life*, for example, recounted his anticipatory enjoyment as he observed two women engaged in "flat" intercourse with each other, content in the knowledge that he as a man could do things better (1966). It was probably from similar male erotic fantasies that various houses of prostitution staged exhibitions of lesbian lovemaking, or in their pornography delighted in portraying butch-type lesbian women (Fraxi, 1962).

The point to emphasize is, however, that lesbian communities have existed even in the most repressive of communities, and have existed unsuspected by the community. I think also that similar male groups existed, although they probably had to exercise even greater caution or adopted the protective coloration of marriage or the swinging bachelor. Unfortunately it is difficult to document these except when materials have survived accidentally. The published literature, however, only touches the tip of an iceberg. Though two males living together might have aroused suspicion, males living in groups such as in a boarding house, a dorm, or a bunkhouse roused little suspicion. Probably because of the greater difficulty in living together, the male homosexual relationship has been somewhat more unstable than the female.

All of this makes it obvious that homosexuality is not a new kind of life style, but one that has been around for a long time. The difference is that what has been kept underground is now emerging, and I suspect this is true of other life styles as well. When the pressures to remain underground are removed, however, I think there will be a greater increase in more stable relationships, and the homosexual patterns will closely resemble those existing among heterosexual couples or lesbian women. The difficulties with much of the past research into the area is that the researchers have concentrated on those who were unable to adjust or who were unhappy and discontented with their existence. My own research would indicate that the overwhelming majority of homosexuals never came to the attention of a psychiatrist. None of my Salt Lake City sample did, for example. In short, homosexuality, I think, is an alternative life style that has lost many of the disadvantages for those who opted for this life style in the past. It is not a new life style — just a more public one. Hopefully, also, those engaged in it will suffer less personal fears of exposure than in the past.

REFERENCES

Acton, William. *The Functions and Disorders of the Reproductive Organs*. 1857.
Anonymous. *My Secret Life*. 11 vols. London, 1966. Reprinted New York: Grove Press.
Augustine, St. *The Good of Marriage*, 11:12, 16:18, translated by Charles T. Wilcox in vol. 15, *Fathers of the Church*. New York: Fathers of the Church, 1955.
Augustine, St. *Soliloquies*, I, 10 (17), translated by Thomas F. Gilligan, in vol. I, *Fathers of the Church*. New York: Cima Publishing Company, 1948.

Bailey, Derrick Sherwin. *Homosexuality and the Western Christian Tradition*. London: Longmans, 1955.

The Bible. Any edition.

Bullough, Vern. "Homosexuality and the Medical Model." *Journal of Homosexuality* 1 (1974): 99–110.

Bullough, Vern. "Sex and the Medical Model." *Journal of Sex Research* 11 (November, 1975): 291–303.

Bullough, Vern. *Sexual Variance in Society and History*. New York: Wiley, 1976.

Bullough, Vern *The Subordinate Sex*. Champaign-Urbana: University of Illinois, 1973.

Bullough, Vern and Bullough, Bonnie. "An Early Lesbian Community." *Signs*, in press.

Corpus Juris Civiles. 3 vols. Berlin: Weidman, 1959.

Fraxi, Pisanus. *Bibliography of Prohibited Books*. Reprinted 3 vols. London: Jack Brussell, 1962.

Gigeroff, Alex K. *Sexual Deviations in the Criminal Law*. Toronto: University of Toronto Press for the Clark Institute of Psychiatry, 1968.

Gratian. *Decretum, Pars Secunda, Causa XXXIII, Questio* vii, c. 11, in *Juris Canonica*, edited by Emile Friedberg, 2 vols., Leipzig: Bernard Tauchnitz, 1879–81.

Hansard, *House of Lords Debates*, vol. 46, cols. 567–77 (August 15, 1921).

Heald, Henry T., and Finley, Mary K. "Alienation and Sexuality: A Comparison of Homosexual and Heterosexual Women." Paper given at the American Sociological Association, 1975 meeting in San Francisco. Unpublished.

Hooker, Evelyn. "The Adjustment of the Male Overt Homosexual." *Journal of Projective Techniques* 21 (1957): 18–31.

Hyde, H. Montgomery. *The Love That Dare Not Speak Its Name*. Boston: Little, Brown, 1970.

Jahrbuch für Sexuelle Zwischenstufn. A yearbook devoted to homosexuality, edited by Magnus Hirschfeld and published, mainly in the first decade of the twentieth century.

Kinsey, Alfred C., Pomeroy, Wardell B., Martin, Clyde E., and Gebhard, Paul H. *Sexual Behavior in the Human Female*. Philadelphia: W. B. Saunders, 1953.

Levitt, Eugene E. and Classen, Albert D., Jr., "Public Attitudes Toward Homosexuality." *Journal of Homosexuality* 1, (1974): 29–44.

McNeill, John T. and Gamer, Helena M. *Medieval Handbooks of Penance*. New York: Columbia University Press, 1938.

Marcuse, Herbert. *Eros and Civilization*. Boston: Beacon Press, 1955.

Money, John and Ehrhardt, Anke A. *Man and Woman Boy and Girl*. Baltimore: Johns Hopkins Press, 1972.

Shurtleff, Nathaniel B., ed. *Records of the Colony of New Plymouth*. Boston: William White, Printer to the Commonwealth, 1851–61.

Stephen, Sir James Fitzjames. *Digest of Criminal Laws*. St. Louis: F. H. Thomas & Company, 1878.

Sussman, Marvin B., et al., editor, "The Second Experience: Variant Family Forms and Life-Styles," a special issue of *The Family Coordinator*, 24 (1975): 391–576. This issue, including articles by many of the contributors to this forum, concentrates on heterosexuality.

Theodosian Code. Edited and translated by Clyde Pharr. Princeton: Princeton University Press, 1952.

Thomas Aquinas, St. *Summa Theologica II-II* Q. cliv, 11 and 12, translated by the Fathers of the English Dominican Province. New York: Benziger Brothers, 1947.

Wolfenden, John, et al. *Report of the Committee on Homosexual Offenses and Prostitution.* London: Her Majesty's Stationery Office, 1957.

Coming Out: The Gay Identity Process

MICHAEL P. BURK

Preface

WHEN I first became aware of the work that Elisabeth Kübler-Ross had done with terminally ill patients, and her book, *On Death and Dying*, it occurred to me that some of her basic findings might also apply to homosexuality in a general way. I felt that the five stages that she found her patients experienced in coming to accept the reality of their situation might basically apply to the process that many homosexuals go through in coming to accept the reality of their situation; this process is called "coming out." After several years of probing my own experience, by conversations and reading, and by probing the experience of others who have come out, I find that using these five stages is a most helpful schema in gaining a total look at the process of coming out.

In looking at coming out in the same basic framework that Elisabeth Kübler-Ross uses in her work, there is the imminent danger that some will feel I am drawing a connection between homosexuality and disease. I am not. What is common to both experiences is not the presence of any disease but the social stigma and the probability of great personal

and social loss involved in both identities. Both situations do, furthermore, present a dilemma that those affected must deal with, whether
they accept or reject their situation. Their future reactions will be
determined by how they emerge from this process.

I would like to state at the outset that my use of entirely masculine
pronouns does not necessarily indicate that these descriptions of the
experience of coming out do not also apply to women. However, since I
am not a woman and since I have not discussed the experience of
coming out in these terms with very many lesbians, I shall confine my
discussion to male homosexuality and not attempt to make any
generalizations relating to the area of lesbianism.

I should also explain that this discussion is not the result of any
massive quantitative study; I have no hard research data to fall back
upon. This discussion emerges from my own experience, my own
participant-observation findings, conversations with friends and counseling clients, reading the work of others, talking with associates,
talking with people in other fields, etc., etc. Some may object to my lack
of scientific objectivity and method but this is not a scientific study or
survey, and does not purport to be.

What I am trying to do is to show why I feel Kübler-Ross's framework
applies to the experience of coming out. I feel that she has developed a
valid scheme and that it applies well to other areas of human
significance—in this instance, homosexuality. More than anything I
want to bring order to our conceptualizations of this experience as a
holistic process, affecting more than just a person's sexuality. It is my
hope that this view of coming out may help to shed a healthier, more
positive light on homosexuality by dispelling some of the haze that has
in the past clouded this issue.

Coming Out as an Identity Process

Coming out for a gay person is the process whereby he achieves
an acknowledgment and acceptance of his homosexuality. This process
also implies the achievement of a new openness on the part of the
individual, particularly towards others who share this sexual identity.
Coming out not only involves the identity of the individual but also
affects how he functions in society, as Dennis Altman points out.

Thus, coming out for a homosexual implies a long process whereby he/she
seeks to arrive at a modus vivendi out of the interaction between his/her

sexual and emotional needs, the stigma with which one is branded and the gay world through which one can meet others with similar needs (Altman, 1971, pp. 28–29).

Achieving this "modus vivendi" forces a drastic reassessment of one's self and one's total life style.

The best method I have yet found for looking at this process in a fairly organized fashion is to use the five stages that Elisabeth Kübler-Ross provides, plus one called "externalization," which I have supplied. We will be using these six stages as an aid in conceptualizing some of the responses and emotions a person experiences while coming out.

Identity Crisis

It is probably during the period of middle or late adolescence that a person begins to become fully aware of his sexuality. Of course, the experiences of our childhood may contribute to the formation of our sexuality and our total identity. But the period of adolescence brings with it the identity crises which contribute most to the formation of our adult selves. It is a period of experiencing and feeling, and an intense search to find out who we really are.

Adolescence is also, unfortunately, a time when a maximum of social pressure is brought to bear upon us. This is unfortunate because this tremendous pressure greatly inhibits our ability to succeed in finding our real selves. It is nearly impossible for the adolescent to sort through his own feelings and values with every social institution at hand telling him how he should feel and react and what his values should be.

While the adolescent feels pressure from almost every social institution, it seems that the most powerful of these institutions requiring conformity are parents and the peer group. These people put the most direct and powerful pressure on the adolescent to behave and to accept their values as his own; their expectations are the highest. If his behavior or his values do not align with their own they will be the first to rebuke him.

It is interesting in this context to note the language that adolescents frequently hurl at one another. If an adolescent does not conform to his peers' ideas of what is socially acceptable or exhibits behavior which is in some way not very masculine or which is felt to be effeminate, he will probably find himself labelled a "fag," a "homo," a "fairy," a "queer," etc. Working through the identity crises of adolescence and encountering this kind of hostility and alienation from one's peers may be rather traumatic for the individual. The adolescent may postpone dealing with his homosexuality on many levels. He may repress it altogether. Some individuals may go through a type of avoidance overreaction and continually try and assert their masculinity to themselves and others.

Some people repress their homosexuality for many, many years. The main result, however, of all these pressures for conformity is that most individuals aren't able to deal with their own homosexuality or to come out until they are out of high school, or away from home, or in college; i.e., until these pressures have abated to a significant degree. Many emerge into early adulthood still repressing their homosexuality.

Stigma and Loss

The process of coming out is partially necessitated by the social stigma our society attaches to homosexuality. Indeed, our entire Judeo-Christian heritage has consistently scorned all sexual relations or acts which are nonprocreative, looking with particular disfavor upon homosexual relations as being not only wrong but somehow very threatening.

Coming out is a process of coming to terms with the guilt and shame that society has forced upon the homosexual. It is a process of working through this guilt and social stigma. It is seeking the modus vivendi we mentioned earlier; it is facing the odds against oneself.

Our society is structured to give rewards, social and legal, for heterosexuality and to punish homosexuality. Therefore, coming out is also a process in which a person deals with the possibility that he may suffer some great losses. One of the greatest of these losses is simply the loss of personal physical freedom; it is still fairly easy to be arrested on one charge or another in those states where homosexuality remains illegal — although this situation is now beginning to change. Because of the many prejudices against homosexuality, a declared homosexual may lose social acceptability. There is still a high probability that he will lose his job. The only exception to this is when he has chosen a field that is traditionally tolerant of homosexuals and therefore has a disproportionate number of gay people working in it (e.g., fashion, the theater, the arts, etc.). The homosexual may, depending upon his landlord, lose his residence. This is one reason for the formation of "gay ghettoes" in larger metropolitan areas. If he owns a house, it is still likely that he will incur the wrath of neighbors. A declared homosexual may find that his friends are suddenly not his friends. By far, perhaps the hardest loss for most gay people is the loss of family. Some families are able to accept the fact that a son is homosexual; some families accept it to varying degrees. Occasionally one parent can accept it and the other cannot; the same is true of other family members. Often a family cannot accept the fact that a son is gay and will disown him as a family member. Accordingly, most homosexuals are very cautious about letting their families know.

The losses mentioned above are all very large ones, or forms of discrimination which a gay person may expect to suffer. Many gay people, however, do not experience anything quite as disastrous. But a great proportion of gay people do in some way experience what are termed the "subtle oppressions" in Deryck Calderwood's filmstrip, *The Invisible Minority.*

The subtle oppressions are acts committed by well-intentioned liberals or inconsiderate heterosexuals who like to think of themselves as sympathetic towards gays. Examples of these range the entire spectrum of kinds of covert discrimination. One example might be some close friends asking you not to go someplace with them because they are taking their sixteen-year-old son along and they "just don't think it would be a good idea." Or you might be expected to appear at a party with a date of the opposite sex, instead of the person (of the same sex) you have been living with for the past three years and who is your lover. These more subtle kinds of oppression are the results of assumptions, oversights, misunderstandings, etc. which, whether conscious or unconscious, are prejudices and discriminations that do cause pain to the gay person.

While coming out is a working through of the guilt and shame of being homosexual in this society, it just brings the person to a point where he can begin to cope with the stigma with which he will be forced to live. It is in one sense the end of a process and in another sense the beginning of a process.

There are other identities and situations which also involve a high degree of prejudice and social stigma. Elisabeth Kübler-Ross deals with the person who has a terminal illness; the example of the amputee or one who has just become a paraplegic might also be cited. Equally worth considering are those such as the transvestite, transsexual, drug addict, or the alcoholic. Each of these identities is stigmatized and suffers from the prejudices of our society. It seems that each of these may require a process similar to the one we are talking about in order for the person to gain an acceptance of his situation and deal with it in terms of his life. Any one of these would make an interesting study in terms of these stages of coming out.

The Stages of Coming Out

1. DENIAL

The denial response probably begins in middle or late adolescence and may continue as long as the person is capable of and feels the need to deny his homosexuality to himself. This may be a reaction to the social pressure the person encounters from parents, peers, and others. It may involve the repression of homosexual feeling for as long as possible. The person who is having homosexual feelings or experiences really has no choice but to try and deny their validity for him; it may be a matter of psychological survival.

Even after the pressures of adolescence begin to abate, many people continue to deny and repress the part of their sexuality that is homosexual. Many people continue in the denial stage for many years, refusing to acknowledge their homosexuality. Often they try to repress homoerotic responses and to deny them as a part of their total sexuality.

There are certainly enough people seeking counseling in order to try and deal with their homosexuality to indicate that denial cannot last successfully for most people who are gay. Many gay men, in some form of denial, will become involved in a heterosexual marriage and raise a family only to find, years later, that their denial is unsuccessful. This, of course, can result in a great deal of pain for all involved.

Denial is, in essence, a self-rationalization saying, "No! Not me!"

2. ANGER

The continuance of homosexual feelings or experiences may lead the person into the second stage of coming out — anger. The person may continue to have homoerotic feelings or to participate in occasional homosexual experiences which he cannot repress from his consciousness. If these seem to increase in frequency in relation to the person's heterosexual feelings and experiences, they may begin to threaten his heterosexual self-image. The person's homosexuality may become significant enough that he cannot continue successfully to block it from his consciousness. All of this will cause him to become very annoyed and frustrated because he still can't or won't deal with homosexuality in himself. Acknowledgment of his homosexuality will now be blocked by anger.

Generally speaking, anger intensifies as denial becomes inadequate. However, this does not mean that denial ceases; quite the opposite. Thus, the anger and denial stages are very closely linked and may be present at the same time. The person in this second stage may find his anger spilling over into other areas of his life and affecting his general temperament. He may become generally irritable or hostile. The anger stage adds a slightly new dimension to denial and repression of homosexuality within the individual.

Anger may be characterized as a rationalization which says, "No! Why me!?"

HOMOPHOBIA. In accepting their homosexuality, many people never get past these two initial reactions. For some reason, whether it be social pressures or inability to resolve their internal conflicts, they may get caught up in stages 1 and 2. This may result in an overreaction of extreme hostility and prejudice. This overreaction syndrome is called "homophobia" or "queer fear."

George Weinberg deals extensively with homophobia in his book *Society and the Healthy Homosexual*. He says:

> Most men who loathe homosexuals have a deathly fear of abandonment in the direction of passivity. The surrender of control signifies to them a loss of masculinity and in their demand for control produces narrowness . . .
>
> The person I am describing usually feels under tremendous pressure to be the aggressor in sex, and he expects conformity and passivity on the part of his woman. He is easily undone when he does not find it. He inflicts ludicrous role expectations on his children. In some cases the fear of being womanish has so invaded the crannies of the person's mind that it affects his attitudes toward the use of color in his home and in his clothing. He has also defined himself out of existence by the very contrast he is fighting so hard to establish (Weinberg, 1972, pp. 3–4).

Although Weinberg here is describing a person who is in a heterosexual situation, homophobia in the person who is coming out may have a very similar basis and manifestations.

Homophobia may manifest itself in the behavior of the individual in many ways, some of which are almost suggestive of classic paranoia.

The homophobic individual might become a walking encyclopedia of prejudice based upon every fear or myth he has ever known about gay people. He knows every put-down or insult that exists about gays. This might be the person who has an almost unlimited repertoire of "queer" jokes at parties. He may develop the fearful feeling that somewhere, sometime, he will surely be attacked and raped by a homosexual; he is sure that every homosexual is after his body. He may also be the type of individual who is supremely confident of his ability to spot homosexuals in any group of people, and he will not hesitate to tell you "who is and who isn't" on any occasion. At the same time he is careful to be the superior example of the all-American male, exuding masculinity and machismo. People who exhibit these kinds of superficial behaviors seem to be the most deeply insecure about their own sexuality.

Often people who are so filled with fear by homosexuality will react to individuals they suspect of being homosexual with outright hostility and physical force. It is entirely conceivable that the phenomenon known as "queer bashing" may be largely the result of homophobic reactions to adolescent and adult identity crises.

Getting caught up in the mire of guilt conflicts and identity crises that produce denial, anger, homophobia, and their associated behaviors, may repress coming out indefinitely for the homosexual. For the person who is mainly heterosexual or bisexual, homophobia can be viewed as a blockage of healthy psychosexual development. In essence, homophobia can be described as:

> a form of acute conventionality. Ultimately, it condemns because of difference. It has every basic attribute of an irrational social prejudice (Weinberg, 1972, p. 21).

3. BARGAINING

Moving into the bargaining stage of coming out can be seen as a breakthrough in many respects. For the individual who is coming out this may represent the first real and serious consideration he has given to homosexuality in himself. This may be the first time he has been free enough from pressure to think about any degree of homosexuality as being a valid part of his entire sexuality. To do this the individual has had to break through the prejudices, myths, and fears that dominated him in the first two stages.

The individual now begins to try and place his homosexuality in some kind of perspective with his whole self. While maintaining a largely heterosexual self-image, he begins to consider what would result if he tried to give any sort of expression to his homosexual feelings. He is bargaining with himself about whether he can ever feel good about giving expression to the feelings he knows he has. He must weigh this against the heavy sanctions our society puts on any kind of taboo sexual behavior. He has found:

> As the whole structure of socialization acts so as to channel our polymorphous perverse instincts into narrow but socially approved norms, there is not only a repression of general eroticism but also of bisexuality (Altman, 1971, p. 68).

If, in bargaining, he can work through some of the stigma and guilt associated with homosexuality, the individual may find himself at a point where he can, for the first time, view himself as a bisexual being; i.e., not strictly heterosexual. This redefinition of personal sexuality is an important result of the bargaining process because it represents the first real acknowledgment of homosexuality in the individual. It represents a breakthrough in the inner repression he has been maintaining.

The person's defining himself now as bisexual is only a partial lifting of guilt and repression because the individual usually wants to maintain some association with heterosexuality and the larger portion of society. For him there is still a great threat in thinking of himself as predominantly gay, even though he may realize this to some degree.

This is not to say that those who define themselves as bisexual are largely a group of repressed homosexuals. Nor is this to say that people who are, in emotion and practice, relatively bisexual don't exist. What I am saying is that the gay person who is coming out may find that defining himself as bisexual is a very safe and neutral label for him to lean on while he tries to get a better perspective on himself. It may buy some time for him to regroup and deal more fully with the issue. He may stay here until he feels safe enough to proceed.

In the bargaining stage the person rationalizes to himself, "Well, maybe I do have homosexual feelings, but. . . ." or "Yes, me. But. . . ."

4. DEPRESSION

As the individual begins to face the full impact of his homosexuality, he enters the fourth stage, which is usually marked, at some point, by a period of depression. This stage is the last major battleground that must be crossed on the way to full personal acceptance. Here the person must work through the major feelings of guilt and anxiety that still block his ability to accept his homosexuality. The person openly confronts himself with all his defenses and inner repressions lowered.

The depression also serves a preparatory purpose. It helps prepare the individual to face the stigma that is associated with homosexuality in this society. It helps him psychologically to deal with the losses he may have to face as a result of this stigma and discrimination. It helps him to gain a realistic view of his position as a homosexual in this society.

The real main characteristic of this stage is an intense search for self-acceptance. The individual seeks to learn if he can ever lead a happy and meaningful existence as a gay person in our straight (heterosexual) culture. An intrinsic part of this search is the search for others who share his sexual orientation. There is a basic need to see that there are other people living in the real world who are homosexual and who are not the group of miserable degenerates that myths have led him to believe.

The gay person who is coming out will often develop a great curiosity about famous personages who are or supposedly were homosexual. This kind of "gay history" will help to reassure his knowledge that being gay will not somehow destroy his character or ability to make a contribution to humanity. Later it may act as good ammunition to throw at people in order to dissolve some of the myths that exist about homosexuals being degenerate, promiscuous do-nothings.

It is in this stage of coming out that supportive and nondirective counselors or friends are very beneficial. During the depression stage, when anxieties and inner conflicts really bear down upon the individual, counselors or friends who have a healthy attitude and understanding about homosexuality can most help the gay person. With their support and empathy it is much easier for the person to find self-acceptance.

In the depression stage the gay person may be said to realize to himself, "Oh, yes. Me."

5. ACCEPTANCE

This is the final stage in the resolution of guilt, fear, and anxiety within one's self. People reach the acceptance stage with differing degrees of self-awareness and consciousness, and this is a factor in the total health of the gay individual. By this time the person may be said to have greatly resolved within himself the societal guilt and stigma attached to his sexual orientation.

This stage represents a holistic integration of sexuality and total life style. For some gay people this may be the first time in their life that they haven't actively repressed a full awareness of their sexuality. Sexuality becomes integrated into the whole identity, as Dennis Altman explains:

> Perhaps the most sensible conclusion is that there are many reasons that may account for an individual's homosexuality, that this aspect of behavior becomes part of his or her total concept of identity, and that it is almost impossible to eradicate it without damaging the whole personality (Altman, 1971, p. 6).

Reaching the acceptance stage of coming out can be viewed as Abraham Maslow viewed the process of growth from neurosis into health. This holistic integration makes available the total, healthy self to be actualized. With acceptance, the person is healthy enough within himself to be able to deal with most of the encounters he will experience in gay or straight society. This is not to say that the person can cope with anything and everything, or that he will live happily and healthily ever after. But he is now in a better position to become a productive self-actualized person than he has been previously.

In this stage, for the first time, the full person speaks and says, "Yes, me. And I am O.K."

6. EXTERNALIZATION

The homosexual who has achieved a comfortable degree of self-acceptance and a good amount of inner security will be able to move into the sixth stage, which is that of externalization. He may first identify himself as a homosexual within the gay community. This might involve the traditional first visit to a gay bar, coffeehouse, gay liberation meeting or function, etc. The person may be honest about his homosexuality only with those gay people with whom he associates. Some people are not very honest even with other homosexuals, using a false name because they fear the possibility of being publicly exposed; often this fear is justified. Because of the risks still involved in being gay, many persons who comprise the gay community are forced to live a sort of double life. They feel they cannot afford to risk being known in the larger society as a homosexual, so while interacting with the gay community they are open and comfortable. When they return to the world of their family, office, or straight friends they interact as though they were heterosexual.

One who is more secure or feels he has less to lose may begin to externalize his gay identity to others close to him who are not gay. He may find this a healthier stand to take in his interactions with others and find that it promotes better relationships with those who are important to him. Sidney Jourard discusses some of the reasons for this.

> . . . Disclosure of the truth, the truth of one's being, is often penalized . . . Yet, when man does not acknowledge to himself who, what, and how he is, he is out of touch with reality, and he will sicken . . . . And it seems to be another fact that no man can come to know himself except as an outcome of disclosing himself to another person, he learns how to increase contact with his real self, and he may then be better able to direct his destiny on the basis of this knowledge . . . .
>
> Self-disclosure, however, requires courage. Not solely the courage to be, as Paul Tillich wrote of it, but the courage to be known, to be perceived by others as one knows himself to be (Jourard, 1964, pp. 6–7).

This act of self-disclosure for the healthy homosexual is usually brought about in interaction with those who represent significant others for that person. Transparency to others is most self-actualizing when it is disclosure to those people who give the most meaning to one's life.

For the healthy gay person who weighs the risk and makes the choice, externalization with his significant others can put his relationships with them on a more meaningful plane. Of course, he must take into consideration the reaction the person might have to his disclosure. He might lose that person altogether; or he might foster a new depth of meaning in that relationship—each person in one's life requires this individual decision. The decision of self-disclosure to another is usually to help promote openness and honesty in the interaction between those people. The more a gay person chooses not to be transparent to his significant others, the more he has to hide from them and the more he has to play self- (and other) destructive games. Again Jourard has some applicable comments.

> Self-disclosure is a symptom of personality health and a means of ultimately achieving healthy personality. When I say that self-disclosure is a symptom of personality health, I mean a person who displays many of the other characteristics that betoken healthy personality will also display the ability to make himself fully known to at least one other significant human being. When I say that self-disclosure is a means by which one achieves

personality health, I mean it is not until I am my real self and I act my real self that my real self is in a position to grow. One's self grows from the consequence of being . . . .

Alienation from one's real self not only arrests personal growth; it tends to make a farce out of one's relationships with people . . . .

. . . Every maladjusted person is a person who has not made himself known to another human being and in consequence does not know himself. Nor can he be himself. More than that, he struggles actively to avoid becoming known by another human being (Jourard, 1964, pp. 32-33).

In a sense this helps to indicate that the decision to come out and the decisions of externalization, while they involve the risk of loss and discrimination, are basically decisions for the existential freedom and the self-actualization of the total person. To decide not to take the risks is a decision to hide from a self, which one can then never fully know, and to cripple one's self in interactions and relationships with others.

When a gay person "comes out" (i.e., externalizes) to those people who are significant to him, he may initiate in them a process similar to the one he has just gone through. They may experience several of the stages of coming out. This is particularly so in the case of parents of gay people. Their parental sense of responsibility adds to the feelings of guilt they may have to work through; they may feel that they somehow "caused" their child's homosexuality. Significant others must also come out. They must work through their feelings about homosexuality in those to whom they are close. The process is no easier for them than it is for the gay person.

Coming Out and Human Variety

Speaking about coming out, or about homosexuality, is rather difficult simply because of the variety of experience enountered in any portion of the human milieu. Because of this variety of experience, no two gay people will experience the process of coming out in exactly the same way. There is as much variety of personalities in any group of gay people as there is in any group of heterosexuals. Gay people don't all come out to the same extent and they don't all view their homosexuality in the same way. Dennis Altman explains:

It would be possible to graph homosexuals according to the extent that they are prepared to come out openly. At one extreme are those who seek to maintain a self-image of heterosexuality, engaging in homosexual sex furtively, with hostility, and often when drunk; at the other are those who are open both to themselves and to others about their homosexuality (Altman, 1971, pp. 13-14).

Part of the reasons for the great variety in the way people progress through these stages and the different lengths of time each person may take in coming out is the fact that homosexuality itself may be hidden or repressed to a great degree. If a person belongs to an ethnic minority he is constantly made aware of that. If one is a homosexual, however, he may very successfully suppress his own awareness of this and he can hide it from others. Therefore, a person's coming out may be a rather stop-and-go process spanning a period of many years. One of the inherent frustrations of the gay liberation movement is that homosexuals are a hidden minority. A large number of gay people simply refuse to "come out of the closet," preferring to deny their homosexuality to others and sometimes even to themselves.

There is a vast number of gay people who come out but externalize their gayness to very limited extents. I briefly mentioned these people earlier in talking about gay people who are open about their homosexuality only to certain people or in specific settings. These are persons who almost lead a double life; they are gay to the homosexual community at the gay bar but when they go home, or to friends, or to work, they are straight. They live in and out of the "closet" of covertness, opening the door and coming out of the closet upon occasion and stepping back in, closing and locking the door behind them when they want to be safe.

Some people gain a certain amount of self-acceptance but can never be open about being gay for a number of reasons. They may feel that they don't want to risk being stigmatized; or they feel that somehow they just can't integrate being gay into the rest of their life—that it is a very separate matter and no one else should know about it. Many men just can't deal with the guilt they feel; they can't ever feel that being a homosexual is O.K. Some have simply accepted society's view of them—that they are somehow not "normal"; therefore, they strive to hide that which makes them feel abnormal.

Often they take these feelings to professionals for help in coping with themselves or for help in personal adjustment. Often they have not received very healthy reactions from those professionals. Many have insisted that first the gay person must be changed or "cured" before there can ever be any hope for them to lead a healthy and fulfilling life. The attitudes of professionals are now beginning to change as they become more comfortable with and educated in areas of human sexuality.

Concluding Remarks

In presenting this overview of the process of coming out I have attempted to look at it as a process of growth into a more integrated and healthier human being. I think the process should be viewed as holistically as possible; the process and the experiences and decisions encountered in it affect the whole individual, not just his sexual behavior.

Using Elisabeth Kübler-Ross' framework of five stages, plus the sixth which I have added, is the most useful method I have yet found for conceptualizing this total process. It is very helpful in describing the emotions and experiences a person encounters while coming out. Most of all, it helps to form a clear picture of this process for others.

It is important to bear in mind that these terms or stages are, indeed, generalizations and, therefore, subject to the same attacks that may be made on any generalization. Not every person who comes out goes through all of these stages and not necessarily in this same order. Although coming out is usually a relatively long process, it seldom takes the same length of time for any two people. Likewise, a person may experience a great variance in the length of time he spends in any of these stages. Also, as mentioned earlier, the process may be postponed and taken up again according to each individual's needs. For some people coming out may take many, many years; for some it can take a few weeks or months. Some people even claim to have come out when they were seven years old, or some to have been "out" for as long as they can remember.

I stated at the outset that I wanted to dispel any connection that someone might draw between homosexuality and any disease concept. However, on a totally different plane, I think that coming out may be seen allegorically as death and resurrection. The gay person, upon coming out to his family, may find a complete lack of understanding on their part; they may reject him completely. The family may treat him as if he had died, even going into a metaphoric state of mourning. Coming out is the death of an imposed identity; one that society places upon people and takes for granted. Coming out is the death of this imposed straight identity and the resurrection from its ashes (just as the phoenix) of a totally new and rejuvenated person.

I believe that coming out is a necessary process for the homosexual. It is a process which makes possible a new, positive, and healthy self. I also believe that the externalization of being gay is self-actualizing (or helps the individual to be) and can aid the person's awareness of himself. It also helps facilitate the ability to integrate personal situations into broader social and political concepts of liberation. Personhood cannot be full if portions of the person are segregated or denied and repressed.

It is my hope that what I have presented here will help bring more understanding to an area of human experience which has long been blocked from sight. Speaking metaphorically, I hope these concepts can help to unlock one of the doors to the closet in which homosexuality has been kept for too many years. It is our duty as people engaged in any form of helping relationship, and as people who share this planet together, to promote understanding and openness.

REFERENCES

Altman, D. Homosexual Oppression and Liberation. New York: Outerbridge & Dienstfry, 1971.

Clark, L., and Nichols, J. I Have More Fun with You Than Anybody. New York: St. Martin's Press, 1972.

Fisher, P. The Gay Mystique: The Myth and Reality of Male Homosexuality. New York: Stein & Day, 1972.

Frankl, V. E. Man's Search for Meaning. New York: Washington Square Press, 1963.

Hoffman, J. The Gay World. New York: Basic Books, 1968.

Humphreys, L. Tea-Room Trade: Impersonal Sex in Public Places. Chicago: Aldine, 1970.

Jourard, S. M. The Transparent Self. New York: Van Nostrand, Reinhold, 1964.

Kübler-Ross, E. On Death and Dying. New York: Macmillan, 1969.

Marmor, J. Sexual Inversion: The Multiple Roots of Homosexuality. New York: Basic Books, 1965.

Maslow, A. H. Toward a Psychology of Being. New York: Viking Press, 1971.

McCaffrey, J. A., ed. The Homosexual Dialectic. Englewood Cliffs, N. J.: Prentice-Hall, 1972.

Miller, M. On Being Different: What it Means to Be a Homosexual. New York: Random House, 1971.

Murphy, J. Homosexual Liberation: A Personal View. New York: Praeger, 1971.

Rogers, C. On Becoming a Person. Boston: Houghton Mifflin, 1961.

Weinberg, G. Society and the Healthy Homosexual. New York: St. Martin's Press, 1972.

FILMSTRIP

Calderwood, D., and Skodzinsky, W., producers. The Invisible Minority: The Homosexuals in Our Society. Boston: Beacon Press, 1973.

THE FUTURE

[11]

THE CONCLUDING PAPERS attempt to peer into the future, but a reasonably immediate future. You may not agree with all of what they say, but much of it, as demonstrated by Ramey's statistics, is already happening. What is predicted, therefore, in the immediate future is a greater realization of the new flexibility in relationships rather than the appearance of dramatically new kinds of relationships.

Many of the common interpersonal relationships and behavioral patterns of today were violently attacked and scoffed at for many years. Bertrand Russell wrote about cohabitation in the 1920s, but it took another forty years for cohabitation to become a visible phenomenon in the United States. Judge Lindsey opted for "no-fault" divorce at the same time but didn't live until the 1960s to see it occur. But attitudes are changing more rapidly today. Gallup reported an astonishing change in attitudes toward premarital sexuality from a poll taken in 1969 when 68 percent thought it wrong to 1973 when only 48 percent were of that mind. What was especially newsworthy, in addition to the remarkable change of the attitudes of 20 percent of the population in the space of only four years, was the fact that this change occurred not only for the young, which might have been expected, but for the old as well. It was, in short, an across-the-board change of heart. That being the case, we should not be surprised if within the space of a few years attitudes toward marriage undergo differentiation and change as well.

Life Styles of the Future

JAMES W. RAMEY

F UTUROLOGISTS have developed several techniques for predicting what we will find over the next hill. The most widely used technique for such projections is probably the Delphic method, in which experts pool their guesses based on present trends. Such projections are virtually useless beyond about twenty years, however, because experts have no way of taking account of "breakthroughs." Breakthroughs are usually thought of in the context of technology, but similar effects occur in behavior. Diffusion of innovation has been shown to apply to behavior as well as to the adoption of new technology. For example, women have smoked for generations, but it was not until after World War II that the diffusion curve suddenly turned upward and it became commonplace for women to smoke. This process of diffusion breakthrough seems to occur at the point at which about 8-10 percent of the population are involved in a particular practice.

I believe we should stick to known events and statistics relating to actual behavior in our future predictions about life styles. This means giving up the *ought* and sticking with what *is*. As Cuber (1970) said,

> In many ways, people in America function in two separate and often contradictory spheres. One consists of a set of prescriptions concerning what behavior *ought* to occur and *why* it should follow the outline prescribed. The other consists of what people *actually* do in concrete instances when overt behavior is observed. The two are in direct conflict in almost every aspect of sex, marriage, and family life.

In addition to sticking to the facts, we should also avoid projections beyond the next decade or so, especially in light of several breakthrough

274

type changes that are now in progress which make projection extremely difficult. Some of these breakthrough changes in the way we live have been presented elsewhere in this book, notably in chapters by Macklin and Knapp. But there are other myths about the present that also should be dispelled.

Perhaps the most important of these has to do with the prevalence of the monogamous nuclear family, which most people assume is the predominant family form in the United States. Actually, it is very much a minority family form, practiced by fewer than one in ten adults today. A nuclear family consists of a breadwinner-father, a housewife-mother, and children. Many people may have spent some part of their lives in such a family unit but few have spent a lifetime in one. According to the Bureau of Labor Statistics (April 1977) adult households were distributed as follows:

Adults heading single-parent families	16%
Other single, widowed, separated, or divorced adults	21
Adults living in childfree or postchildbearing marriages	23
Adults living in extended families	6
Adults living in "experimental" families	4
Adults living in dual-breadwinner families	16
Adults living in single-breadwinner nuclear families	13
Adults living in no-breadwinner nuclear families	1
	100%

Furthermore, as lifespan increases, fewer and fewer people will conform to the ideal nuclear family form. Today the average couple lives about thirty-six years *after* their children leave home. During this period they no longer constitute a nuclear family. Furthermore, even among those with children in the home, fewer and fewer families have a single breadwinner. The shift toward the nuclear family, which began just after the Civil War, has been reversed in recent years. Today approximately 60 percent of wives with husband present and children in the home are working wives, and today only 34 percent of all husband-wife couples constitute single-breadwinner marriages (Hayghe, 1976). Single-parent families are growing at three times the rate of dual-parent families, and there has been a 71 percent increase in the number of women heading single households since 1970 (Census Bureau, 1976).

Even the 18 percent figure for adults living in single-breadwinner nuclear families is not the "bottom line," however, for both the law and the "ideal" say that these should be monogamous nuclear families. The evidence suggests strongly, however, that they are not. Kinsey, in 1948 suggested that 50 percent of husbands and 28 percent of wives engaged in extramarital sex by age forty-five. Gebhart suggested in 1968 that the current figures for all marriages were 60 percent of husbands and 40 percent of wives involved in extramarital sex by age thirty-five. Constantine (1974), quoting the Research Guild survey for 1968, points out that there was more extramarital sex reported during the first two years of first marriage for those in the twenty–twenty-four age group than for the entire married lives of all married individuals in all other age groups.

Today, more than a decade later, assuming these trends have continued, and there is no reason to believe otherwise, it is entirely reasonable to assume that less than half of the people in nuclear families are monogamous, particularly when one takes into account that these are precisely the people most likely to be affected by the Guild Study figures—those in their twenties and early thirties.

The fact is that we already live in a pluralistic life style society. Few individuals alive today have not lived in several different life styles, and such an occurrence will be even more rare for those born into our society in the future. What is new is that we are now undergoing a pluralistic revolution in life styles which is inevitable and irreversible—because a technological revolution, a demographic revolution, and a biological revolution preceded it. The demographic revolution has almost doubled the lifespan since 1900, while cutting the childbearing years in half. The technological revolution has made it possible for single individuals to maintain their own households, thus reducing the dependence of women on finding a husband as a means to survival. The biological revolution, beginning with the widespread distribution of the Pill in the early 1960s, has freed women from the capricious dominance of men and fate, through pregnancy.

In a scant ten years, since the introduction of the Pill, it has already been replaced as the most widely practiced means of medically adequate contraception by sterilization. As of 1973, sterilization was the preferred method of contraception for all married couples over age twenty-four, and in the three years since 1970, even those in the fifteen–twenty-four age group had tripled their use of sterilization for contraceptive purposes. This presages such a profound change in our society that Westoff (1976) predicts the end of unintended pregnancy among married couples by the end of the 1970s.

Other chapters in this book have considered some of the life styles that now have become practical as a result of the several revolutions we have mentioned. What has not been mentioned is the change in the pace of communication. Change spread rather slowly fifty years ago. People had adequate time to assimilate change, whereas today, in the light of our extraordinary communications ability which allows us to view events in China or on the moon as they are occurring, they have difficulty simply recording change, much less assimilating it. Social scientists are also seriously hampered by inability to keep up with change in our society. Note, for example, that the sterilization figures Westoff reported in the spring of 1976 relate to data collected in 1973 in the Nation Survey of Family Growth.

Nevertheless, even though the figures are fragmentary, it is obvious that something momentous is happening. First marriages are being put off by a year, children by two years. Divorces passed the 1,000,000 mark in 1975, and even in Florida, amounted to 66 percent of marriages. Marriage has become a matter of choice for the first time, rather than an imperative. More people are choosing not to get married. Since 1970, for the fourteen–twenty-four age group, 78 percent more females are living alone and for the twenty-five–thirty-four age group 106 percent more females are living alone, while over this same period there has been an increase of 29 percent and 46 percent respectively for these two age groups of women living with nonrelatives (Census Bureau, 1976). Not only are more people staying single longer—those who get divorced are also postponing remarriage longer.

What about predictions for the near future? Based on current evidence, it is reasonable to assume that:

1. The trend will accelerate among women either to postpone marriage or remain single, perhaps cohabitating from time to time. A similar but less pronounced trend may be expected among men.
2. The marriage rate will continue to drop and the divorce rate will continue to increase until divorces level off at about two for every three marriages.
3. The trend toward sterilization as the preferred form of contraception in the United States, as in the rest of the world, will continue to grow, thus lowering the birth rate further and helping to end unintended pregnancies.
4. The trend toward sexual pluralism will continue both in and outside marriage.

5. The focal family will replace the nuclear family as the "here and now" family unit.

6. Marriage will increasingly become a peer relationship wherein the partners try to achieve and maintain a morphogenic relationship rather than revert to the traditional "female as possession" pattern.

7. The trend toward cohabitation rather than marriage will continue as an alternative primary relationship pattern, especially on a short-term basis.

8. Rapid growth will occur in deliberately childfree primary relationships.

9. The trend toward sexually open marriages in which intimate friendships are viewed as positively supportive of the primary relationship and of personal growth will continue.

10. Intimate networks, growing out of sexually open marriages, will take on many aspects of kinship networks and may indeed include kin as well as intimate friends.

11. The barriers between the married and the unmarried will significantly erode, especially as more of the unmarried live in primary relationships, and sexual intimacy will increase across this barrier, particularly between the unmarried and childfree or post-child couples.

12. Today, nineteen states have "consenting adults" acts on the books. Ten states have passed such acts in the past year. Most states will pass such laws in the future.

13. There will be considerable growth of the current trend toward live-in situations involving a couple and a single or two couples.

14. There will be further relaxation of the promotion of monogamy by organized religion as the only acceptable type of primary relationship or marriage, and an increase in the active exploration of alternatives to marriage and monogamy by organized religious groups.

15. There will be some acceleration of the establishment of multiadult households as a means of securing economic advantages, broadening sexual access, and replacing the extended family, with many of these groups growing out of intimate groups and networks or of senior citizen groups.

16. There will be tacit recognition that the various types of complex living groups involve a number of positive aspects, and gradual legal recognition of at least certain types of complex living arrangements.

The demise of the family is unlikely in the foreseeable future, but its shape is changing. We are slowly beginning to realize that the nuclear family has serious flaws, and that it is at best a transitional family form that many people have used during the childbearing years. Look for a dawning recognition that the focal family must replace the nuclear family if we are to deal with reality. The practice of serial monogamy has overlaid sets of in-laws, children, and ex-mates to such an extent that we now have lateral extended families in which may be embedded a number of focal families, i.e., households that may include both adults and children who may or may not be currently legally related although they may have been legally related at some time in the past. It is an easy step from the focal family involving only those who are or have been legally related to one in which some may not be or have been legally related. Nevertheless, the important binder in such a family group is commitment—willingness to accept unlimited liability for—regardless of the legal nature of the relationships. This commitment need not be predicated on the existence of one or more primary relationships but certainly does not preclude such relationships.

The important point about the concept of the focal family is the looseness of the definition itself. By letting people self-define who is in the family, as we traditionally have done in the United States for two hundred years, informally, we escape the legalisms that have grown up in the past thirty-five years, especially with respect to the function of the human service delivery systems that have divided us all into irreducible units of one father-breadwinner, one mother-housewife, and a parcel of kids. Even though we knew in our hearts that this was not reality, we have allowed it to happen, and we have all suffered as a result, especially blacks, hispanics, and farm families, groups that traditionally have included many people in the family who were not actually members either by consanguinity or affinity.

We accepted self-definition of the family in the past. We may well be forced to do so again in the near future, as some families become so legally complex after two or three marriages as to make the current definition ridiculous. The children have no problem with this concept. As far as they are concerned, there just isn't any problem. They adapt to the current situation quickly, and are not overly concerned with the fluidity of family forms so long as they are secure in their feeling of being loved and wanted for themselves.

The interesting aspect of accepting the idea of the focal family is that it immediately allows for pluralistic family forms within a single framework. Society has a way of coopting or normalizing innovative behavior by shifting definitions. This may well be the mechanism by which we make acceptable the shift away from the monogamous nuclear family ideal. This is not to say that everybody will forsake the monogamous nuclear family. Many people will of course continue to strive toward this ideal. But already we see articles in the press about the impossibility of keeping up with the Jones' when the Jones' have two breadwinners in their family, unless one also has two incomes.

We may be closer than we think to reserving legal marriage for parenting. If our focal families begin without formal marriage for many, as a living together arrangement, which indeed seems to be happening, we learn how to manage a household, how to live in a primary relationship, how to be a functioning adult, without the burden of legal marriage and marriage roles. Today we find the lines blurring between living alone, cohabiting, dating, and childfree or postchild marriage. Whether the individuals in one or another of these life styles are serially monogamous or nonmonogamous, their living arrangements are quite similar. The nonmonogamous ones, in particular, move freely between these life styles in the establishment of their various relationships.

The increase in networks of love relationships that are specifically nonparenting relationships can be expected to hasten the social and legal differentiation between marriage for love and marriage for parenting. It is well known that cohabiting couples who become pregnant or plan pregnancy almost always get married (or have an abortion).

The focal family, then, may include married and/or unmarried adults. If children are involved, they are included not on the basis of legal relationships to any of the adults involved, but rather on the basis that the adults in the group are willing to accept and perform the parenting role with respect to these children. If, however, adults in the group wish to conceive children, the state should, and I believe eventually will, stipulate that if unmarried, they should marry for the purpose of parenting. In this age of positive contraception, the issue of sexual freedom among adults in such a group should remain a private concern, since the danger of unanticipated pregnancy is very unlikely, as is the question of paternity.

We are not suggesting that most focal families will involve more than one primary relationship or even more than one male and one female adult. It is much more likely in the future, as today, that one or more of the children in the family will be unrelated or that the adults will be unmarried. Typically such a group might include a woman and her child by a previous marriage, a man with whom she is cohabiting and may eventually marry, and a child by her ex-husband's first marriage, actually unrelated to anyone else in the family, for example. It is not unusual for the ex-husband to live with such a focal family temporarily from time to time, while visiting his children. It is also not unusual for sexual relations to occur at such times between ex-mates. There are endless variations on this theme, and we all know of at least several examples among our friends.

Some of us also know of less common arrangements involving three adults or two couples. These seem to be among the fastest growing of the various types of complex living groups, perhaps because they are the easiest to form and maintain and because they cause the least stir among friends, neighbors, and family. The couple that adds a single to the relationship may do so because of an interest in three-way intimacy, to relieve the pressure of childrearing, or to ease the economic burden, but many appear to do so simply because of situational factors, such as divorce crisis, death, loss of a job or the like. When the third party is already a good friend, such temporary arrangements sometimes become permanent, and even when they do not, a surprising number of people who have had such an experience actively seek to repeat it until a permanent arrangement is found. Such threesomes do not necessarily constitute group marriages, although some do. Generally the primary relationship commitment is strong only between two of the partners, less often it exists between each same-sex partner and the cross-sex partner, and in a few instances it also exists between the same-sex partners. Such groups of three or four adults constitute a very small but slowly growing minority.

Larger complex living groups are also flourishing, especially in urban settings. These usually involve seven or eight adults and they appear to be particularly important as a form of social support for some single people, although they often involve married couples as well as singles. Most of these groups do not involve children. Participants usually join such groups for economic reasons, to find order and regularity, and friendship and support from caring people in a noncaring world. It is a way to make the transition from parents to adulthood, to break with the past, to have new experiences, to live with a lover, or to live in a single state but in the company of others.

Most people living in complex living groups are steadily employed, lead normal lives, and are not freaks or drop-outs. In a current study of such groups it has been found that the activities most often cited as being made easier by living in such a group are: (Zablocki, 1976)

To be cared for when physically ill	82%	(N=478)
To solve emotional problems	81	
To relate to people openly and spontaneously	80	
To meet new people	77	
To find out who you are	74	
To meet financial emergencies	72	
To be the kind of person you want to be	72	
To find out what you want in life	70	
To be single	70	

In a study by Bardford and Klevansky (1975) of fifteen middle-class complex living groups in the San Francisco area, each involving five to fourteen people (average eight), the answers to a similar question, i.e., why live in a complex living group were:

Interpersonal contact and relationship to others

Sense of community, belonging to a larger group

Chance for personal growth

Better setting for children to grow and develop

Chance for deep intimate relationships

Most of the members of these groups were single men or women who were lawyers, therapists, school teachers, engineers, computer programmers, professors, ministers, managers, or salespersons. Most joined in search of community.

I have suggested (Ramey, 1976a) that the individual rather than the family is the basic building block of American society today. Paradoxically, many of the same forces in our society that make it possible for the individual to operate a self-contained household also make households of three or more adults more desirable.

The number of single adults in our country is growing daily. Already more than one out of every three adults is single, separated, widowed, or divorced. The unmarried are putting off marriage. The separated, widowed, and divorced are putting off remarriage. One out of every five households in America is a single or nonrelative household, and while 90 percent of these are singles living alone, the rest (two million) live in nonrelative households (Census Bureau, 1976).

Complex living groups represent a way of finding community and economic sharing without making a commitment to marriage or cohabitation for many people who have not yet experienced such a commitment or who do not wish to make such a choice, as well as for many older people who are under pressure from their children (heirs) and the government not to remarry (women who marry lose their social security benefits). For those who have already tried marriage or cohabitation and found these arrangements too constricting—not providing freedom to grow and develop—a form of withdrawal from society, complex living groups, also promise a way to remain single, but within the structure of a strong support group. This is especially true for divorced women with small children. Finally, there are happily married or cohabiting couples who want to open up their marriages even more than would be the case if they practiced open marriage—by actually sharing living quarters with other married and/or unmarried adults.

It has been argued that the very complexity of group marriages, communes, and all other forms of complex living groups is such that most people will never be attracted to them. We should not forget, however, that in different social and cultural settings people have and do live in very complex groups. The question is not one of capability but of desirability. In a society that has pushed the notion of independence for centuries, it is easy to equate autonomy with personal growth and commitment with stagnation, and to suggest that the two cannot exist side by side. History suggests, however, that it is in *groups committed to personal growth* that the most growth occurs, not in individuals committed to autonomy.

My research suggests that the greatest growth of complex living groups will occur in groups of eight or fewer individuals living together, and that many of these households will grow out of intimate groups and networks. Larger commune-type groups usually develop out of religious and/or utopian convictions, and they generally occur at an earlier stage in life, whereas the type of group I have in mind generally involves people over thirty.

The likelihood of significant growth of religious or utopian complex living groups is limited because they require radical departure from mainstream culture. Small groups of the type I have described elsewhere (Ramey 1976a, 1976b) are, on the other hand, solidly in the mainstream tradition of the American dream, i.e., banding together in order to optimize ability to compete within the system. The outcomes associated with such groups are prized in our society, e.g., enhanced economic status, better child nurturing, and greater personal freedom because of the economic and numerical enhancement of the focal family unit. We can reasonably expect this type of multiadult household to show a gradual increase over the next two decades, but the number of such households is not likely to become a significant factor before 1990, based on present law and custom. *Unless:* If the focus does indeed shift from the "ought" to the "is," from nuclear family to focal family, in general usage and in our dealings with governmental agencies, then the lines could blur much more quickly between various focal family configurations. This shift could be speeded by de facto approval of the sexual aspect of such relationships through the speedy enactment of consenting adults acts throughout the remainder of the states. It could also be speeded up by the cumulative effects of positive contraception, especially sterilization, and by the increasing independence of women as the impact of equal employment opportunity spreads, and women invade more traditionally male professions.

Another factor that cannot be predicted is the governmental position on marriage for parenting. Current legal opinion suggests that private marriage contracts, when tested in court, will be able successfully to abridge every provision of the State's public marriage contract excepting those having to do with the rights of children. When that happens, as it surely will, we will be very close to having substituted the right to contract marriage privately for the public contract, *providing conception is specifically prohibited.* Thus the public marriage contract would become, in effect, a parenting contract. Those who wished to could still use the public contract form whether they planned to have children or not, but it would be *required* of everyone who wishes to have children.

The logical next step, once it became established that one could marry either under the public contract or could write a private agreement to suit the needs of the parties at the moment, would be the introduction of a requirement for public contract that the parties show satisfactory evidence of having successfully operated under a private marriage contract for a reasonable length of time, say two years. The object would be to prevent parenting before the parties had at least demonstrated that they could establish a viable primary relationship. Pregnancy without a parenting license may ultimately carry a legal penalty in addition to the requirement that the pregnancy be automatically terminated by abortion unless this would endanger the life of the woman. We need to have an end to unwanted and/or unplanned babies. Life is too precious to allow people to whelp like animals, without the emotional, economic or childcare commitment and preparation, and childrearing ability to give the child an even break in the world.

Too many children born today are either unplanned, unwanted, or both, due to external pressure from potential grandparents, church, and society. We appear to be more concerned about supervising the birth of dogs than of people in this country. It would only be a matter of time, given the scenario I have sketched, before the State would add emotional, economic, and childcare requirements to the parenting marriage contract, similar to the requirements for adoptive parents today.

In this manner much of the difference between various types of private relationships would slowly disappear, as indicated earlier. A private marriage contract would not be that different from cohabitation, or other forms of relating that do not involve marriage, and there would be nothing to prohibit more than two adults from entering into such an agreement, thus legalizing a variety of possible focal family forms.

Having legally established this watershed between making love and making babies, we would expect that many individuals would never trade in their private contract for a parenting contract. Private contracts would not have to be registered with the State, but simply notarized, as are private contracts today for other purposes, and they could be renegotiated or dissolved at the will of the parties, as is the case with other contracts. The number of people opting for parenting public marriage licenses would steadily decline, as has been the case in Sweden, where there has been a 50 percent decline in marriage since 1966. As in Sweden, the various government and business agencies, in their transactions that involve recognition of marriage, could just as easily accept the word of the parties that the private contract exists as they do today with respect to nonmarital contracts.

Since private contracts would *be* private, they could as readily specify sexual nonexclusivity as they could sexual exclusivity. Moreover, being private, they could also involve parties of the same sex, or a specific time frame, as well as more than two contracting parties.

How soon is this all likely to happen? Sooner than we expect, in all likelihood, given the pace with which the pluralistic revolution is sweeping away cherished givens with respect to sexual behavior and marriage and the nature of the family.

REFERENCES

Bardford, P., and Klevansky, "Middle-Class Communes." In P. Stein, *Single in America*. Englewood Cliffs, N.J.: Prentice-Hall, 1976.

Constantine, L. L. Plenary Session, Future Families of the World Conference, University of Maryland, April 1975.

Cuber, J. F. "Alternate Models from the Perspective of Sociology." In *The Family In Search of a Future*, edited by H. Otto. New York: Appleton-Century-Crofts, 1970.

Gebhard, P. quoted by Morton Hunt. *The Affair*. New York: World, 1969.

Hayghe, H. "Families and The Rise of Working Wives—an Overview." *Monthly Labor Review* 99 (1976): 18.

Kinsey, A. C., Pomeroy, W. B., and Martin, C. E. *Sexual Behavior in the Human Male*. Philadelphia: W. B. Saunders, 1948.

Ramey, J. W. *Intimate Friendships*. Englewood Cliffs, N.J.: Prentice-Hall, 1976.(a)

Ramey, J. W. "Multiadult Households: Lifestyle of the Future? "*The Futurist* 10 (1976): 78-83.(b)

U.S. Bureau of the Census. *Current Population Reports*, Series P-20, Nos. 212, 218, 287, and 291. 1976.

U. S. Bureau of Labor Statistics, News Release, March 8, 1977.

Westoff, C. F. "Trends in Contraceptive Practice: 1965-1973." *Family Planning Perspectives* 8 (1976): 54-57.

Zablocki, B. "Preliminary Report on the Urban Commune Study." In P. Stein, *Single in America*. Englewood Cliffs, N.J.: Prentice-Hall, 1976.

EPILOGUE

[12]

WE HAVE COVERED a wide array of different intimate life styles. Some readers may find a few styles interesting, one or two exciting but perhaps a little too daring, and others rather "sick." What each of the life styles discussed has in common is that to a greater or lesser degree they are outside the pale of normative monogamy. Which, if any, are destined to survive and flourish and which to disappear or dwindle? I believe that an historical perspective can be illuminating. Let us start by listing some givens in today's society: (1) "Love" marriages; (2) easy divorce; (3) free choice in marriage; (4) women's liberation; (5) dating; (6) small family; (7) monogamy.

It may come as a surprise to some, but none of these phenomena except monogamy has been part of our history for very long. The idea that marriage should occur for reasons of love seems to have been more or less coterminous with the publication of Richardson's novel *Pamela* about the middle of the eighteenth century. However, the relationship of love to marriage was not perceived as it might be today. In the late eighteenth and nineteenth centuries it was believed that desirable spouses were those with desirable traits.

An ideal husband, for example, was religious, sound of wind and limb, and not given to "idleness, intemperate use of intoxicating drinks, smoking, chewing, sniffing tobacco . . . taking . . . opium, licentiousness, gambling, swearing and keeping late hours at night" (Fowler, 1855, p. 131). An ideal wife embodied the virtues of piety, purity, submissiveness, and domesticity. Thus, one chose a partner because of his or her possession to greater or lesser degrees of these qualities, and one then loved him or her because of these qualities and

287

because it was the individual's role as a spouse to do so. The idea of love and compatibility of personality as a reason for marriage, without undue emphasis on qualities possessed in the abstract, seems to have arisen around the turn of the twentieth century in the ladies' magazines (Preston, 1905; McCall, 1911).

Easy divorce is surely a twentieth-century phenomenon, as is free choice in marriage, if we mean by "free choice" freedom from economic and parental pressure in choosing. The women's liberation movement in the United States dates officially from the Seneca Falls Convention of 1848. The first hundred years or so seem to have focused almost exclusively on political and legal equality, which were hammered out slowly decade by decade. Although this struggle is not over yet, the gains have been impressive. The more subtle social and economic struggle accelerated with the publication of Betty Friedan's *The Feminine Mystique* in 1963.

Dating is largely a twentieth-century phenomenon, originating in increased mass education, reduction of child labor, urbanization, improved means of transportation such as the safety bicycle and the automobile, and improved communication such as furnished by the telephone. The small family has been evolving for several hundred years, but has become especially pronounced in the past decade or two as the Pill, increase of married women in the labor force, and concern over the population explosion have begun to influence the birth rate.

Only monogamy can be said to have much longevity among the phenomena we have traced, and this leads me to my main thesis: That change in the way we relate to each other in intimate relationships has always been with us and so has monogamy. I believe that future intimate relationships must take account of these twin facts.

Monogamy has endured from the earliest records of history, and even in polygynous societies it is much more frequent than polygyny. Of course, there have been violations of the monogamic code all along, sometimes with the full approval of society as in the kingly prerogatives, sometimes more surreptitiously as for commoners. Yet despite the continued infractions of the monogamic code, for the most part violations have not been societally sanctioned and still are not. Why has monogamy survived when it seems to be a detriment to the pleasures of so many?

It has been said that society has a vested interest in its children and in preserving the family as its basic economic unit. It can be argued also, with some justification, that until recently there was little knowledge of effective contraception, and that monogamy was essential for the support of women who, in the midst of continuous pregnancies, were hardly in a position to support themselves. It can be argued further that the reality of the economics of living meant that few men could support more than one woman.

But to focus on the physical and societal rationales for monogamy is to say that we eat *only* to make our bodies grow, to fabricate waste products to excrete, and to avoid dying from starvation. Even a simpleton knows better than that — that we eat because we *feel hungry*. In like manner, monogamy has evolved out of the basic human need to love and to be loved, to confide and to be confided in, and to counteract the threat of loneliness and inevitable death in a meaningful intimate relationship. Dyadic love has generally been fused with exclusive dyadic sexuality, but this is not a logical necessity, merely a convenient marriage of two important drives: intimate pairing and sexuality.

Let me further admit that joining intimacy and identity in a unit larger than oneself does not have to be limited to one other person. It can be achieved in triads, quartets, communes, groups, and in multiple relationships. Yet the frequency of all these other arrangements accounts for but a small fraction of the world's population compared to those involved in monogamy. Moreover, in many of these non-monogamic arrangements, whether in accord with the "house rules" or not, monogamic pairing often occurs. Throughout the course of history, so far as we have records, through monarchies, dictatorships, republics, clans, patriarchies, and kibbutzim, monogamy has survived and flourished. And if and when the institution of marriage as we know it should ever die, *Brave New World* and *1984* notwithstanding, some form of monogamic relationship will survive.

Does this mean that the various types of nonmonogamic relationships that we have examined in this book are no more than a safety valve for mavericks or misfits, a small but manageable segment of the population? I think not. To understand their role in the future and also in current living, we must disencumber ourselves of some epiphenomena of monogamy which unfortunately confound and confuse many people. First on this list is sexual exclusivity, sometimes referred to as sexual "fidelity." It is argued by many that the true monogamist desires only his partner, or, if like Jimmy Carter (and the rest of us), he lusts after "forbidden fruit" in his heart, he at least never acts on these lustful feelings.

The annals of history, not to mention the preceding pages of this volume, have amply documented that many people are not sexually monogamous. The sinners of history have been stoned, burned, castrated, branded, and ostracized for their nonmonogamous sexuality, without any noticeable degree of success. Moreover, most of these "adulterers," despite the burden of guilt inculcated in them by society, have loved their spouses and never desired to break up their monogamic relationships. Perhaps, therefore, it is time to rid ourselves of the idea that monogamy and involvement in other intimate relationships are incompatible.

It has been part of folklore that it is not possible to love more than one person at a time, but there are a goodly number who report that they have done so. I believe that the number so reporting would be in the majority if these individuals had had the opportunity to do so without suffering from societal sanctions.

More than one hundred years ago John Humphrey Noyes shocked many readers with this bold sally:

> All experience testifies (the theory of the novels to the contrary notwithstanding), that sexual love is not naturally restricted to pairs. . . . Men and women find universally (however the fact may be concealed), that their susceptibility to love is not burnt out by one honeymoon, or satisfied by one lover. On the contrary, the secret history of the human heart will bear out the assertion that it is capable of loving any number of times and any number of persons, and that the more it loves, the more it can love. . . .

Please note the line "the more it [the heart] loves, the more it can love." This line is in accord with the principles of learning theory which hold that the repetition of successful and rewarding responses should lead to greater response generalization — to loving more persons. This observation clearly flies in the face of the conservative marriage counselors' dictim that it is neurotic to be in love with someone else than one's spouse.

There is yet another reason why individuals may readily love more than one person at a time. I believe few would quarrel with the observation that no one person can satisfy all of another person's needs. We may readily love two people if they satisfy different but important needs. We may of course elect not to label the satisfactions provided by the nonsocietally approved person as "love," but that may be more a function of avoiding culturally prohibited acts (labeling a nonspouse as a loved one) than of representing the actual feeling tone engendered by the rewarding acts of the person.

If the experience of loving two or more people at a time is not an everyday occurrence, it is because societal mores are so constructed as to minimize the opportunity for the development of extramarital love relationships. Socially, two married persons are really one — the "couple." Most *soirées* given by couples are for other couples. Although Mr. Smith does not sit down next to Mrs. Smith at a dinner for twelve, the opportunity for development of extramarital relationships is limited by the nature of the event. The mores of dinner parties usually dictate a stereotyped impersonal cant to the evening discussions.

Even if Mr. Smith found Mrs. Jones charming, he would be unlikely to feel comfortable enough to call her up to invite her out to lunch while excluding their respective spouses. The average individual, therefore, may relegate the task of need satisfaction to his fantasy life, and shrug his shoulders and rationalize that "no marriage is perfect."

Another factor to be considered is that an individual may be involved in activities outside the marriage which prove so rewarding that the dissatisfactions of marriage are more than compensated for by the rewards of the outside activity. A football coach involved in game plans and competition may demand very little of his spouse. Further, some individuals' tolerance of frustration is greater than others because of low self-esteem or realistic or unrealistic perceptions of themselves as incapable of attracting others. Others, particularly women, may be locked into the house by their roles as mother and housewife and have neither sufficient opportunity nor sufficient energy to develop potential, nonhousehold love relationships. In sum, multiple love relationships do not occur very often, but this does not mean that there is a lack of interest in developing such relationships. Neither does it signify that people are very content with the present style of monogamy.

Is there a solution? I would like to argue the thesis that monogamy *is* the best form of relationship for most individuals, but that to maximize its true potential it must be made much more flexible than has been the case heretofore. How can this be achieved? I would start by saying that most persons need to feel that there is at least one significant person in their lives whom they can trust, confide in, with whom they can make love, share experiences, perform capably in a variety of activities, and share a number of common interests. Certainly, theoretically, this compatibility could be shared with two, three, or more. But as the number of persons in this hypothesized group increases, the likelihood of their satisfying all of their needs in conjunction with one another decreases. It is the major reason that successful three or four person marriages are a rarity.

The demands of time schedules and money will often preclude more than two people from engaging in enjoyable activities together at a given time. Regarding sexual expression, most people find two an ample number. Some might argue that this should not be the case, that these individuals don't know what they are missing by avoiding group sex, and that sexual conservatism, fear of the unknown, and competitiveness ought to be overcome. Perhaps so, but I would submit that an innovation that bears some continuity with present mores is more likely to be accepted than an innovative activity like group marriage and/or group sexual relationships which violate mores regarding extramarital behavior and extradyadic behavior simultaneously.

The new monogamy of which I speak would retain the primacy of the main monogamic relationship (usually between the married couple) vis-à-vis other relationships, as Burt and Wendy, and James Ramey have indicated earlier. It is difficult to conceive of a monogamic relationship surviving if it must often play second fiddle to other dyadic relationships, unless there are nondyadic factors such as money, property, children, and social network keeping the couple together.

I would go further and say that in the case of two different dyadic groups involving a common person (Mr. A, Mrs. A, and Mr. B, Mrs. A), greater harmony might prevail within both relationships if the needs that Mr. A. and Mr. B satisfied in Mrs. A were qualitatively different. If both Mr. A and Mr B serve as kindly father surrogates, if they both love Italian opera and dancing along with Mrs. A, then the possibility of competition between them is maximized. It would be better if they appealed to complementary aspects of Mrs. A and vice-versa. If Mrs. A loved dancing, Italian opera, parties, and books, it might be better if Mr. A loved Italian opera and books, and Mr. B dancing and parties.

The new monogamy must deal with other thorny issues than competition of needs. There are also the twin issues of sexual fidelity and jealousy. It should be reiterated that the primary relationship must come first. That a married person may prefer to do something with a person other than his spouse when his spouse is willing to engage in the same activity with him is conceivable. But if that is his preference, in good conscience he ought not to expect his spouse to remain married to him. But what if his spouse is away on a trip and he wants to go to bed with a friend? The acceptability of such action obviously goes beyond right or wrong. It is for the couple to decide on the issue of fidelity and indeed whether sexual jealousy might prove disruptive to the viability of the marriage. It would seem advisable for the couple composed of the married and "outside" person to also consider the effects of various actions on their own relationship and on their other intimate relationships.

But sexual jealousy is not endemic to the human condition. Extramarital sex is condoned in a goodly number of societies. However, those cultures that officially accept extramarital sexuality generally do so under prescribed conditions. The so-called Eskimo wife-lending, for example, occurred only when a male eskimo needed to take a long trip and his wife was pregnant or nursing a child. He might then substitute the wife of a willing neighbor. Reciprocally, the neighbor might take the first eskimo's wife on a trip at a later date.

I believe that couples will decide in the future as now what "depth" of extramarital relationships will be permitted and under what conditions. What will be different from current mores is that fidelity will be interpreted as a commitment to the relationship above all other relationships. It will not necessarily include exclusive sexual access to the partner nor exclude other intimate relationships.

In the past revered marriage writers have written that sexual monogamy was an evolutionary phenomenon, and some even professed to see man's simian cousins, the primates, as also having arrived at monogamy. But more careful observation revealed that the primates were not so faithful after all. Although females might have a favorite "lover" they often took sex where they could find it and, like man, sometimes did not even blush at incest.

In fact, there is no evidence of man having been biologically programmed for monogamy. A better case, indeed, could be made for the belief that man is biologically polygamous since, despite stern laws against adultery, man has always engaged in it. The presence of condoned extramarital sex in some cultures, however, is proof enough that sexual monogamy is a learned phenomenon. It is understandable if unfair that for thousands of years men often used their greater physical strength and freedom from the probability of conception to reduce women to the status of valued property. Sexual fidelity was reserved primarily for women. "Valued property" should not be demeaned by the introduction of spurious issue through adultery. It remains to be seen whether sexual exclusivity can survive the era of contraception and women's economic independence.

At the present time, many individuals have opted for sequential monogamy both of the premarital and marital variety. But there is much to be said for long-lasting, fulfilling relationships in which the partners, nevertheless, are not committed to the burden of forswearing other meaningful relationships. Although in the near future some individuals will opt for complete and total monogamy, many, as today, will continue to mix monogamy with occasional clandestine or semiclandestine extramarital activity in which the partner "officially" does not know that his partner engages in sporadic sexual sallies.

An increasing number of persons will seek new structured extramarital relationships such as group marriage and swinging. However, the sharpest increases will occur for couples, married or unmarried, who decide to maintain and further develop extradyadic relationships, acting as individuals rather than as a couple. In these open or, more correctly, "semiopen" marriages or relationships, some degree of extramarital friendships will be tolerated so long as they do not threaten the marriage. In the near future, sexuality will be more largely stripped of its symbolic value as proof of possession or of undying monogamic love. It will be seen as of value in its own right as a joyous activity, but even richer when it involves union with a loved person. In such a climate, lovemaking with the spouse, a spouse who no longer is viewed as an inhibitor of other relationships, will be an especially satisfying experience in which basic compatibility is welded with increased acceptance of the right of the other to function as an individual. There is already ample evidence that among swinging marriages that survive any length of time, extramarital sexual experience rather than detracting from sexual satisfaction in marriage, actually enhances it. Probably the same will be found for successful open relationships.

Which of the numerous options to choose? I think that I would be foolish to predict the best choice. The couples involved will often not really be able to predict the ultimate consequences of the choices they make. What will be different about future relationships will be lessened state regulation with more choice as to the nature of the relationship left up to the participants. And for the first time in history, the partners will come to the discussion table with approximately equal assets. Thus almost everything will be fodder for negotiation: kitchen work, care of children, whose career takes priority, whether to practice sexual exclusivity, and tens of other variables now largely avoided. A world in which sex roles will be weakened in favor of androgynous approaches may seem threatening to some, but in the long run it should lead to improved communication, better relationships, and the satisfactions inherent in being in a relationship in which roles have been chosen instead of assigned.

REFERENCES

Fowler, L. N. *Marriage: Its History and Ceremonies.* New York: S. R. Wells, 1855.

McCall, A. B. "The Tower Room". *Women's Home Companion* 38 (Sept. 1911): 34.

Noyes, J. H. *History of American Socialisms.* New York: Hillary House, 1961.

Preston, A. "The Ideals of the Bride to Be". *Ladies' Home Journal* 22 (March 1905): 26.

INDEX